RITUAL, POLITICS,
THE CITY IN FATIMID CAIRO

SUNY Series in Medieval Middle East History
Jere Bacharach, Editor

RITUAL, POLITICS, AND THE CITY IN FATIMID CAIRO

PAULA SANDERS

State University
of New York
Press

Published by
State University of New York Press, Albany

Printed in the United States of America

For information, address State University of New York Press,
State University Plaza, Albany, N.Y., 12246

Production by Susan Geraghty
Marketing by Fran Keneston

Library of Congress Cataloging-in-Publication Data

Sanders, Paula.
Ritual, politics, and the city in Fatimid Cairo / Paula Sanders.
p. cm. — (SUNY series in medieval Middle East history)
Includes bibliographical references and index.
ISBN 0–7914–1781–6 (hc acid free). — ISBN 0–7914–1782–4 (pb acid free)
1. Cairo (Egypt)—Social life and customs. 2. Cairo (Egypt)--Court and courtiers. 3. Festivals—Egypt—Cairo—History.
4. Rites and ceremonies—Egypt—Cairo. I. Title. II. Series.
DT146.S26 1994
962'.16—dc20 93–22317
CIP

10 9 8 7 6 5 4 3 2 1

In loving memory
Theresa and S. D. Goitein

CONTENTS

ABBREVIATIONS, ACRONYMS, AND SHORT TITLES

b.	ibn
d.	died
fl.	flourished
K.	Kitāb
Q.	Qur'an
r.	reigned

AO	Acta Orientalia
BIFAO	Bulletin d'Études Orientales de l'Institut Français d'Archéologie Orientale
BSOAS	Bulletin of the School of Oriental and African Studies
EI	Encyclopaedia of Islam
EI2	Encyclopaedia of Islam, 2nd edition
IJMES	International Journal of Middle East Studies
JAOS	Journal of the American Oriental Society
JASP	Journal of the Asiatic Society of Pakistan
JESHO	Journal of the Economic and Social History of the Orient
JNES	Journal of Near Eastern Studies
JRAS	Journal of the Royal Asiatic Society
ZDMG	Zeitschrift der Deutschen Morgenländischen Gesellschaft

Daʿā'im al-islām	Daʿā'im al-islām wa-dhikr al-ḥalāl wa'l-ḥarām wa'l-qaḍāya wa'l-aḥkām
Himma	K. al-himma fī adab ittibāʿ al-a'imma
Ittiʿāẓ	Ittiʿāẓ al-ḥunafā bi-akhbār al-a'imma al-fāṭimiyyīn al-khulafā
Khiṭaṭ	K. al-mawāʿiẓ wa'l-iʿtibār bi-dhikr al-khiṭaṭ wa'l-āthār
Nujūm	Al-Nujūm al-zāhira fī mulūk miṣr wa'l-qāhira
Rusūm	Rusūm dār al-khilāfa

Subḥ	K. Ṣubḥ al-aʿshā fī ṣināʿat al-inshā
Supplément	Supplément aux Dictionnaires Arabes
Tāj	K. al-tāj fī akhlāq al-mulūk
Vêtements	Dictionnaire détaillé des noms des vêtements chez les Arabes

ACKNOWLEDGMENTS

This project could not have been completed without institutional support from a number of different sources over the years, beginning with the Departments of History and Near Eastern Studies of Princeton University and the Mrs. Giles Whiting Foundation. In 1987–88, the American Research Center in Egypt funded research in Cairo for an ongoing study of Mamluk ritual and economy that also gave me the opportunity to re-think many parts of this project while walking the Fatimid procession routes as often as I liked. The Dean of Humanities and the History Department of Rice University have been exceptionally generous with both funding and leave time. The staff of the Rice University Library, and particularly Jennifer Geran and Doug Klopsenstein of Interlibrary Loan, provided indispensable assistance.

No scholar, least of all me, works in a vacuum. I view this book as the product not only of my own research and thinking, but also of countless collaborations, large and small, occurring over many years. At each stage in its development, colleagues and friends have intervened in important ways, always for the better. I am grateful for all of these interventions, in whatever form they came—conversation, written critique, questions, comments, references, even occasional asides and afterthoughts.

The influence of A. L. Udovitch and Bernard Lewis, who guided my first ventures into Fatimid history at Princeton, will be apparent to all who know their work. I would not know how to repay the debt I owe them, one that has only increased with time. I owe a similar debt of gratitude to Jacob Lassner and Carla Klausner for the many years of friendship, encouragement, and good counsel they have given me.

At different stages, Jere Bacharach, Irene Bierman, Fred Denny, R. Stephen Humphreys, Bernard Lewis, Avrom Udovitch, and Lucette Valensi read the entire book. Fatma Müge Goçek, Jacob Lassner, Laurie Nussdorfer, and Leslie Peirce offered comments on particular chapters. I thank all of these colleagues for their generosity in providing such careful readings and thought-provoking critiques. I would also like to thank Peter Brown and Roy Mottahedeh for the many conversations from which I have benefitted so much. Three close friends have played an especially important role in the shaping of this book: Shaun Marmon, my companion in Islamic history (and other adventures), Michael Maas, and Carol Quillen. They have listened to, read, and commented on nearly every part of this book in many different incarnations, in addition to providing constant support. It is no exaggeration to say that without them I could not have finished. These friends and colleagues, as well as anonymous press readers, saved me from many errors and pushed me in directions I might otherwise not have gone. The errors that remain are entirely my own.

Barry Bergen, Judy Coffin, Edward Douglas, Grace Edelman, Willy Forbath, Paul Lerner, Matt Mancini, and Dan Sherman provided encouragement, hot meals, and diversions when they were most needed. Susan Lurie occupies a special place among these friends for her emotional support. My parents, grandparents, sisters, and brothers have encouraged me at each stage of my career, but I must thank especially my mother, Lilian Kranitz, for her complete confidence and unfailing support in everything I have undertaken.

The earliest version of this book was written during my years in Princeton, when I worked as research assistant to the late S. D. Goitein and was a visitor almost every day at his home. Scholars familiar with Professor Goitein's work can imagine what it meant to a young historian to observe, on almost a daily basis, the unique combination of gentleness and rigor that he brought to his scholarship. The long hours of quiet, intense work with Professor Goitein were punctuated by late afternoon breaks for coffee and sweets with Mrs. Goitein, during which I enjoyed their full attention. To this day, I feel their remarkable presence in my life and work.

CHAPTER 1

Introduction

FATIMID HISTORY: AN OVERVIEW

The Fatimids came onto the scene in the Islamic world when both the political hegemony and the religious authority of the Abbasid caliphate were being challenged. Some of the most serious challenges to Abbasid religious authority came from various Shiʿis, groups who insisted that ʿAlī b. Abī Ṭālib should have succeeded the Prophet as head of the *umma* (community of believers). These partisans (*shīʿa*, hence the term *Shiʿi*) of ʿAlī eventually argued as well that the headship of the Islamic community should rest with the descendants of ʿAlī and his wife Fāṭima, the daughter of the Prophet Muhammad; the partisans believed these descendants had inherited spiritual authority. The disputes between different groups of Shiʿis often centered around genealogy, and the Ismaʿilis asserted that the line of the imamate should be traced to Ismāʿīl, the son and designated successor of Jaʿfar al-Ṣādiq (d. 148/765). The Ismaʿilis maintained that even though Ismāʿīl had predeceased his father, the imamate remained in his line and was passed to his son Muḥammad. The founder of the Fatimid dynasty, ʿUbayd Allāh, thus claimed direct descent from Muḥammad b. Ismāʿīl and, ultimately, from the Prophet Muḥammad through ʿAlī and Fāṭima.

Although ʿUbayd Allāh's origins are obscure (and his lineage hotly contested by medieval polemicists), his history is known from the year 286/899, when he assumed leadership of the Ismaʿili movement in Syria. At that time, the movement acknowledged Muḥammad b. Ismāʿīl as the hidden imam and believed that he had not died but gone into concealment and would reappear as a messianic figure called "the rising" (*al-qāʾim*) or "the guide" (*al-mahdī*). According to early Ismaʿili doctrine, this messianic figure would abrogate the external religious law (*ẓāhir*) and reveal instead the esoteric and inner truths of true religion (*bāṭin*). Some considered ʿUbayd Allāh's claim to be the imam, and his assumption of the messianic title *al-mahdī*, as fraudulent. These dissenters considered ʿUbayd Allāh to be a usurper and split off under another leader, Ḥamdān Qarmaṭ; they became known as the Qarmatians.

ʿUbayd Allāh was then compelled to leave Syria, and he headed for North Africa, where an Ismaʿili missionary, Abū ʿAbd Allāh al-Shīʿī had already successfully proselytized the Kutāma Berbers of Ifriqiyya (modern-day Tunisia). With the support of the Kutāma, ʿUbayd Allāh al-Mahdī established the Fatimid state in North Africa in 296/909. He was succeeded by his son, who took the regnal title al-Qā'im, in 322/934. Al-Qā'im (r. 322–34/943–45) consolidated Fatimid power in North Africa by concluding an alliance with another Berber group, the Ṣanhāja. These were relatively quiet years, with the exception of a Berber rebellion led by the Kharijite insurgent Abū Yazīd; this was finally crushed by al-Manṣūr (r. 334–41/945–52), the third Fatimid caliph.

The accession of al-Muʿizz in 342/953 marked a turning point in the history of the Fatimid dynasty. After three previous attempts (twice by ʿUbayd Allāh, once by al-Qā'im), al-Muʿizz succeeded in conquering Egypt in 358/969. The relatively bloodless campaign was led by his general Jawhar, who founded a new capital city, Cairo. Several years later, al-Muʿizz moved his court from North Africa to Cairo, and Egypt remained the center of the Fatimid empire until the end of the dynasty.

Soon after the conquest, al-Muʿizz appointed Yaʿqūb b. Killis, a Jewish convert to Islam, as his chief administrator. He introduced a series of far-reaching administrative and fiscal reforms that included the establishment of a centralized system of tax collection. Al-Muʿizz also carried out a successful program of propaganda in the holy cities of Mecca and Medina, where local rulers recognized Fatimid rule until the eleventh century. However, he continued to face challenges from both the Qarmatians and the Buyids in Syria, and shortly before his death in 365/975, Syria fell to the Buyids.

The reign of his successor al-ʿAzīz (r. 365–86/975–96) was dominated by the ambition to control southern and central Syria, and in this period the Fatimid empire reached its greatest extent. In addition, Egypt itself flourished under al-ʿAzīz, who also introduced a series of military reforms. He fixed the rates of pay for his army and court personnel, and he brought Turkish slave troops into the army. These Turkish troops rose to prominence at the expense of the Berbers who had brought the Fatimids to power.

The Turks were often at odds with both the Berbers and new regiments of black slave troops, and factional strife continued to plague the Fatimid army.

Al-ʿAzīz was succeeded by al-Ḥākim (r. 386–411/996–1020), perhaps the best known Fatimid caliph. His reign has been the object of much study, and modern scholars have puzzled over his often erratic behavior. In a state that had been marked by its tolerance of Jews, Christians, and Sunnis, al-Ḥākim introduced numerous repressive measures against those groups. However, he often repealed those measures as suddenly as he announced them. His eccentricities were a source of encouragement to a small group who believed him to be an incarnation of divinity. This group, the Druze, believed that when he disappeared in 411/1020, he had gone into concealment and would return at a later time. It appears, however, that al-Ḥākim was the victim of a murder planned by his own sister, Sitt al-Mulk. She acted as regent for his son al-Ẓāhir (r. 411–27/1020–35), whose reign was marked by famine and unrest internally and by a series of foreign relations failures, most notably with the Byzantines.

The exceptionally long reign of al-Mustanṣir (r. 427–87/1035–94) did not provide much relief from the empire's problems. During his rule, Egypt was plagued by a series of low Niles resulting in intermittent famine for nearly twenty years and compelling the caliph to appeal to the Byzantine emperor for grain. These years also witnessed the eruption of Turkish and Sudanese slave soldier rivalry into open warfare, forcing the caliph to sell the contents of his treasuries in order to placate the troops. By 465/1073, the situation had deteriorated so much that al-Mustanṣir asked for help from the governor of Acre, Badr al-Jamālī, who held the title *amīr al-juyūsh* (commander of the armies).

Badr, a freed slave of Armenian origin, arrived in Egypt in 466/1074 and restored order in a matter of months. His arrival inaugurated the long period of rule by military wazirs that characterized the second century of Fatimid rule. Badr assumed leadership of the civil bureaucracy, the military, and the propaganda mission. After Badr, Fatimid wazirs were almost exclusively military officers, and they were the real rulers of the state.

Badr died in 487/1094, only a few months before the caliph al-Mustanṣir, and was succeeded in the wazirate by his son al-Afḍal. Al-Afḍal installed the younger son of al-Mustanṣir as the caliph al-Mustaʿlī (r. 487–95/1094–1101), and the supporters of the dispossessed elder son Nizār broke with the state. The Nizārīs never accepted the legitimacy of the Musta'lian line, and they worked actively (but unsuccessfully) to overthrow the Fatimid government. The short reign of al-Musta'lī was dominated by the Nizārī threat and by al-Afḍal's relatively successful attempts to recapture lost territories. In 495/1101, al-Afḍal raised a five-year-old son of al-Musta'lī to the throne. This caliph, al-Āmir (r. 495–524/1101–30), remained under the thumb of al-Afḍal until the latter's death in 515/1121.

The reign of al-Āmir saw the restoration of some of the power of the caliph, and al-Āmir ruled directly after imprisoning his wazir al-Ma'mūn al-Baṭā'iḥī in 519/1125. But al-Āmir's rule was challenged constantly by the Nizārīs, as well as by marauding Berber tribes. In 516/1122, he issued a public proclamation that asserted the legitimacy of the Musta'lian line, but in 524/1130 he was assassinated by the Nizārīs. At his death, al-Āmir left an infant son, al-Ṭayyib. A cousin of the late caliph, 'Abd al-Majīd, was named as regent by factions of the army. However, the son of al-Afḍal, Abū 'Alī Kutayfāt, overthrew the government, confiscated the palace treasuries, and imprisoned 'Abd al-Majīd. He also deposed the Fatimid line in favor of the expected imam of the Twelver Shi'is. Abū 'Alī Kutayfāt remained in power for a little over a year and was murdered in 526/1131. At that time, 'Abd al-Majīd was restored as regent; but the infant al-Ṭayyib had disappeared, and there was no apparent heir. 'Abd al-Majīd thus proclaimed himself the imam with the title al-Ḥāfiẓ (r. 524–44/1130–49). His authority was contested both by the Nizārīs, who opposed the Musta'lian line altogether, and by the Ṭayyibīs, who maintained that al-Ṭayyib was in concealment in the Yemen.

The last three Fatimid caliphs, al-Ẓāfir (r. 544–49/1149–54), al-Fā'iz (r. 549–55/1154–60), and al-'Āḍid (r. 555–66/1160–71), came from the Ḥāfiẓī line. All were children, and the state was controlled by powerful wazirs. The last few years of Fatimid rule were essentially a contest for power between generals and wazirs. The last wazir of the Fatimid caliphs was Saladin, best known to modern readers as the heroic figure who successfully fought the Crusaders. But he also dealt the final blow to the Fatimid caliphate. In 566/1171, Saladin had the name of the Abbasid caliph read in the mosques of Cairo for the first time in over two hundred years. A few days later, the last Fatimid caliph, al-'Āḍid died.

APPROACHING FATIMID RITUALS

This book is about Fatimid political culture in Egypt as it can be reconstructed from court rituals. Ritual stands at the center of this book. Although it is commonly said of Islam that it is an "orthopraxic" rather than an "orthodox" religion, few scholars have dedicated their energy to studies of Islamic ritual in the premodern period. To the extent that such studies have been undertaken, they have tended to focus on the prescriptions found in legal literature. The day-to-day ritual practices of Muslims have thus received little attention, and when they have been studied, it has ordinarily been from the point of view of "popular religion." This state of affairs is, on some level, understandable. The sources are generally unyielding when it comes to the daily lives of ordinary men and women. We might expect, then, that the situation would be different with respect to the history of the caliphates, where there are many court histories that record the details of the daily lives of men in power. And yet it has not been so.

The modern historiography of Islamic dynasties has had surprisingly little to say about ritual of any kind and almost nothing to say about political ritual. This may be because our understanding of political legitimacy in Islamic dynasties has been focused on the formal claims in investitures and proclamations that can be recovered in written documents. Thus, for example, we may look at polemics over genealogical claims or dream prophecies that we understand to be implicitly political. Or, we might look at certain prerogatives like naming the ruler in the Friday sermon (*khuṭba*) and minting coins (*sikka*) that explicitly assert a ruler's political claims. But we have not, by and large, looked at other ways in which a ruler's or dynasty's claims to authority might be articulated.

This book approaches ritual as a dynamic process through which claims to political and religious authority in Islamic societies may be articulated and in which complex negotiations of power may take place. Therefore, I am not looking at ritual in terms of its role as the vehicle for the fulfillment of the individual believer's obligations to God. Religious rituals in a political setting do, of course, fulfill such obligations. My interest here, however, is to discuss the ways in which ritual at the court was embedded in changing social and political realities and how court rituals responded to those changes. I will thus be arguing throughout this book that rituals have a multiplicity of meanings and functions that may conflict without being mutually exclusive and that change over time.

The study of political culture through ritual and ceremony is not new. Beginning with Marc Bloch and Ernst Kantorowicz, European historians recognized that ritual could articulate claims to royal authority, assert royal power, and express changing conceptions of the character of kingship.[1] As subsequent studies focused on the political functions and meanings of ritual symbols at court, historians began to question the meaning of religious symbols and the relationship between the sacred and social life.[2] Even more recently, historians have asked how ritual might express urban concerns.[3]

We may ask the same questions about Islamic dynasties, but we must do so in a very different context. European historians discuss ritual and ceremony in the context of a set of formal institutions and associations that provided stability and continuity in medieval and early modern European societies. Building blocks of the European sort, often described in terms of corporate identities, were generally not present in medieval Islamic societies. The continuity of social and political life in medieval Islamic societies, as Roy Mottahedeh has shown for the Buyid period, depended largely upon mutual ties of loyalty and obligation between individuals.[4]

How are we to understand court rituals in this context? First, we may look to ceremonies as a source of information about relationships of loyalty and obligation that are not discussed explicitly elsewhere. The tenth and eleventh centuries in the Islamic world were a time when men began to write systematically about the sources of political and religious authority. Al-Māwardī (d. 450/1058), for example, wrote *al-Aḥkām al-Sulṭāniyya* (The Rules of Government) in response to a compelling set of political circumstances: the fragmentation of the Abbasid empire, the rise of the petty principalities, and the loss of the caliph's political and military power. His work is an attempt to create a systematic framework for the delegation of political power, one that would preserve the religious authority and prestige of the caliphate. However, al-Māwardī does not discuss explicitly the formal ties between individuals that Mottahedeh distills and extracts from the historical chronicles. The actual operation of government depended upon those relationships of loyalty that cannot be accounted for in a work like *al-Aḥkām al-Sulṭāniyya*.

The writing of political theory was not the primary way in which medieval Muslim bureaucrats and administrators dealt with the problems of political authority and power. Relationships of authority were elaborately articulated in ceremonies. Ceremonies worked within a complex system of references that included both the theoretical sources of a ruler's authority (whether caliph, sultan, or amir) and the particular network of loyalties that made it possible for him to exercise his authority. Symbolic expressions of authority in ceremonies could take into account what a theoretical work (often written after the fact as an apologia) could not: the fluidity of social and political boundaries and commitments. And ceremonies could do what systematic theoretical accounts could not: negotiate power relationships and reshape political configurations. Thus, while we can learn from *al-Aḥkām al-Sulṭāniyya* about the theoretical structure of Abbasid government in the Buyid and Seljuk periods, we will probably learn more from *Rusūm dār al-khilāfa* (Protocol of the Caliphal Court), written by his contemporary Hilāl al-Ṣābi' (d. 448/1056), about how the caliph actually exercised his authority and wielded the power left to him.

The Fatimids shared the same cultural assumptions as other medieval Islamic rulers about the workings of government and, in particular, the obligations of the ruler to his subjects. As Isma'ilis, however, the Fatimids challenged the hegemony of the Abbasid caliphate, and they therefore had a stake in appropriating its most visible signs of authority. Fatimid insignia of sovereignty and protocol look very much like Abbasid insignia and protocol. The protocol of both caliphates asserted their claims to political and religious leadership of the community of believers as well as established the relative ranks of men at court who stood beneath the caliph. These contingent hierarchies, and the symbols of rank and authority that expressed them, are the primary focus of chapter 2.

For the Abbasids and the Fatimids both, the multiplication of symbols of authority occurred in a political context in which the relationship of religious and political authority was becoming increasingly complex. Whereas earlier in the history of the Islamic empire, contests for power occurred among dynasties with competing claims to caliphal authority, now these contests took place between caliphs and military powers who could make no claims at all to religious leadership. This contest over authority and power was played out in the Abbasid lands with the Buyids, Ghaznavids, and Seljuks. For the Fatimids, as for the Abbasids, the struggle to assert authority was directed not only against rival pretenders to the caliphate, but also against the military powers upon whom they relied and who relied, at least in theory, upon them for legitimacy. What emerged was a symbiosis in which the tensions inherent in this contest for power were never fully resolved. To be sure, many disputes were quite open. But they were as often lying just beneath the surface, operating as a sort of subtext to any ceremony and percolating to the surface as powerful men at both the Abbasid and the Fatimid courts attempted to appropriate ceremonial prerogatives and space for themselves.

If Fatimid and Abbasid insignia and ceremonial resemble each other so closely, then what made Fatimid ceremonial "Fatimid"? To begin with, it was the Fatimids who were doing it. This is by no means an obvious answer, for it tells us something about how generalized the symbols of authority were in the medieval Islamic world. Prerogatives, insignia, and protocol were appropriated by men who claimed political authority. The real question for us, then, is, how did the Fatimids invest these symbols with a meaning that was particularly their own? For the Isma'ili Fatimids, the world could be interpreted on many different levels. This is most often expressed in the tradition of allegorical interpretation of the Qur'an (*ta'wīl*) by the terms *ẓāhir* (external manifestation of phenomena) and *bāṭin* (esoteric meaning). As I will be discussing throughout this book, the Fatimids invested their ceremonies with multiple meanings that did not have to be, indeed were not intended to be, understood by all. We can see these multiple meanings at work most clearly in the celebration of the festival of Ghadīr Khumm. The Fatimids' formulation of a new relationship to their history and the distant 'Alid past in that ceremony is the central concern of chapter 6.

The most striking difference between Abbasid and Fatimid ceremonial, however, is the urban and processional character of Fatimid ceremonial. Abbasid caliphal ceremonies were static; they took place almost entirely in the palace. In fact, the two accounts we have of urban processions in the city of Baghdad are both processions of wazirs. The Abbasid caliphs clearly had a different conception of their capital city than did the Fatimids. From the beginning of the Fatimid period, Cairo was a setting for ceremonial. Although the Fatimids declared their aspirations to have the Friday sermon (*khuṭba*) read in their names in Baghdad, it is clear that Egypt was not merely a way station for them. This declaration has been taken literally by modern historians, who argue that the Fatimids never intended for Cairo to be their permanent capital. There is compelling evidence, however, to support a view that the Fatimids always intended Cairo to be their permanent capital. The desire to exercise the caliphal prerogative of *khuṭba* in Baghdad should not be taken as a statement of intent to move their capital. It means, simply, that the Fatimids challenged openly the authority of the rival Abbasids. Every caliphal dynasty had established its own capital in a geographically distinct region of the Islamic world: the Umayyads built Damascus, the Abbasids built Baghdad. There is no reason to think that the Fatimids would have felt any particular need to establish themselves in Baghdad. It was far more consistent with the culture of their times, and far more expeditious, for them to build a new capital that would, by definition, embody their authority.

The primary focus of chapter 3, therefore, is how the Fatimids articulated their claims to political and religious authority in the physical setting of their capital Cairo. By studying the history of the celebration of Ramaḍān and the Two Festivals, I argue that the Fatimids consciously constructed Cairo as an Isma'ili ritual city in the early years of Egyptian rule. This ritual city was constructed not only architecturally and topographically, but also ceremonially. The landscape could be, and was, reinterpreted as the Fatimids responded to changing political, religious, and social concerns. Thus, I would argue that Fatimid "court" ceremonies were as deeply embedded in the social and religious life of Cairo and Fustat as they were in more narrowly conceived concerns for political legitimacy, and by the twelfth century they had developed into a complex urban language.

This "urbanness" was equally characteristic of the ceremonies for the New Year and the inundation of the Nile. Chapter 4 discusses the history of the urban procession of the New Year in the twelfth century in terms of changes in the composition of the Fatimid army and the structure of Fatimid administration. Chapter 5 deals with the processions to cut the canal and perfume the Nilometer during the inundation of the Nile. In these processions, the Nile was incorporated into the urban landscape and commercial centers of Cairo and Fustat.

Fatimid ceremonies had other meanings, as well. They might communicate very particular pieces of information about individuals or groups in power. Or, as discussed in chapter 4, they could involve complicated negotiations of power. Even when there were no apparent changes in the organization of a procession, for example, new political configurations could change the meaning of a ceremony dramatically. The historicity of Fatimid ceremonial is, therefore, an important underlying theme of this book.

Each of the three major Mamluk historians of the Fatimid period wrote about ceremonies in a different context. Al-Qalqashandī (d. 821/1418) embedded his descriptions of Fatimid ceremonies (based entirely on the late Fatimid-early Ayyubid historian Ibn al-Ṭuwayr) in his systematic discussion of the organization of the Fatimid state.[5] Al-Maqrīzī (d. 845–46/1442), on the other hand, wrote about Fatimid ceremonial in his monumental topography,[6] where people and events, institutions and ceremonies, were incidental to street plans and buildings. Although he authored a chronicle of the Fatimid dynasty,[7] the long descriptions of ceremonies that he included in his topography are almost entirely missing from his history. Ibn Taghrī Birdī (d. 874–75/1470) reported these ceremonies in an abbreviated and rather unreliable account within the obituary of the caliph al-Muʿizz, whom he mistakenly credited with establishing them.[8]

Thus, the most important texts upon which this study depends reflect the sensibilities of men who wrote nearly three centuries after the fall of the Fatimid dynasty, and the original context of the descriptions has been lost. We do not know how the Fatimid historians themselves might have structured their discussion of court ceremonies. The longest and most detailed descriptions are those of Ibn al-Ṭuwayr, but we do not know how he organized his history of the Fatimids, what place ceremonial occupied in it, or what he thought the appropriate context for its discussion. What we do know is something of the Mamluk context in which these descriptions found a readership. The Mamluks had an intense and abiding interest in the ceremonial of previous Egyptian dynasties that matched their preoccupation with the ceremonial of their own court. But the social and political structure of the Mamluk empire differed dramatically from that of the Fatimids, and their understanding of Fatimid ceremonial must also have been very different. Most of what we know about Fatimid ceremonial has come to us from Mamluk texts that decontextualize and depoliticize the ceremonies, as they do much of Fatimid history.

A modern historian who wishes to repoliticize these ceremonies is working at cross-purposes with the Mamluk sources.

For this book is about how deeply political these rituals and ceremonies were. In other words, it is about precisely those things that made Fatimid ceremonial "Fatimid." Thus, it is an attempt to understand, through these rituals, something of how the Fatimids saw themselves in relation to other Islamic political powers, to the population they governed most directly in Cairo and Fustat, and to their own history; to discuss the character of the Fatimids' capital city, Cairo, in terms of social and political changes that left their mark on the city; and finally, to understand the dynamic relationship between politics, ritual, and urban life that gave shape and meaning to Fatimid rule.

CHAPTER 2

The Ceremonial Idiom

PROTOCOLS OF RANK

In the year 296/908–9, the Fatimid missionary (*dāʿī*) Abū ʿAbd Allāh al-Shīʿī conquered Ifriqiyya. He remained there for about three months to establish the administration before setting out for Sijilmāsa, whose governor was holding the Imam ʿUbayd Allāh al-Mahdī captive. The imam had sent one Abu'l-Qāsim al-Muṭṭalibī to identify Abū ʿAbd Allāh, whom he had never met. Abū ʿAbd Allāh and al-Muṭṭalibī besieged Sijilmāsa and demanded the imam's release. The governor refused and attacked, and another siege was staged. When he could hold out no longer, the governor sent out Ibn Bisṭām, a merchant, to negotiate an accord. Jaʿfar al-Ḥājib, the source for this story, describes how the negotiation began:[1]

> When Abū ʿAbd Allāh saw [Ibn Bisṭām] he dismounted, thinking him to be [the Imam ʿUbayd Allāh] al-Mahdī. Ibn Bisṭām also dismounted [out of respect] for the dismounting of Abū ʿAbd Allāh. Upon seeing this, Abū ʿAbd Allāh mounted his horse again and ignored him. Then Abū ʿAbd Allāh summoned Abu'l-Qāsim and said to him, "Stay at my right side and do not leave me, because this is why the Imam sent you to me. Had you been with me, I would not have dismounted for a common man."

Ibn Bisṭām assured Abū ʿAbd Allāh of al-Mahdī's well-being, but the siege continued until the governor released the Imam:

> As soon as the Imam al-Mahdī appeared, Ibn al-Muṭṭalibī said to Abū ʿAbd Allāh, "This is my master and yours, and the master [*mawlā*] of all the people." Abū ʿAbd Allāh then dismounted, and so did Ibn al-Muṭṭalibī and the troops. He kissed the ground and they did also; he continued kissing the ground, and [the troops] kissed the ground behind him, until he had prostrated himself before the hoofs of al-Mahdī's horse. Then he lifted up his head and kissed the stirrup of al-Mahdī.[2]

This episode was an elaborate dialogue in which the relative ranks of the parties involved were ascertained and acknowledged. Dismounting as a sign of respect was a well-established Near Eastern tradition. When Abū ʿAbd Allāh dismounted in expectation of seeing the Imam, Ibn Bisṭām also dismounted, revealing that Abū ʿAbd Allāh had humbled himself to a man who was his inferior. When al-Mahdī finally appeared, Abū ʿAbd Allāh, having found the proper object of veneration, became the model of a man paying homage. But this dialogue was carried out in silence, and the language that was used was not speech but protocol.

There was a rich vocabulary available in Arabic to express the ideas inherent in the notion of protocol. The term *rusūm*, meaning "protocol" or "ceremonies," is fundamentally something that is prescribed; it is also the term used for the portions that officials at court received on festivals.[3] Hilāl al-Ṣābi' used the terms *rusūm* and *marāsim* in his account of the rules, regulations, and protocol of the Abbasid court,[4] where they had a range of meanings that reflects other usages. By far the most common term, however, is *adab*, the ubiquitous and comprehensive Arabic term that reveals a preoccupation with all of the forms of human behavior.

As a concept of human behavior, *adab* found expression in a genre of literature called by the same name.[5] This literature ranged from manuals of instruction for judges, scribes, and wazirs to treatises on the manners, morals, and customs of kings and caliphs.[6] As a section of a larger work (e.g., of jurisprudence), it might comprise regulations for those aspects of daily life in which one's comportment was most on display: eating, drinking, or dressing. There was nothing that a man did that did not, in some way, reveal his innate character as well as his station in life. In societies where social and political continuity depended largely on the personal bonds established between individuals, *adab* played a critical role as a means of determining character, forming social relationships, and negotiating political bonds.[7]

At court, the gestures, salutes, and acts of homage dictated by protocol were the building blocks of ceremonies: prostration, kissing the ground, addressing the ruler in the prescribed manner, mounting and dismounting at designated places and times. These highly disciplined and prescribed acts composed an idiom that was used by all Islamic dynasties of the time in conjunction with prerogatives like naming the ruler in the Friday sermon (*khuṭba*), minting and inscribing the ruler's name on coinage (*sikka*), and titulature to lay claim to both political and religious authority. What we would call "formal political theory" was never a privileged genre of writing in the Islamic world, and such treatises often did not reflect actual changes in political culture. But men of letters continued to write *adab*, and changing ideas about rulership were articulated in the idiom of protocol and ceremonial.[8] The protocol of the courts expressed symbolically a developing set of assumptions about authority, rule, and rulers that was not fully articulated in written texts until the eleventh century. Even after the formal theories of political authority had been elaborated, they did not displace the importance of protocol.

One of the fundamental assumptions of Islamic protocol was the notion that God was the only absolute ruler, before whom all believers were equal. But the spiritual egalitarianism of Islam carried no expectation of social equality. Among believers, differences in social station and rank were assumed to exist, yet after God, all rank was understood as being relative. It was critical that people knew and acknowledged these differences in rank. Thus, protocol communicated critical information about the structure of society and hierarchy at its center, at the court.[9] This information was encoded not only in markers like titles, but also in the elaborate protocol of homage and salute, which signified both the position of the caliph above all other men and the ranks of individuals relative to each other.[10]

In general, the phrases *al-adab fi'l-salām* and *adab al-khidma* designate in the broadest sense the protocol to be observed in the presence of the caliph or king. More specifically, the two terms *al-salām* and *al-khidma* denote a disciplined sequence of gestures that can best be rendered as "salute" or "homage." The two terms almost always appear in the texts in this more specific sense. Although the sources discuss the general requirements of protocol in chapters on saluting and paying homage, they are also treated in detail separately.[11]

The *adab* or "protocol" of the Fatimid court was much like that of contemporary Islamic dynasties, most particularly that of the Abbasid caliphs. The prescribed deportment of those attending the caliph is almost identical in the three major *adab* works of the Abbasid and Fatimid periods. Those in attendance are exhorted to stand up straight and still, not to fidget, and to maintain absolute silence unless spoken to by the caliph.[12] Then they are to answer in a low, but clear, voice.[13] They must fix their attention on the caliph, not allowing anything to distract them.[14] They must maintain a dignified bearing at all times, refraining from laughter even if there is cause for it.[15] They must not say or do anything to annoy or offend the caliph.[16] On the other hand, they are to avoid praising those in the caliph's disfavor.[17] There may not be any arguments or disagreements in the caliph's presence, nor may there be any response to a slanderous remark.[18] The caliph's mistakes are not to be corrected except by allusion, and while it is permissible to recite the good qualities and deeds of previous caliphs, kings, and imams, there can be no implicit criticism of the present ruler in doing so.[19] No one should share a secret with someone else, nor should anyone else allow himself to overhear a confidence of the caliph.[20] Finally, ignorance of the rules of protocol is no excuse for violating them.[21]

Although Fatimid and Abbasid practices were nearly identical, they were not interpreted in the same way. The Abbasid treatises *Kitāb al-tāj* and *Rusūm dār al-khilāfa* view strict protocol in the presence of the caliph or king as a necessary and desirable form of respect. In Isma'ili thought, the well-established rules of protocol assumed an additional dimension. Al-Qāḍī al-Nu'mān (d. 363/974), the Fatimid jurist and ideologue, places protocol squarely in the context of religious devotion. In his treatise, *Kitāb al-himma*, al-Qāḍī al-Nu'mān likens standing before the imam to prayer, thus raising it to the level of a religious duty. It is not surprising, then, that the postures permissible in the presence of the imam were the postures of prayer. His chapter on standing and sitting in the presence of the imam opens: "Standing before the imams who are the friends [*awliyā'*] of God for one who recognizes their rightful position, believes in their imamate, and believes that standing before them glorifies them and exalts their rank is a religious devotion ['*ibāda*] by which one comes nearer to God, who has made glorification and exaltation [of the imams] an obligation, just as standing in prayer before God on high glorifies him."[22]

Thus, the protocol that in an Abbasid context symbolized merely the relative ranks of men symbolized in a Fatimid Isma'ili context the glorification of God. In contrast to the explicit directions that open the chapters of the Abbasid texts *Kitāb al-tāj* and *Rusūm dār al-khilāfa* dealing with protocol in the ruler's presence, the corresponding chapter in the Fatimid *Kitāb al-himma* opens with the Isma'ili prescription that glorification of the imams is a form of obedience to God.[23] This was the primary argument advanced by Al-Qāḍī al-Nuʿmān to defend the custom of kissing the ground before the imam: "Glorification of the Imams, blessings of God upon them, is a form of glorification of God, provided the intent in glorifying [the imams] is obedience to God and its aim is the pleasure of God, who has no partner."[24] Al-Qāḍī al-Nuʿmān went further in his argument:

> We have seen the legates and crown princes [of the imams] kiss the ground as a salute to them, revering them, knowing their rank, and understanding what God has made incumbent on their behalf. Their adherents are the most worthy of whomever imitates them in that practice and seeks God's favor by glorifying his friends [*awliyā'*] and they are neither haughty nor arrogant. The rabble and the riffraff and the masses of people reject this, regarding it as a prostration to them, not to God [*sujūdan min dūn allāh lahum*] . . . Prostration has an essence [*ḥaqīqa*] beyond kissing the ground. He whose study comes from [real] knowledge . . . does not regard whoever kisses the ground in his prayers as having prostrated himself until he comes to the essence of the prostration [*sujūd*], that is, until his nose and forehead [touch the ground], his having declared his intention to perform the prostration. Therefore, if someone prostrated himself before one of the friends [*awliyā'*] of God, [intending it to be] a glorification of God, that would not be wrong [*munkar*].

He specified, however, that certain prostrations (for example, those of Zoroastrians) were forbidden because these people did not acknowledge God. Al-Qāḍī al-Nuʿmān continued, "We are not saying that we [should] prostrate ourselves before [the imams], nor that they have commanded us to prostrate ourselves before them, but rather that kissing the ground upon which they tread is a greater glorification of them than kissing their hand."[25]

If the imam ordered one to sit, he should accept it as a sign of the imam's beneficence toward him, not as his due.[26] Standing before the imam was itself a great honor, and sitting in his presence was neither preferable nor more intimate, at least in theory. The posture was like that of prayer: one bent forward and cast his glance to the ground as a mark of awe and respect.[27] He let his hands either hang down at his sides or placed the left inside the right, just under the chest.[28] He was not to look around, fidget, or play with his hands.[29] If the imam ordered him to sit down, he did so in an alert posture, neither firmly seated nor cross-legged.[30] It was permissible, however, for him to raise one leg while sitting on the other and to support himself with his hands, placing them on his knees.[31]

In theory, it was incumbent upon anyone entering the imam's presence first to salute him and then to kiss the ground before him (*yabda'a bi'l-salām ʿalayhī thumma yuqabbilu al-arḍ bayna yadayhi*). Al-Qāḍī al-Nuʿmān prescribed not only the salute, but also its meaning: one must believe this to be a glorification of the imam and a way of seeking God's favor. The salute consisted of the formula, "Peace be upon the Commander of the Faithful, and God's mercy and blessing" (*al-salām ʿalayka yā amīr al-mu'minīn wa-raḥmatu allāh wa-barakātuh*). If the person saluting was in a position to hear the imam return the greeting (*radd al-imām ʿalayhi al-salām*), he did not kiss the ground until the imam had finished speaking; then he would fall to the ground, kiss it, and stand up.[32]

Actual practice at the Fatimid court, however, indicates that different forms of salute and homage were tied to rank. The verbal salute seems to have been limited to the highest ranking officials, and in the late Fatimid period, the formula was apparently reserved for the exclusive use of the chief qadi.[33] The most complete information about the meaning of the term *al-adab fi'l-salām* in late Fatimid times appears in Ibn al-Ṭuwayr's description of the general audiences held on Mondays and Thursdays by the caliphs:

> When everything was in order and everyone was in his place, the chief qadi and the witnesses paid homage first by offering the salute [*li'l-khidma bi'l-salām*]. The chief chamberlain (lit., "master of the door") brought the qadi across [the threshold] without his entourage [*yūjizu ṣāḥib al-bāb al-qāḍī dūn man maʿahu*] and the qadi saluted in the manner prescribed by protocol [*fa-yusallimu muta'addiban*] and stood close by. The meaning of *al-adab fi'l-salām* is that he raises his right hand, points his index finger and says in an audible voice, "Peace be upon you, O Commander of the Faithful, and God's mercy and blessing (*al-salām ʿalā amīr al-mu'minīn wa-raḥmatu allāh wa-barakātuh*)." He alone is distinguished by this formula among those who may salute the caliph.[34]

A similar formula was reportedly used by the chief qadi during the Ramaḍān prayer. After the call to prayer for the noon prayer, the qadi entered the caliph's prayer chamber (*maqṣūra*),[35] saying, "Peace be upon the Commander of the Faithful, the descendant of the Prophet, the judge (the preacher), and God's mercy and blessing; to prayer, may God have mercy upon you [*al-salām ʿalā amīr al-mu'minīn al-sharīf al-qāḍī (al-khaṭīb) wa-raḥmatu allāh wa-barakātuh; al-ṣalāta yarḥamuka allāh*]."[36] Finally, in the palace procession on the occasion of Ghadīr Khumm, a late Fatimid ceremony, the qadi emerged from the gate of the Martyrium of Ḥusayn (*al-mashhad al-ḥusaynī*) after the caliph arrived there for "the salute and homage" (*li'l-khidma wa'l-salām ʿalayhi*) by offering the salute and then kissing the foot nearest to him.[37] On the Festival of Fast Breaking (*ʿīd al-fiṭr*), the qadi ascended the minbar, kissing each step as he proceeded, until he reached the third step and waited for further instructions to continue. When summoned, he removed a scroll from his sleeve, kissed it, and placed it on his head to ascend to the top of the minbar.[38]

The wazir offered both verbal salutes and physical demonstrations of homage, although we are not told precisely what formula he used. In the audiences held on Mondays and Thursdays, the wazir saluted after entering, then kissed the caliph's hands and feet, retreated about three cubits, and after standing for a while was ordered to sit on the caliph's right. He repeated the same sequence when leaving.[39] On other occasions, he might kiss the ground,[40] the caliph's feet,[41] or his stirrup,[42] either as a single act of homage or as part of a series of acts of homage.

The wazir's salute could indicate not only his rank relative to other men at court, but also his power vis-à-vis the caliph. In the twelfth century, when the wazir's power eclipsed the caliph's authority, wazirs paid homage on some occasions by making gestures almost as minimal as the caliph's. In the New Year's procession, for example, he is reported as having paid homage by touching the ground (or gesturing toward it) three times.[43] In the same procession, he bowed his head toward the caliph in salute when passing him. Similarly, he gestured as if to kiss the ground during the Nile procession. In both of these cases from the late Fatimid period, the caliph returned the salute with a slight gesture.[44] Thus, the wazir's position as well as his power were expressed through what was almost an abstraction of kissing the ground.

Lesser officials were allowed on occasion to kiss the threshold of the caliph's audience hall (*majlis*), perhaps indicating that they were not actually admitted into the room.[45] Byzantine ambassadors usually paid homage by kissing the ground.[46] In the late Fatimid period, when audiences were held to receive embassies of foreign powers, envoys were met and hosted by the chief chamberlain (*ṣāḥib al-bāb*) and his lieutenant (*nā'ib*).[47] They prevented anyone from meeting with them. When he received permission to present the envoy, the chief chamberlain escorted him, holding his right hand, while the lieutenant held his left.[48] One hundred years earlier, al-Musabbiḥī (d. 420/1029) reported the reception of an envoy from Khurasan:

> On Saturday . . . the Commander of the Faithful [al-Ẓāhir] sat in state in the Gold Hall after it was decorated and carpeted with brocade drapes and beautiful gold curtains. All of the galleries were hung with drapes and covered with rugs. The amirs and the Turks were summoned and ordered to put on their finest clothes, all of gold embroideries and precious brocades. The Kutāma and the soldiers [*junūd*] were ordered to bear their special ceremonial arms. As the people entered together, the Amir Shams al-mulk stood to the right of the throne; the rest of those attending and the slaves of the dynasty stood, as did the nobles. No one sat before the caliph . . . The envoy from Khurasan arrived with a small son of his. He entered and kissed the ground [in deference] to the Commander of the Faithful, who ordered that he be taken all around the palaces, and it was done. The caliph rose, and the people left.[49]

Public homage was both a sign of reverence for the caliph and a mark of rank. Ibn ʿAmmār, wazir to the caliph al-Ḥākim, held audiences in which the people received are described as "being among those who virtually kiss the ground, those who kiss the stirrup, and those who kiss the knee."[50] Officials who carried the insignia of sovereignty had the particular distinction of being summoned by their epithets and kissing the ground.[51] Those of high rank received the privilege of humbling themselves before the imam. Even then, ranks or degrees were observed in keeping with a man's status. An even greater privilege could be granted, however, by allowing a particularly eminent official to pay homage in private. The Fatimid wazir al-Ma'mūn b. al-Baṭā'iḥī paid homage to the caliph in private. This concession to the wazir's high rank actually highlighted the caliph's dependence upon his court officials, the real governors of his state.

Rank and power were also indicated by proximity to the caliph. Proximity to the ruler was a way of establishing authority.[52] Ibn Muyassar, reporting on the events surrounding the Nizārī schism, relates:

> They [the supporters of al-Mustaʿlī] also pointed out that when al-Mustanṣir, at a perilous juncture of his reign, sent his sons to the army, he took care to make the following arrangement: Abū ʿAbd Allāh was sent to Acre to the army commanded by Amīr al-juyūsh [Badr al-Jamālī]; Abū al-Qāsim to Ascalon; and Nizār to the port of Damietta: the higher the rank of each son, the nearer to the capital he was to be stationed. And on this occasion, al-Mustaʿlī was not even allowed to quit the palace.[53]

In view of both the honor and the significance inherent in proximity to the caliph, the powerful wazir al-Afḍal must have felt bold, indeed, when he moved his residence from Cairo to Fustat in 500/1106–7. There could not have been a more blatant assertion of his independence as a ruler. He even presumed to call the new residence "Seat of the Kingdom" (*dār al-mulk*). His sons broke with him and remained in "Seat of the Wazirate" (*dār al-wizāra*), the Cairo residence that their grandfather, Badr al-Jamālī, had occupied.[54] In a show of modesty, the Christian scribe, Abū Naṣr ibn ʿAbdūn, reputedly rode at the end of a caliphal procession rather than closer to the imam (as he was entitled), and justified his action by saying, "The likes of me should not accompany the Commander of the Faithful any closer than that."[55] In each of these cases, proximity to or distance from the caliph signified something slightly different. For Mustaʿlian apologists, al-Mustaʿlī's confinement in the palace provided necessary proof that he was the legitimate heir to al-Mustanṣir's authority. For the wazir al-Afḍal, distance from the palace was necessary to assert his own authority. For the Christian scribe, self-imposed distance from the caliph in a procession allowed him both to honor the caliph and to avert the conventional complaint that Jews and Christians had risen too high in the Fatimid government. Thus, broader social tensions could also be articulated in the protocol of the court.

Proximity was not the only consideration in spatial arrangements. Wazirs and qadis, heirs apparent and lesser sons, were usually stationed at the caliph's side during audiences and processions. Sitting on the caliph's right was a privilege of the highest order. It was so important that in the epistle written during the reign of al-Āmir to refute the Nizārī claims to the imamate, the major piece of evidence introduced to prove the legitimacy of al-Mustaʿlī's succession was the fact of his having been seated on the imam al-Mustanṣir's right during his (al-Mustaʿlī's) wedding celebration.[56] Changes in seating to the right of the caliph also indicated broader shifts in the configuration of political power during the course of the two Fatimid centuries. In the first audience held by the imam al-Mahdī in North Africa, his successor al-Qā'im was seated to his right, while Ṭayyib and Muslim, two fellow prisoners in Sijilmāsa, stood removed at the left and right by two paces.[57] By the late Fatimid period, when wazirs had assumed political power, they had all but displaced members of the caliph's family in the honored position to his right.

Like the protocol of homage and spatial relations, riding mounts also asserted the superiority of the caliph while marking differences in rank among his followers. For most men, the price of a horse was prohibitive, and ordinary men generally rode mules.[58] Riding horses was a prerogative of the elite, and mounts—like clothing, jewels, and other precious objects—often were given to favored officials. Gifts between rulers usually included several horses with heavily ornamented saddles. Riding a horse that had been ridden by the caliph, receiving a mount from his stable, or receiving permission to enter the city gates mounted were all prerogatives granted and revoked by the ruler.[59]

Dismounting in the presence of a superior was a one-sided act of homage that acknowledged the existing hierarchy. When the Buyid amir ʿAḍud al-dawla received the title *Tāj al-milla* (crown of the religious community) from the Abbasid caliph in 367/977, he requested the following privileges: to enter the courtyard of the palace mounted on his horse "as a special mark of distinction by which his honored position would be known; for a curtain to be hung so that no one would see the caliph before he did. But what was intended by that was that no one should see him kiss the ground before the caliph." The caliph granted these bold requests: the curtains were hung and the amir paid homage in private. But the request to enter the courtyard mounted was too audacious to be allowed in fact, even if granted in principle, so the caliph had a barrier of baked brick and clay built across the threshold of the courtyard, forcing the amir to dismount before entering.[60] Even when the caliph intended to honor a man of especially high status or achievement, dismounting within the palace grounds was *de rigeur*. When the Fatimid amir ʿAbd Allāh, a son of the caliph al-Muʿizz, returned to Cairo after a successful battle against the Qarmatians in Ramaḍān 363/973–74, he was shaded by a parasol (*miẓalla*), ordinarily a caliphal prerogative. Al-Muʿizz received him sitting under a dome (*qubba*) over the gate of the palace. As soon as ʿAbd Allāh saw his father, he dismounted and kissed the ground, and his troops dismounted. In this instance, as in others, the troops always dismounted along with their commander, but they were not given the privilege of kissing the ground.[61]

On occasion, the caliph conferred the prerogative of having others dismount for a high dignitary or official. When Ibn ʿAmmār was invested with the office of intermediary (*wasāṭa*) in 386/997–98, people were ordered to dismount for him.[62] The following year, Ibn ʿAmmār entered the palace mounted, crossed the hall of the ministries and entered the door at which the caliph's personal servants sat, and rode to the door of the room in which al-Ḥākim himself sat, where he dismounted. While it was the custom under the Fatimids for wazirs to ride into the palace and dismount at a designated spot (called the "passage of the wazirate" [*maqṭaʿ al-wizāra*]), it is unusual for this place to have been so close to the caliph. Once again, proximity to the ruler, combined with another prerogative, that of remaining mounted, became a powerful statement of rank.[63] But the honor was as precarious as the office; in the same year, Ibn ʿAmmār was dismissed from his post, banished from Cairo, and placed under house arrest.[64] His successor, Barjawān, abolished the practice of dismounting for the wazir.[65] Near the end of the reign of al-Ḥākim, there was a general prohibition against anyone entering the city of Cairo mounted.[66] Later in the Fatimid period, the intense rivalry between the wazir al-Afḍal and Abū al-Manṣūr Nizār, which resulted in al-Afḍal's raising Nizār's younger brother to the imamate as the caliph al-Mustaʿlī, was expressed on one occasion in a hostile encounter between the two men over the issue of riding on the palace grounds. Upon seeing al-Afḍal enter one of the palace gates mounted, Nizār shouted contemptuously, "Dismount, you dirty Armenian!"[67]

SYMBOLS OF AUTHORITY

Insignia of sovereignty, as symbols of the caliph's authority, were significant not only because of the complex associations that their histories had given them.[68] They were special because they touched the caliph, and objects belonging to the caliph were accorded the same respect as the caliph himself. The close association between the insignia of sovereignty and the person of the caliph is also emphasized by the fact that these objects do not seem to have been used to stand in for the caliph. That is, much of their signficance lies in the fact that they were used in association with the caliph, in his presence.

There does not seem to have been a distinctive set of principles or theory guiding the use of the insignia of sovereignty, which are referred to by different terms in the sources.[69] The Mamluk author al-Qalqashandī (d. 821/1418), in a section entitled "The Signs of Caliphate" (*Shiʿār al-khilāfa*), lists the following insignia of sovereignty of the Abbasid caliphs: the seal (*khātam*),[70] mantle of the Prophet (*burda*),[71] caliphal garments (*thiyāb al-khilāfa*), the staff (*qaḍīb*),[72] and color (*lawn*). In the eleventh century Abbasid text *Rusūm dār al-khilāfa*, however, there is no chapter dealing with a single category of objects associated with the caliph's authority. What later writers call the "insignia of sovereignty" are mentioned there in a chapter entitled, "The Audiences of the Caliphs; What They Wear in Processions; and What Dignitaries and All Other Classes Wear When they Enter into Their Presence."[73] This chapter discusses in detail the costume of the Abbasid caliph. It mentions the Prophet's sword (*sayf al-nabī*), mantle (*burda*), and staff (*qaḍīb*) as part of his costume, which also consisted of a long-sleeved black garment, a black high tiara (*ruṣāfiyya*) on his head, and red boots. In front of him, there was a copy of the Qur'an of ʿUthmān. In Abbasid times, the objects that were later referred to as "insignia of sovereignty" were classified as a part of the entire costume of the caliph. The seal (*khātam*) was not considered to be part of the caliph's costume, and it is mentioned only in the chapter "The Paper Used in Writing to or from the Caliphs, the Envelopes Used to Hold Letters to or from [them], and the Seals Used in Them."[74] Other prerogatives, such as pronouncing the caliph's name in the Friday sermon (*khuṭba*), beating drums at prayer time, titles, and various formulae used in correspondence, were discussed separately in the Abbasid manual. The last category, epistolary formulae, receives a disproportionate amount of attention, since much of the discussion of court protocol was embedded in encyclopedic literature produced by and for scribes (*kuttāb*).

Al-Qalqashandī's discussion of the Fatimid insignia of sovereignty is equally problematic. His account relies exclusively on late Fatimid sources, and like his descriptions of ceremonies, is organized by anachronistic Mamluk categories. His "systematic" discussion appears in the section entitled "On Royal Instruments Especially for Grand Processions."[75] The term *royal instruments* reflects al-Qalqashandī's perception of the Fatimids as temporal rulers with no claims to religious authority, although he refers to them often as *al-khulafā'* (caliphs). His comprehensive list includes the crown (*tāj*), staff (*qaḍīb al-mulk*), sword (*al-sayf al-khāṣṣ*), inkstand (*dawāt*), lance (*rumḥ*), shield (*daraqa*), *ḥāfir* (crescent-shaped ruby placed on the head of the caliph's mount), banners (*a'lām*), flywhisks (*midhabba*), various arms (*silāḥ*), drums (*naqqāra*), and tents (*khiyām, fasāṭīṭ*). He makes no distinction among different types of symbols, makes no mention of titulature or the prerogatives of pronouncing the caliph's name in the Friday sermon (*khuṭba*) and inscribing his name on coins (*sikka*), and does not discuss caliphal costuming or color in this section, which is dedicated to insignia of sovereignty. In fact, the available descriptions from earlier Fatimid sources raise questions about the reliability of al-Qalqashandī's discussion of insignia. His discussion is based on Ibn al-Ṭuwayr's (d. 617/1220) descriptions of late Fatimid New Year's and Nile inundation processions. Although it is not possible from the fragmentary evidence of earlier sources to establish a reliable chronology of early Fatimid insignia, it is clear that not all of these symbols appeared in every procession or audience.

The Fatimid *tāj* was not a crown per se but rather a turban (*'imāma*) wound in a distinctive fashion.[76] The style in which it was wound was as significant as the material used, a fact reflected by vocabulary. It is described as the "noble crown" (*al-tāj al-sharīf*) and the "winding of majesty" (*shaddat al-waqār*).[77] This crown was surmounted by a solitaire (*al-yatīma*).[78] The servant who wound this turban was called "winder of the crown" (*shādd al-tāj*), a particularly high rank ("[because he] touches what surmounts the crown of the caliph") that was always held by a eunuch.[79] The term *tāj*, however, is often not used in early descriptions of Fatimid ceremonies. The historian al-Musabbiḥī (d. 420/1029), for example, invariably uses the term *'imāma* when referring to the caliph's turban.[80]

The parasol (*miẓalla*), also a symbol of majesty, always matched the fabric of the caliph's costume.[81] The use of the parasol seems to have been associated particularly with lineage and succession. After defeating the Qarmatians, 'Abd Allāh, the son of the caliph al-Mu'izz paraded past the gate of the palace under the parasol.[82] When al-Mu'izz died, his death was concealed until the Sacrificial Festival (*'īd al-naḥr*), when his successor al-'Azīz rode in procession to the mosque under the parasol and pronounced the Friday sermon (*khuṭba*) in his own name.[83] The parasol was carried over the heir apparent Manṣūr during the Ramaḍān procession of 383/993, while the caliph al-ʿAzīz rode without its shade.[84] The parasol seems also to have symbolized the palace, which was itself associated with the Fatimid lineage. Within the confines of the palace walls, no parasol was carried.[85] However, when the caliph left the palace in procession, he carried the parasol, and upon his return, he inevitably entered the dynastic tomb (*al-turba al-muʿizziyya*). He would have visited it, then, on the two festivals, i.e., the Festival of Fast Breaking and the Sacrificial Festival, and the Fridays of Ramaḍān (mentioned explicitly in al-Maqrīzī) and, by implication, after the processions on the New Year and the Opening of the Canal.[86]

The insignia of sovereignty did not always appear together, and the textual evidence of their use is uneven. It is difficult to determine whether the inconsistencies reflect different practices, textual corruptions, or simply a certain arbitrariness in the reporting of insignia. For example, the account of the caliph al-Ẓāhir's procession to the Azhar Mosque on one Friday in Ramaḍān 415/1024–25, includes a description of his costume and parasol but does not mention any other symbols of authority.[87] In an account of his procession two weeks later, to the Anwar Mosque (known also as the Mosque of al-Ḥākim), not only are the costume and parasol described, but a jewelled staff (*al-qaḍīb al-jawhar*) is also mentioned.[88] On the first of Shawwāl 415/1024, the caliph rode in procession to the open prayer ground (*muṣallā*) under a parasol with heavy gold fringes, and he carried a staff, sword, and lance.[89]

By the late Fatimid period, there appears to have been a more explicit hierarchy of insignia, and these symbols of authority appeared together in the processions for the inundation of the Nile and the New Year, in a review the day before the processions, and on other occasions. According to the account of Ibn al-Ma'mūn al-Baṭā'iḥī (d. 588/1192) the caliph rode in procession to the prayer ground (*muṣallā*) in costume with a banner, a turban surmounted by a jewel, and the staff; the wazir carried the sword and the lance. The selection of the costume was now incorporated into the ceremonial. The entire outfit would be brought out, including the caliph's costume, the parasol, standards and banners, the sword and lance, the shield. On the day of the procession itself, the most important insignia would be assembled and given to their porters: parasol, sword, and inkstand. These three insignia were carried closest to the caliph during the procession. The caliph carried the staff (*qaḍīb al-mulk*) himself.[90]

All things associated with the caliph were accorded the same reverence as the caliph himself. This included all of the material signs of authority like the insignia of sovereignty, the gates and doors of the palace, and the palace grounds. We have seen, for example, how officials might dismount and kiss the palace gates. During the New Year's and Nile processions, the bearers of some of the insignia of sovereignty lowered the tops of their turbans in deference to the caliph.[91] The same respect extended to the caliph's name. Several caliphal prerogatives involved inscribing or publicly pronouncing his name: *khuṭba, sikka*, and *ṭirāz* (inscribing the ruler's name in textiles). Although it is not prescribed in protocol manuals, there are at least three instances in the literature of qadis who kissed the ground upon hearing the name of the caliph while proclamations of appointment were being read aloud.[92] Officials also kissed the caliph's signature in documents.[93]

Also like material symbols of authority, the use of the caliph's name was restricted in his presence.[94] It is common to read in manuals of protocol that one should not use a man's personal name (*ism*) if it is the same as the caliph's. Since names in Islamic societies are complex constructions, usually with five distinct parts, it is possible to address men in several different ways. Furthermore, a man was not to use his *kunya* (a name designating a person as father [*abū*] or mother [*umm*]) in the caliph's presence unless he was of very high rank and the caliph had honored him with permission to use his *kunya*.[95] The *kunya* was often used as an honorific name by elites. Thus, restricting use of the *kunya* in the caliph's presence reproduced more general social differences and further marked the contingent hierarchy in which the caliph stood at the top.[96]

Certain titles, like *al-sayyid* and *al-sharīf* (both used to refer to members of the Prophet's family) were restricted only to the caliph in his presence. In the year 363/973–74, the caliph al-Muʿizz held an audience with the descendants of the Prophet (*ashrāf*, sing. *sharīf*), governors, commanders, and the rest of the notables of Kutāma. Someone addressed one of the *ashrāf*, saying, "Sit down, O Sharīf," to which one of the Kutāma replied, "Is there anyone else in the world besides our master (*mawlāna*) who is noble (*sharīf*)? We will kill whoever claims it."[97] However many other men may have used the same name or title as the caliph when removed from his presence, it was exclusively his when he was present.

The prerogatives that belonged to the caliph were also his to confer on others. His symbols of authority could be used, like protocol, to establish differences in rank among elites, and between elites and common men. In this society, symbols of authority were self-referential in terms of the relative hierarchy. Powerful wazirs thus enjoyed some of the symbols of authority and high rank. They had their own banners and ceremonial weapons, rode horses outfitted with heavily ornamented saddles and stirrups, and wore ostentatious costumes. In the later Fatimid period, as in the later Abbasid period, some of these prerogatives became so diffuse that it is easy to forget the original intent in conferring them. Officials were laden with robes of honor (*khilʿa*, pl. *khilaʿ*) on almost every ceremonial occasion, had access to the caliphal treasuries, and enjoyed a multitude of titles. By the eleventh century, political observers lamented that titles had become so devalued that high officials often carried as many as a dozen to reflect their rank.

People coveted these objects belonging to the caliph not only for the honor and rank that they conferred, but also for their power to transmit blessing and grace (*baraka*). From the beginning to the end of the Fatimid period, in North Africa and Egypt, elite and common people alike sought some share in the caliph's *baraka*. Proximity to the caliph was one way of receiving some of his *baraka*. The homeless mother of a Fatimid adherent requested permission to buy a home close to the caliph's residence because of the *baraka* in being near to him.[98] The sight of the caliph also conveyed *baraka*: when the wazir al-Afḍal died, his successor, al-Ma'mūn b. al-Baṭā'iḥī, advised the caliph to appear before the army, seated in the belvedere above the gate of the palace, because of the *baraka* that would accrue to the troops.[99]

Food was an even more potent instrument for transferring *baraka*. During the banquet for the New Year, the caliph distributed food with his own hands, the recipient kissed it, made a gesture as if to eat it, and then placed it in his sleeve for the *baraka*. When all those present had filled their sleeves, the wazir said, "There is no fault in anyone taking anything from this place; rather, he will derive honor and distinction from it (*al-sharaf wa'l-*

mīza)."[100] In an account of the procession at the inundation of the Nile, *sharaf* (honor) and *baraka* are associated again in relation to food taken from the caliph's palace.[101] An even wider distribution of the food from the caliph's table occurred after the banquets during Ramaḍān, when those present took food from the banquet table (*simāṭ*) and distributed it to the people of Cairo.[102]

The ruler's clothing also conveyed *baraka*. A man asked for a garment (*thawb*) of the caliph's to use as a funeral shroud, because of its *baraka*.[103] Later, the caliphal *ṭirāz* factories mass-produced textiles, many inscribed with the caliph's name, to be given to officials at their investiture, as well as the costumes (*kiswa*) distributed on ceremonial occasions to the caliph's entourage, his family, the amirs, and the troops.[104]

The caliphs shared the general attitude of the population that clothes were a visible sign not only of wealth, but also of God's favor to human beings. This attitude characterized both the Jewish and the Muslim populations of medieval Islamic societies, and there is ample material in the literary and religious texts to support such a view. Al-Dimashqī echoes this sentiment in his twelfth-century treatise on commerce, stating that "[the merchant] possesses many thousands and is not compelled to wear mediocre clothes" (*lā yuḍirruhu an yakūn thawbuhu muqāriban*).[105] The extravagant costumes of the caliphs and their entourages were a sign of the beneficence God bestowed upon them; through costumes, they asserted their rule and staked a claim to their legitimacy.

A direct challenge to the caliph's authority, however, was more likely to be made by appropriating one of the insignia of sovereignty than by wearing a particular fabric. When the rebellious Banū Qurra raised a pretender to the caliphate, he paraded with a parasol (*miẓalla*) over his head.[106] In addition, the Qarāfiyya sent this pretender four robes of a very precious stuff; these he wore on procession. He asserted sovereignty by appropriating one of the caliph's insignia of sovereignty. The Qarāfiyya acknowledged his claim by giving him an elaborate costume that was associated with wealth and power, although such fabrics were by no means the exclusive province of the caliphs.

Clothing symbolized authority, conveyed information about rank at court, and could also be used to negotiate power. A certain Ḥassān who aspired to a larger land grant (*iqṭāʿ*) and greater prerogatives requested a robe and skullcap from the caliph (*thiyāb min thiyābih . . . wa-shāshiyya min shawāshīh*). This was a distortion of the custom of investiture, which was normally initiated by the ruler. But Ḥassān specified that he wanted something that the caliph himself had worn (*thiyāb min thiyāb mawlānā . . . allatī yalbis-hā*). At a time when *ṭirāz* factories mass-produced robes of honor for distribution, this upstart wanted the genuine article. In the eleventh century, people still had a clear sense of just what the relative values of these costumes were. This particular case was more one of extortion under the threat of rebellion than anything else, but the caliph complied.[107]

For the caliphs, the cash value of clothing was as important as its symbolic value. Clothing constituted wealth in the economy of Fatimid Egypt, and expensive textiles were as good as gold at all levels of society, inside and outside of the court. The clothing that a bride brought into marriage was an economic safeguard and often formed the major part of her trousseau.[108] Her dowry consisted not of money but rather of jewelry, clothing, furnishings, and housewares.[109] Even at the court, textiles provided an economic safeguard for the caliph. The vast storehouses of the palace, including the wardrobe (*khizānat al-kisawāt*), were opened and their contents sold when the dynasty fell on hard times during the period of drought and famine under the caliph al-Mustanṣir.

Under such circumstances, it is not surprising that large numbers of textiles originally manufactured for the court entered the general market and came into the hands of quite ordinary, if well-to-do, people. Elites outside of court circles coveted these robes of honor or garments. They imitated court practices and fashions, and they aspired to the prestige conferred by either giving or receiving one of these prized garments. By the eleventh century in Fatimid Egypt, the upper classes enthusiastically imitated the practice of the court by giving one another robes of honor, elaborate costumes that had been specially produced for this purpose.[110] The ancient custom of bestowing honor on a valued member of the caliph's entourage by giving him a piece of the ruler's own clothing (hence, the original meaning of the term *khilʿa* [castoff], usually translated as "robe of honor") had been transformed so that large numbers of these costumes were being produced in the caliphal *ṭirāz* factories expressly for distribution. The importance of wearing something that had actually been worn by the caliph was replaced by the practice of wearing something the production of which the caliph controlled and prescribed.

This is quite unlike the situation of the Fatimids' contemporaries in Byzantium, where the court held a monopoly on the production, sale, and right to wear certain fabrics.[111] The Byzantine emperors of the early Middle Ages controlled the supply of silk, of purple, and of gold embroidery. These goods were all unavailable to the Byzantine lower classes not only because of economic inequality, but also because of the strict social hierarchies that permitted these goods only to the emperor or the aristocracy. These cloths were symbols of authority and were protected from debasement by laws that prohibited their use by the lower classes.[112]

In the Fatimid state, however, the hierarchy of costuming that reflected rank was not legislated. The caliph and his court did not have exclusive control over the production or distribution of certain fabrics, and no textiles or other materials, as far as we know, were mandated only for the ruling dynasty. They became associated with the wealthy and powerful members of the court by virtue of their use of these textiles, not by legislation or regulation. There were some restrictions introduced in the rules of protocol on costuming. Under the Abbasids, for example, the prerogative of wearing the dynastic colors was reserved to the caliphs, their families, their retinue and the highest officials of the bureaucracy and court. In addition, wearing the color red was considered to be a caliphal prerogative.[113]

These prerogatives, like other prohibitions regarding dress, seem to have been widely disregarded. The most notable example of this is the widespread disregard for the restrictions on the dress of non-Muslims (*dhimmīs*), who were technically prohibited from wearing certain types of clothing and were enjoined to wear distinguishing marks. But proclamations reiterating these prohibitions abound in the historical record,[114] a sure sign that they were honored primarily in the breach. Furthermore, there is positive evidence from the Judeo-Arabic documents of the Cairo Geniza that it was, in the Fatimid period at least, difficult to tell Jews, Christians, and Muslims apart in the streets.[115] No comparable proclamations restricting color or costume appear in the manuals of protocol. And the evidence from the literary sources seems to confirm that the elites, if no one else, developed their own fashions with a considerable amount of latitude. The most popular color mentioned in the Geniza, for example, is white, the Fatimid color.[116]

The imitation and appropriation of symbols of authority among the social classes occurred in other ways, as well. Among those of the middle class, men addressed their superiors as "my master" (*mawlāyya*) and referred to one another respectfully using their *kunya*s. Among Jews, the Hebrew honorific titles granted by the yeshivas (academies) of Baghdad, the institutions of religious authority, were eagerly sought. But in the eleventh and twelfth centuries, Jews also coveted the Arabic titles that had proliferated in the government bureaucracy, and which were now used by non-court elites. In the academies, both titulature and spatial arrangements signified rank; as a member was promoted, he advanced forward by rows.[117]

The symbols of the caliph's authority were thus gradually extended to his subordinates as special marks of favor and status. Whether material objects or prerogatives (like titulature), some of them eventually found their way into the middle classes. This does not, however, indicate an attempt by common men to usurp the authority or prerogatives of the court, or to defy hierarchies. Quite the contrary, common men, like men at court, believed that social hierarchy was the natural order of things. A just society did not have to be egalitarian; indeed, it should not be egalitarian. The aspirations of these men for marks of dignity in fact expressed their investment in a social and political order with the caliph at the top. The hierarchies in Fatimid society were contingent, and without the ruler's presence, such symbols of status and rank among ordinary men would be meaningless. The caliph was an accumulation of the dignities that marked social differences, and therefore implied social order, at all levels of society.[118]

THE CALIPH AS CENTER

Collectively, the protocol of the court and the symbols of authority placed the caliph at the top of a hierarchy that established all rank as relative to the caliph and, in some way, contingent on his authority. Ceremonial also placed the caliph at the center, a position that was established by the spatial arrangements of both palace audiences and processions.[119] We can see in the audiences that were held on Monday and Thursday how the caliph's position at the symbolic center of Fatimid society was expressed spatially.[120] When he decided to hold an audience, the hall was hung with drapes and covered with carpets,[121] and his throne (*sarīr al-mulk*) was covered in precious fabrics. After these preparations, the wazir was summoned from his residence and he hurried to the palace with his retinue. His amirs dismounted at the gate of the palace, while the wazir entered the palace grounds mounted and rode down a long colonnade to the first door in the vestibule (*dihlīz*). He dismounted there and continued on foot to his designated place (*maqṭaʿ al-wizāra*).

Once the caliph was seated on his throne, the wazir was summoned from his place to the door of the audience hall (*majlis*), surrounded by the amirs of the collar (*al-umarāʾ al-muṭawwaqūn*), other high dignitaries (*arbāb al-khidam*), and the Qur'an reciters (*qurrāʾ*). The door to the audience hall was closed, and a curtain was suspended in front of it. Outside the door, the majordomo (*zimām al-qaṣr*) and the director of the treasury (*zimām bayt al-māl*), both eunuchs, stood to the right and left. Inside, the chief chamberlain (*ṣāḥib al-bāb*) and commander of the army (*isfahsalār*) stood to the right and left. From the threshold to the end of the arcade (*riwāq*)[122] stood the commanders of the Āmirī and Ḥāfiẓī regiments, other amirs, the staff bearers (*arbāb al-quḍub wa'l-ʿamāriyyāt*), and other ranking army officers. Various assistant chamberlains stood facing the door of the audience hall.

The master of the audience hall (*ṣāḥib al-majlis, ṣāḥib al-sitr*), also a eunuch, placed the inkstand on the platform in front of the caliph, then left by an aisle (*fard al-kumm*). Upon his signal, the majordomo and the director of the treasury each took a corner of the curtain covering the door and raised it. The caliph's throne (*sarīr, kursī*) was at the end of the audience hall, facing the entrance.[123] The caliph sat immobile on his throne, facing the audience, and the Qur'an reciters began to recite. The wazir entered the audience hall, while his amirs stayed in their designated places, apparently outside the audience hall. In order to approach the caliph, he would have walked through a human corridor formed by the commanders of the regiments. He saluted, kissed the hands and feet of the caliph and retreated a distance of about three cubits where he stood for a moment. A cushion was brought out and placed at the caliph's right, and the wazir was invited to sit down.

The chief qadi was waiting with his witnesses. The chief chamberlain (*ṣāḥib al-bāb*) escorted only the qadi across the threshold so that he could pay homage to the caliph.[124] He raised his right hand, pointed with his forefinger, and said, "Peace be upon the Commander of the Faithful and God's mercy and blessings." Then the head of the caliph's relatives (*al-ashrāf al-aqārib*) and the head of the ʿAlids in general (*naqīb al-ashrāf al-ṭālibiyyīn*) saluted the caliph. This all took several hours. Finally, the governors of the four major provinces of Egypt (Qūṣ, Sharqiyya, Gharbiyya, and Alexandria) were allowed to kiss the threshold.

If the wazir had something to discuss with the caliph, he rose from his place, approached him bending over his sword, and spoke to him. Then he ordered those present to leave. The wazir was the last to leave, and he exited after kissing the caliph's hand and foot. He returned to the vestibule (*dihlīz*) where he had dismounted, mounted, and rode to his residence, attended by his retinue. The caliph entered his private quarters with his personal slaves, the door of the audience hall was closed and the curtain lowered until the next audience (*mawkib*).[125]

The description of this audience demonstrates how spatial arrangements, material objects, and protocol all functioned to construct the caliph as a permanent and immobile center. The caliph appeared in full regalia, seated on his throne. There was no visible formal procession to the throne. The audience saw none of the preparations.[126] He was never seen moving from one place to another without great solemnity, and he was usually concealed while in transit, either by curtains or his bodyguard; he was never seen while he ate, slept, or spoke.[127] Whatever movement he might make was distinguished by its economy, and on the rare occasions when he personally returned the salute of one of his officials, it consisted in the slightest of gestures.[128]

Of the insignia mentioned by al-Qalqashandī, only one, the inkstand, appeared, but the authority of the ruler was projected onto the audience hall: the curtain concealed not just the caliph, but the entire room. When the curtain was raised, the wazir beheld not only the caliph but also the room as a whole. The highest-ranking eunuchs and amirs were grouped not around the caliph but at the threshold of the audience hall. An elaborate ritual surrounded entering the room, which was accessible only to the highest-ranking officials. The wazir took his place to the caliph's right in a ritual that both marked his subordinate relationship to the caliph and presented the caliph and wazir together as the authorities of the state. The fact that the wazir did not conduct any business with the caliph until after the completion of the salutes, a process that could take several hours, indicates that the real business of the audience was, in fact, the ceremonial salutes and not any particular issue that needed administrative attention.

The caliph's entire body did not have to be visible for him to act as the center of ceremony, nor did he have to speak or gesture himself. His eunuchs were so closely associated with him that, in his presence, they could act for him. On the four *layālī al-wuqūd* (nights of lights) in the two months before Ramaḍān, the anniversary festivals of the Prophet (*mawlid al-nabī*),[129] 'Alī's, and the imam,[130] an audience was held at the belvedere (*manẓara*) over the Emerald Gate (*bāb al-zumurrud*) of the palace. The qadi and the witnesses went to the parade ground between the two palaces (*bayn al-qaṣrayn*) with candles and gathered beneath the belvedere in which the caliph sat. One of the windows opened, and he showed only his head and face; a number of his eunuchs could be seen standing around him. One of these eunuchs opened another window, put out his head, pointed with his right hand (which was covered with his sleeve), and said, "The Commander of the Faithful returns to you the greeting." He greeted the chief qadi and the chief chamberlain with their titles. After that, those remaining were greeted without specifying anyone in particular.

When the greetings were completed, the Qur'an reciters began to recite; they stood with their backs to the belvedere, and faced those attending. The preacher of the Aqmar Mosque pronounced the caliph's name in the sermon (*khuṭba*) and preached about the virtues of the month, finishing with prayers for the caliph. He was followed by the preachers of the Azhar and Anwar Mosques. When they all finished, the eunuch who had originally returned the greeting put his hand out of the same window and returned the greeting to the whole gathering. The windows were then closed, and the people withdrew. The qadi and the witnesses went to the wazir's residence, where he held an audience to receive their greetings, and the three preachers delivered sermons but in a more restrained manner than they had for the caliph.[131]

The eunuchs had as much at stake in the observance of these ceremonies as the caliph himself. We learn from al-Maqrīzī that "al-Afḍal b. Amīr al-juyūsh annulled the observance of the anniversary festivals (*mawlid*) of the Prophet, 'Alī, Fāṭima, and the present imam, and maintained this policy until they were forgotten. Then the eunuchs began to talk about them again to the caliph al-Āmir and presented them as a way of opposing the wazir and of restoring the customs and ceremonies."[132] Thus, the restoration of these particular ceremonies not only asserted the caliph's power, but also restored the eunuchs to their former position. Even later in the Fatimid period, the celebration of the birthdays of Ḥasan and Ḥusayn was added to the four birthdays,[133] a consequence of the renewed interest in the distant ʿAlid past by the late Fatimid caliphs following the Ṭayyibī schism.

The palace complex in which these audiences took place was immovable, constructed and located to isolate the Fatimid ruler at the center. Its gates and doors were symbols of sovereignty and authority and were the sites of important ceremonial activity. People mounted and dismounted at gates and doors, belvederes and balconies surmounted them, allowing the caliph to witness parades and processions and, in turn, allowing the people to view him. They marked the boundary between the space of everyday life and the almost sacral quality of the space occupied by the caliph himself. They were rendered homage just as the caliph himself was: when Mālik b. Saʿīd al-Fāriqī was invested as qadi, he paraded from the palace to the Mosque of ʿAmr on an ass, dismounting as he passed each gate of the palace to kiss it.[134] During the procession to the perfuming of the Nilometer, its guardian, Ibn Abi'l-Raddād, dismounted as he passed by each gate the caliph entered and, when exiting from the main gate of the palace, dismounted and kissed it.[135] An embassy of Tughtakīn was received in 517/1123–24, consisting of two envoys who dismounted at Bāb al-Futūḥ (one of the city's northern gates) and kissed it, then walked to the palace, where they kissed the River Gate (*bāb al-baḥr*) and requested permission to see the caliph.[136]

When the caliph emerged from his palace to parade through the space of everyday life, the boundaries created by walls, doors, and gates were maintained symbolically through the protocol of Fatimid processions. Riding in mounted procession with the caliph was the prerogative of an elite few.[137] Whoever went with the imam had to know his rank and his station. Those who walked behind the imam in procession were also required to pay careful attention to maintaining their proper position; this was, in fact, their primary responsibility.[138] The caliph's personal bodyguard surrounded him, always in the positions closest to him. When he sat in the enclosed prayer chamber (*maqṣūra*) in a mosque, he was attended inside by his private guard, while the regular troops assumed their positions outside the structure. The relationships that existed in the palace did not change when he left; they were, in fact, more rigidly enforced outside of the palace. Just as the walls of Cairo and of the palace repelled unwanted visitors from intruding on the caliph's domain (both physical and spiritual), his personal bodyguard of eunuchs preserved that boundary symbolically when the Fatimid ruler ventured into public.[139]

The caliph was the pivot of the procession. In effect, he moved only in relation to the buildings he passed and the streets he traversed; his own position in the procession never changed. Every move disrupted the order that had been so carefully established. Each time the caliph moved, or one of the officials accompanying him moved in relation to him, the proper relationship between them was reestablished by the constant salutes that are so striking a part of ceremonial. Treating each movement or activity as a unit, marked at its beginning and its end by a salute to the caliph, was a reminder that the power generated at the center by the caliph was the source and the legitimating authority of the flurry of activity surrounding him. It is almost as if to say that without him, there could have been no motion at all.[140]

The illusion of permanence and immobility created by protocol, symbols of authority, and spatial organization all masked a reality marked by constant change. Ceremonial was not static, and it did not merely reflect an unchanging set of social and political relations. Among those men most invested in the idea of hierarchy, there were continual contests for power and prestige. Ceremonial was a fundamental way to renegotiate alliances and to reinscribe men at different positions in the social and political order. In the chapters that follow, we shall see how precarious that hierarchy could be under specific social and political conditions and how court ceremonial could be used to reconfigure a myriad of contingent relationships in Fatimid society.

CHAPTER 3

The Ritual City

The previous chapter argued that the Fatimids articulated claims to authority and negotiated contingent relationships through protocol and symbols of authority, and it discussed how the spatial arrangements of ceremonies helped to construct the illusion of the caliph as a permanent and immobile center. This chapter analyzes the growth of Cairo, the capital of the Fatimid empire, in terms of Fatimid ceremonies. It may be argued that one should begin by discussing topography as the physical context in which ceremonies are properly interpreted. Such an approach, however, often assumes that the meaning of the city is not itself at issue. I assume, instead, that the relationship between the growth of the city and the elaboration of ceremonial inform each other and that their meanings change in relation to one another over time. Therefore, I look at how Cairo was constructed through topography and ceremonial as a ritual city, how that ritual city was transformed over time, and how the new meanings it acquired were in turn exploited to articulate changing ideological and political commitments.

In the first years of their caliphate in Egypt, the Fatimids created an Isma'ili ritual city in Cairo. They accomplished this through the manipulation of topography and inscriptions, as well as through ceremonies that linked the ritual centers of Cairo. Under the reign of the caliph al-Ḥākim, these ceremonies also integrated the ritual centers of Fustat into the Isma'ili ritual city, even while Fustat remained a distinct urban center. This Isma'ili ritual city was eventually reinterpreted and its meaning transformed in the late eleventh and twelfth centuries, when the Fatimids deliberately created a ritual *lingua franca* that was systematically articulated through ceremony, which emphasized those aspects of ritual that could be conceived of as broadly Islamic and that were not explicitly embedded in Isma'ilism. Cairo became the site on which this ritual *lingua franca* operated as an urban language, thus blurring the boundary between Isma'ilis and Sunnis and mitigating urban religious tensions.

THE BEGINNINGS OF THE RITUAL CITY

Cairo was first established by the general Jawhar, who conquered Egypt on behalf of al-Mu'izz. Like the North African Fatimid capitals of al-Mahdiyya and al-Manṣūriyya, Cairo was a palace city separate from an existing commercial center. In North Africa, that center was Qayrawan; in Egypt, it was Fustat. The new Egyptian capital shared not only the architectural style and general layout of the North African capital, but also its name: it, too, was called "al-Manṣūriyya" (the new city was not renamed al-Qāhira until al-Mu'izz arrived).

At the heart of Jawhar's military encampment stood the palace complex, the center of the Isma'ili city that was being constructed in both topography and thought in the early Fatimid period. The presence of the imam and his sanctity conferred a particularly exalted position on both the land and the physical structure in which he resided. When the Fatimid caliph 'Ubayd Allāh al-Mahdī took up residence in 308/920 in al-Mahdiyya, the first North African capital of the dynasty, the poets of Ifriqiyya extolled both him and his new capital:

> My congratulations, O generous prince, for your arrival upon which our epoch smiles
> You have established your camp in a noble land, prepared for you by glorious angels.
> The sanctuary and its environs, its lofty shrines are exalted
> And in the West is an exalted residence where prayer and fasting are accepted:
> It is al-Mahdiyya, sacred and protected, as the sacred city is in Tihāma.
> Your footsteps make the ground wherever you tread like the Maqām Ibrahim
> Just as the pilgrim kissed the [sacred] corner, so do we kiss the walls of your palace.
> Through the course of time, an empire grows old, its foundations crumble under the test of time
> But your empire, O Mahdī, will always be young, Time itself will serve it

> The world belongs to you and your descendants wherever you may be;
> It will always find an imam in you![1]

These sentiments were echoed by the court poet, Ibn Hānī' (d. ca. 362/973), in praise of 'Ubayd Allāh's great-grandson al-Mu'izz, the architect of Cairo:

> We are brought by noble camels in pilgrimage to the sanctuary (*ḥaram*) of the imam, across vast expanses of desert
> Our dust-covered locks are anointed by our coming to kiss the corner (*rukn*) [of his palace] . . .
> Will Paradise be permitted to me, now that I have seen one of its open doors?[2]

The imam's presence had a transforming power over even the best of creation:

> Awe of you causes the sun to forget where it rises, the mere mention of you makes the angels forget their hymns of praise
> You have been formed as an image of your lord's kingdom, to which he gave the knowledge (*'ilm*) whose soul you are.[3]

Even the heavens are not what they appear to be when the imam is on earth:

> The [true] heaven of God isn't the one you see, the earth which contains him [the imam] is [truly] heaven.[4]

The imam was the terrestrial incarnation of the universal intellect, the first principle emanating from the Creator himself, the "cause of the world, which was created by him."[5] He was considered to be an emanation of the divine light, and numerous epithets described his brilliance and luminousness: *al-agharr, al-azhar, al-mutalliq, al-mutadaffiq, al-mutaballij, al-waḍḍā'*.[6] As the construction of Cairo continued, new mosques would come to be known by names evoking this special quality associated with the imam: al-Azhar, al-Anwar, al-Aqmar. The imam stands at the center of an Isma'ili's fervent faith: to praise the imam is to praise God; to believe in him is to believe in God and his Prophet; to obey him is to obey God and his Prophet.[7]

Because the palaces and their inscriptions are lost,[8] we cannot say if these ideas about the sanctity of the imam and the ground upon which he tread, so sublimely articulated in poetry, found material expression in architecture, or if this spiritual topography found its way into the actual topography of the city. Historical and topographical sources reveal little of the intentions of al-Mu'izz and his general. Ibn Duqmāq (d. 790/1388), for example, tells us only that Jawhar built the palace for his master "so that he and their friends and armies were separate from the general public."[9]

We do know that al-Mu'izz supposedly drew the plan for the palace himself and that the palace city was modeled on the existing North African capital of al-Manṣūriyya.[10] Two of the city's gates, Bāb Zuwayla (Zuwayla Gate) and Bāb al-Futūḥ (Conquest Gate), bore the same name as the city gates of al-Manṣūriyya and stood in the same relation to each other as in the North African city, leading directly into the city's major thoroughfare and widening in the center to form a parade ground, the *bayn al-qaṣrayn* (lit., "between the two palaces," i.e., the parade ground between the Eastern and Western Palaces). This thoroughfare was the axis of Cairo, its major processional route. It defined the center of Cairo and continued as the main commercial artery of Fustat.

There were things other than theology, panegyrics, and the similarity of the town plans to reinforce the special position of the palace at Cairo. The southern section of the Eastern Palace housed the tomb of the Fatimid caliphs (called "the Tomb of al-Mu'izz" or "the Saffron Tomb").[11] Al-Mu'izz carried the coffins of the first three Fatimid imams across the North African desert and reinterred them in his new capital. We know almost nothing about the actual transfer of these coffins, but even the terse description preserved by al-Maqrīzī suggests that it was one long procession, connecting the new and the old al-Manṣūriyyas. In a profound sense, al-Mu'izz had brought his genealogy with him, the proof of the direct and unbroken line through which the imamate passed to him.[12] But the tombs were not merely reminders of a glorious past or symbols of legitimacy; they were thought to have real power. When al-'Azīz set out to recapture Aleppo in 386/996, he took along the coffins of his ancestors.[13]

In addition to being the repository for the corporeal remains of the line of imams, the palace was also the repository of the spiritual knowledge (*'ilm*) that resided in the imam of the time. It housed the renowned Fatimid library, whose books had a particular significance in Isma'ili thought; they were part of the rightful inheritance of the imams, symbols of his spiritual authority.[14] The palace was therefore the appropriate place for the dissemination of knowledge. The chief qadi Muḥammad b. al-Nu'mān lectured there on the sciences of the Family of the Prophet.[15] The chief missionary (*dā'ī*) also delivered lectures there, as well as at the Azhar.[16] Even at the end of the Fatimid period, the chief missionary was still delivering lectures in the palace: in the Iwan for the men, in his audience hall (called *"al-muḥawwal"*) adjoining the Gold Hall (*qā'at al-dhahab*) for the women.[17]

Though a spiritual center from the first, the palace did not originally have an administrative function. After Cairo was established, government administration continued to revolve around the two congregational mosques of Fustat, the Mosque of 'Amr (also called *al-jāmi' al-'atīq*, "the old congregational mosque") and the Mosque of Ibn Ṭūlūn. They exemplified the association of politics and religion in a single center that had characterized many of the early mosques built by Arab conquerors.[18] When 'Amr b. al-'Āṣ conquered Egypt and established his garrison at Fustat, he built his mosque on the plan of the mosque in Medina, with the administrative complex (*dār al-imāra*), adjoining it.[19] Ibn Ṭūlūn, unlike earlier rulers, did not reside in the residence (*dār*) adjoining his mosque. But he symbolically preserved the strong association of politics and religion by building his administrative complex on the *qibla* side of his mosque, with an entrance that led directly to the prayer enclosure (*maqṣūra*). The ruler entered to change his clothes for prayer and then entered the mosque unseen.[20] For both the Tulunids and Ikhshidids, Ibn Ṭūlūn's administrative complex and mosque were the real governmental center of the city, although the Mosque of 'Amr continued to serve administrative functions. The public treasury (*bayt al-māl*) was housed there even in Fatimid times.[21] In 378–79/988–89, al-'Azīz installed a running fountain underneath the dome (*qubba*) that surmounted it.[22]

If the palace was not at first an administrative center, neither was it a ritual center. Instead, the Mosque of 'Amr remained the center of ritual and cermemonial activity for all of the communities of Fustat.[23] The Mosque of 'Amr had a noble and ancient history. Long before the Fatimid conquest, it had become a center of urban life responding to the rhythms of the Coptic calendar as well as those of the Muslim calendar. It was the Friday mosque for the Muslim population of Fustat, but it was also the terminal point for parades on Nawruz, the Coptic New Year.[24] As a center of political and religious activity, it was often the site of disorder and dissension as well as of peacemaking and reconciliation.[25]

Standing at the heart of Fustat in the old al-Rāya district, the Mosque of ʿAmr was also at the center of economic and commercial life.[26] Jews, Christians, and Muslims often crossed each other's paths here. It is no wonder, then, that when Jawhar came to Egypt in 358/969, he and his troops bypassed the larger Mosque of Ibn Ṭūlūn, the administrative seat of Fustat, and went instead to the Mosque of ʿAmr for the Friday prayer. The commander and his vast army distributed alms (*ṣadaqāt*) at the city's oldest and most venerable mosque, where they would be seen not only by the Muslim population, but also by the multitudes of Jews and Christians who also lived and worked in this densely populated area.[27]

On this first Friday of Fatimid hegemony in Egypt, Hibāt Allāh b. Aḥmad, the lieutenant of the preacher (*khaṭīb*) of the Mosque of ʿAmr, wore white (the Fatimid color) while delivering the sermon (*khuṭba*) in the name of the Fatimid caliph.[28] When it was time to recite the invocations, he read from a prepared text, asking for God's blessing upon al-Muʿizz and his assistance to "make clear his proof, gather together the Muslim community (*umma*) in his obedience, and hearts in friendship and comradeship . . . and to bequeath to him East and West . . . For you have said in your True Speech (Q. 21:105) 'The earth shall be the inheritance of my righteous servants.'"[29]

The audience for this sermon and invocation must have been as diverse as the population of Fustat itself. This may account for the curious absence of any specifically Shiʿi formulae in the prayer. In the letter of safety (*amān*) given to the Egyptian population upon his conquest, Jawhar had, among other things, agreed to repair and furnish mosques and to pay the local muezzins and imams. He also guaranteed the integrity of local religious practices.[30] But in doing so, he asserted that Islam has one custom (*sunna*) and that practice should be according to the ancestors of the Islamic community (*salaf*). He seems to have made no attempt to impose Ismaʿili doctrine on the local population, emphasizing instead ritual practice.[31] Jawhar recognized implicitly how deeply entrenched local religious practices were, while laying claim at the same time to the authority of the distant past by invoking the practice of the ancestors (*salaf*). And so, Jawhar did not attempt at first to integrate Fustat into a new Isma'ili ritual map; rather he tried to reinscribe local practices in a new context that, by definition, would be considered as Isma'ili.

Jawhar did, however, proscribe some Sunni practices upon his arrival. He suppressed the recitation of sura 87 as well as the pronouncing of the formula "God is most great" (*takbīr*) after prayer.[32] But he did not impose the Isma'ili calendar on the local population.[33] He and his troops celebrated the Festival of Fast Breaking (*'īd al-fiṭr*) that year at the *muṣallā* (open prayer ground) of Cairo without sighting the new moon, while the population of Fustat said the festival prayer the next day at the Mosque of 'Amr.[34] Although the different schools of law (*madhāhib*) disagreed over the proper location for the festival prayers—*muṣallā* or mosque—Isma'ilis agreed unanimously on the *muṣallā* as the appropriate site.[35] There had been *muṣallās* in Fustat, but they were not used in the period immediately preceding the Fatimid conquest for the festival prayer.[36] Jawhar established the *muṣallā* of Cairo in Ramaḍān 358/969, just beyond the northern city wall at Bāb al-Naṣr (Victory Gate).[37]

The *muṣallā* was more than simply a site for festival prayer. The history of Fatimid *muṣallās* infused the Cairo *muṣallā* with both religious and political significance. According to Fatimid sources, when 'Ubayd Allāh al-Mahdī built his capital city al-Mahdiyya, he ordered an arrow to be shot from the wall of the city westwards. He then ordered a *muṣallā* to be built where it landed, saying, "The master of the ass (*ṣāḥib al-ḥimār*) will arrive here," referring to the Kharijite rebel, Abū Yazīd al-Khārijī, an avowed enemy of the North African Fatimid state. The prophecy was fulfilled when Abū Yazīd was stopped at the *muṣallā* when he attacked al-Mahdiyya.[38] Given the amuletic power attributed to the *muṣallā* in this historicized legend, it is probably no coincidence that the *muṣallā* at Cairo was built outside Bāb al-Naṣr, the gate that was the city's most vulnerable point for attack.[39]

Nearly a year later, Jawhar insisted on introducing the Shi'i call to prayer (*adhān*) in Fustat. The muezzins used the Shi'i formula, "Hurry to the best of works" for the first time on 8 Jumādā I 359/970 at the Mosque of Ibn Ṭūlūn.[40] But this first Friday prayer with the Shi'i call to prayer was not without incident. The preacher of the Mosque of 'Amr, 'Abd al-Samī' b. 'Umar al-'Abbāsī (so conspicuously absent the previous year, when his lieutenant delivered the sermon at the Mosque of Ibn Ṭūlūn) led the prayer, reciting suras 62 and 63[41] and performing the *qunūt* in the second cycle of prayer (*rakʿa*).[42] But he "forgot" (thus says the text) the genuflection (*rukūʿ*) before the prostration (*sujūd*) in the second cycle of prayer. ʿAlī b. al-Walīd, Jawhar's army judge (*qāḍī ʿaskar*), declared the prayer null and void (*bāṭil*) and ordered it repeated as a regular Friday prayer.[43]

This was nothing short of sabotage. Ordinary prayers may be made up easily, but the congregational prayer on Friday and the Festival prayers are exceptions. Once missed, or nullified through some error, they must be replaced by ordinary daily prayers; they lose their extraordinary value and efficacy.[44] Our reluctant preacher clearly could not resist the temptation. The Shiʿi call to prayer was proclaimed, but the sermon was delivered in Jawhar's name rather than in the name of the Fatimid caliph. The preacher thus acknowledged the conquering general, but not the Fatimid imam. More important, the ritual prayer itself was utterly devalued. He had managed to negotiate that ambiguous boundary between politics and religion, to acknowledge political hegemony while denying spiritual authority. The preacher was also resisting the implicit claim of the Shiʿi call to prayer that Fustat was an Ismaʿili city. Fustat might be a part of the Fatimid polity, but it was not Ismaʿili and not a part of the Fatimid ritual city, which would be confined to Cairo for another forty years.

In the same month that the Shiʿi call to prayer was introduced in Fustat, Jawhar laid the foundations of the Mosque of Cairo.[45] The first Friday prayer was held there some two years later on 7 Ramaḍān 361/972.[46] The Mosque of Cairo, more commonly known as the Azhar, was the religious center of Cairo, much as the Mosque of ʿAmr had been for Fustat and the Mosque of Ibn Ṭulūn for al-Qaṭāʾiʿ. It never became an administrative center like those other two great mosques, nor was it the nucleus of the new city of Cairo. At least initially, most ritual celebrations took place at the *muṣallā*, just outside the city walls. When al-Muʿizz arrived in Cairo during Ramaḍān 362/973, he did not lead congregational prayer at the new mosque. This should not be read as reluctance to fulfill ritual and ceremonial duties. Al-Muʿizz gave an elaborate audience in the middle of the month, seated upon his gold throne (*sarīr*), in the hall (*īwān*) of his new palace, and allowed the "nobles and friends and dignitaries" to be presented to him.[47] Nor should it be taken as an indication that such ceremonies simply did not exist in his time. In this same year, he rode in formal procession to celebrate the Festival of Fast Breaking (*ʿīd al-fiṭr*) at the *muṣallā*,[48] displayed the ceremonial covering (*shamsa*) for the Kaʿba in his audience hall (*īwān*),[49] and led prayer on the Sacrificial Festival (*ʿīd al-aḍḥā*).[50]

The description of al-Muʿizz's celebration of the Festival of Fast Breaking (*ʿīd al-fiṭr*) is an eyewitness account of the historian Ibn Zūlāq (d. 386/996) and follows closely the prescriptions for festival prayer in al-Qāḍī al-Nuʿmān's compendium of Ismaʿili law, *Daʿāʾim al-Islām* (The Pillars of Islam).[51] Al-Muʿizz recited sura 1 (*al-fātiḥa*) and sura 88 (*al-ghāshiya*) in the first cycle of prayer, then pronounced "God is most great"; in the second cycle of prayer, he recited sura 1 and sura 93 (*al-ḍuḥā*), also followed by pronouncing "God is most great." He performed extended cycles of prostrations (*rukūʿ sujūd*), during which the congregation pronounced the formula "God be praised!" (*subḥān allāh*) some thirty-odd times. Al-Qāḍī al-Nuʿmān himself repeated the formula "God is most great" after it was uttered by the caliph. Ibn Zūlāq notes that some people who did not know that it was the custom of ʿAlī b. Abī Ṭālib to pray in this manner on the Festival criticized the practice.[52] This statement may indicate that some of the general population attended the Fatimid celebration.

After the prayer, al-Muʿizz ascended the minbar and said, "Peace be upon you and God's mercy and blessings."[53] Two banners that hung from the minbar were then unfurled to conceal him, and he delivered the sermon from behind them.[54] A pillow of ornamented brocade (*dībāj muthaqqal*) had been placed on the top step of the minbar for the caliph to sit upon between the two sermons.[55] He began the sermon by saying, "In the name of God, the merciful and compassionate" (*basmala*) and then pronounced the formula "God is most great" (*takbīr*). Jawhar and two other dignitaries, one of them the bearer of the parasol (*ṣāḥib al-miẓalla*), stood with him on the minbar. After completing the sermon, al-Muʿizz, followed by his four sons, returned to the palace in a procession that included two elephants.[56] At the palace, a banquet was served. This was to be the basic form of Fatimid celebrations of the Festival of Fast Breaking (and, with the addition of the sacrifices, of the Sacrificial Festival) until the end of the dynasty. Later caliphs elaborated certain parts and increased or decreased the size of their entourage, the magnificence of their costumes, the guest list at their banquets, the number of robes of honor, and other distributions, but the essential elements remained the same.

THE ELABORATION OF THE RITUAL CITY UNDER AL-ʿAZĪZ

The celebration of the Festival of Fast Breaking (*ʿīd al-fiṭr*) appears to have been well established at the time of the Fatimid conquest of Egypt. In addition to the practices the Fatimids brought from North Africa, there is also evidence that the Festival of Fast Breaking was observed in Egypt with processions, in addition to the prayer, under the Tulunids and Ikhshidids.[57] The texts are silent, however, on the celebrations for Ramaḍān. This is surprising, given the obligatory nature of the fast (*ṣawm*) and the importance of the month itself in Islamic thought. Ramaḍān is the month in which the Qur'an is believed to have been revealed to Muḥammad, and pious acts and benefactions are said to have manifold benefits if performed then.[58] The meritorious qualities and benefits to be derived from pious acts during Ramaḍān also seem to have influenced some political and military maneuvers. There are a preponderance of conquests, foundations of cities, and political changes during these months. The conquest of Egypt by Jawhar took place during Ramaḍān, and it is not a coincidence that the caliph al-Muʿizz, three years after his general had conquered the land, finally made his appearance in Egypt during this "best of all months."

Nonetheless, there is no evidence of a caliphal procession to Friday prayer during Ramaḍān until the reign of al-ʿAzīz.[59] It appears that the addition of Ramaḍān processions was part of a program to elaborate the ritual city. In the year 380/990, al-ʿAzīz rode to the Azhar Mosque under a golden parasol (*miẓalla mudhahhaba*), carrying the staff (*qaḍīb*), wearing a *ṭaylasān*, and girded with a sword.[60] He was accompanied by five thousand men. After delivering the sermon and leading the prayer, he returned to the palace, collecting petitions along the way.[61] Al-ʿAzīz's addition of the procession to Friday prayer during Ramaḍān was the first of several actions that increased the density of the ritual landscape. In the same year, he founded a new mosque outside of Bāb al-Futūḥ (Conquest Gate),[62] known today as the Mosque of al-Ḥākim (after the caliph who completed its construction). This initiated what would come to be a concentration of ritual monuments and life in the northern part of the city of Cairo. The northern walls were the site of the *muṣallā*, and the landscape on which al-ʿAzīz chose to build his new mosque was already suffused with religious and political significance.

The new congregational mosque was integrated into the ritual life of the court when the caliph led prayer there on the first Friday in Ramaḍān 381/991; he led prayer at the new Mosque of al-Ḥākim and prayed at the Azhar Mosque on the following Friday.[63] In 382/992, the chronicles record him praying in only the Azhar Mosque,[64] the following year in his new mosque,[65] and once again in 384/994 in both the Azhar Mosque and the new mosque.[66] However, the new mosque did not displace the Azhar Mosque as the premier congregational mosque in the city, as it would later on during the reign of al-Ḥākim.

Although topographically distinct, the new ritual center in the northern sector of Cairo had to be connected with the palace, the center of the Isma'ili city. Al-'Azīz's procession to the *muṣallā* for the festival prayer in 380/990 demonstrates how the link between the palace and the northern part of the city was created. From that year on, processions on the festivals and during Ramaḍān were not just a means of getting from one point to another: they were meant to connect the points as well. The procession itself was not unusual. The caliph rode with his troops,[67] who wore costumes of ornamented brocade (*dībāj muthaqqal*) and were girded with swords and belts of gold. Horses led by hand during the parade (*janā'ib*) had jeweled saddles of gold and amber.[68] Elephants, ridden by soldiers bearing arms, paraded in front of him. The caliph himself rode under a parasol ornamented with jewels (*miẓalla thaqīla bi'l-jawhar*) and carried the staff (*qaḍīb*) of Muḥammad ("his grandfather") in his hand.[69]

However, the procession route was altered. Al-'Azīz had ordered the construction of benches (*maṣāṭib*, sing. *maṣṭaba*) from the palace to the *muṣallā*.[70] He commanded the Believers (i.e., the Isma'ilis), seated according to rank by the chief qadi, Muḥammad b. al-Nu'mān,[71] to sit on the benches and recite "'God is most great' (*takbīr*), so that it would be continuous from the palace to the *muṣallā*."[72] The benches established a physical link between the palace and the *muṣallā*; the continous recitation of "God is most great" by the Isma'ilis constituted a liturgical link; the procession itself was still another link. The recitation of "God is most great" from the time the caliph left the palace until he entered the *muṣallā* was, it seems, a way of sacralizing the procession route. The prayer for the Festival of Fast Breaking and the Sacrificial Festival has neither a first call to prayer (*adhān*) nor a second call to prayer (*iqāma*); thus uttering "God is most great" (*takbīrat al-iḥrām*) is the beginning of the prayer.[73] In fact, we might say that the festival prayer (*ṣalāt al-ʿīd*) began at the start of the caliph's procession and that the procession itself was now part of the prayer.

The founding of the new mosque, building the benches, and staging processions for Ramaḍān as well as the festival all point to a new conception of the role that ritual was to play in the construction of a fully integrated ritual city. The allegorical interpretation (*ta'wīl*) of the festival in Ismaʿili thought makes the connection among the procession, the prayer, the construction of the ritual city, and the centrality of the imam even more plausible. Two works of the Fatimid jurist and ideologue al-Qāḍī al-Nuʿmān (d. 363/974), *The Pillars of Islam* (*Daʿā'im al-Islām*) and *The Allegorical Interpretation of the Pillars* (*Ta'wīl al-daʿā'im*),[74] designate three festivals, which are Friday prayer (*al-jumʿa*), the Festival of Fast Breaking (*ʿīd al-fiṭr*) and the Sacrificial Festival (*ʿīd al-aḍḥā*).[75] Each festival has an esoteric (*bāṭin*) paradigm: that of the Friday prayer is the call or mission (*daʿwa*) of Muḥammad, which is also the call to the hidden imams; of the fast of Ramaḍān, concealment (*al-kitmān wa'l-satr*); of the breaking of the fast, the *mahdī* (rightly guided one) and the revealing of the hidden mission;[76] of the sacrificial feast, the *qā'im* (riser).[77] These ritual observances thus symbolized the imam himself.

In his *Allegorical Interpretation,* al-Qāḍī al-Nuʿmān makes explicit the connection between the festivals and their paradigms of the *mahdī* and *qā'im*. In the *Pillars,* he prescribes that the prayer for the two festivals should be neither in a house nor in a mosque but in an open place,[78] and he says that one should bring out arms (*silāḥ*) to the prayer.[79] The paradigm (*mathal*) of going out to prayer (*al-khurūj li'l-ṣalāt*) and taking out arms (*ikhrāj al-silāḥ*) is striving against the enemies (*jihād*).[80] He explained this further by requiring that the prayer be held in an "open field" (*al-baraz*), that is, the *muṣallā*.[81] These ideas were current even in the North African period of the caliphate and are probably the appropriate intellectual climate in which the story of the master of the ass (*ṣāḥib al-ḥimār*, i.e., the Kharijite Abū Yazīd) should be viewed.[82] The creation of an historical fiction demonstrating that the *muṣallā* was a symbolic battleground gave the *muṣallā* a particular charge that carried over into the Egyptian period of the caliphate.

If these ideas were current even in the North African period, why did it take nearly twenty years for them to influence the character of Fatimid processions? The answer lies, perhaps, in the changing political circumstances in which these ideas circulated. Al-ʿAzīz, a talented and ambitious administrator, was also an active campaigner.[83] He was preoccupied with securing southern and central Syria, but both the Byzantines and the Qarmatians proved to be formidable enemies. In spite of several humiliating defeats, he persisted; he was restrained only by the influence of his powerful wazir, Ibn Killis.[84] When Ibn Killis died in 380/990, al-ʿAzīz renewed his Syrian ambitions, albeit at a considerable risk. At the same time, he was changing the composition of the army that was to fight those battles. He introduced new Turkish elements into the army, displacing the North African Berber troops that had been traditionally the mainstay of the dynasty, a move that required considerable political maneuvering and a skillfull balancing of conflicting interests.[85]

The newly created urban map provided a landscape on which these complicated political, religious, and military agendas could be integrated and expressed. The formal procession of these diverse troops together with the caliph to the *muṣallā* may well have been intended to underscore their unity in the service of the ruler. Such a procession through the ritual city could serve as a powerful reminder to these troops, who lived in Cairo in quarters named for their regiments, that this was the caliph's city. In Ramaḍān of this same year, al-ʿAzīz had gone in procession with five thousand soldiers to the Azhar Mosque.[86] From 380/990 on, descriptions of Fatimid processions nearly always include detailed information about the composition of the regiments who paraded through the city. On this new urban map, the procession to the *muṣallā* could be read as an assertion of political and military unity and of loyalty to the caliph in the face of external threats to the empire's stability.

Another set of concerns, related specifically to Ismaʿilism, was also being expressed through these urban processions. Just as the imam himself stood at the center of belief, the palace stood at the center of the spatial arrangements of Cairo. From this point of view, the procession could be seen as a relatively faithful representation of the esoteric meaning (*bāṭin*) of the festivals. While creating the ritual city, al-ʿAzīz assured the continued centrality of the palace through a series of physical, liturgical, and processional links between the palace and the ritual centers of the city. In doing so, he asserted the ritual unity of the city of Cairo in specifically Ismaʿili terms.

The Isma'ili ritual city was being created not only in new construction and processions, but also in the increasing participation of the court in the ritual affairs of the residents of both Cairo and Fustat. Al-'Azīz began to provide food for those who attended the Azhar Mosque during the months of Rajab, Sha'bān, and Ramaḍān, when the practice of seclusion in the mosque (*i'tikāf*) was especially commendable. He was also the first Fatimid caliph to lay out a table during Ramaḍān for those people who broke their fast after praying at the Mosque of 'Amr in Fustat.[87] In the years before Fustat became a part of the Fatimid ritual city, these distributions of food helped to redefine the spaces in which popular religious practices were observed. The gradual integration of Cairo and Fustat into a single ritual city did not take place through the imposition of Isma'ili doctrine or practice on the local population, nor did it occur in a strictly linear or evolutionary fashion. The two cities remained distinct in rank, in composition, in religion, in doctrine, and in practice. In Fustat, where the religious practices of Christians and Jews already constituted an important category of difference, the continued ritual practices of the Sunni population may have seemed neither particularly challenging nor problematic. Unlike the explicit resistance of the preacher (*khaṭīb*) who sabotaged prayer in the first year of Fatimid rule in Egypt, the continuation of these local practices did not, in itself, necessarily imply resistance to Fatimid political or religious hegemony. The caliph's recognition and support of these local practices may actually have defined them into the category of the permissible.

THE INTEGRATION OF FUSTAT INTO THE RITUAL CITY

By the time that al-Ḥākim assumed the throne in 386/996 as a boy of eleven,[88] the ritual city was well established and was being used as the stage on which political and religious dramas were played. Al-Ḥākim continued to construct the Isma'ili ritual city by completing the mosque that his father had begun and by building congregational mosques in both Fustat and the Qarāfa cemetery. Al-Ḥākim also elaborated and expanded the caliph's direct participation in the celebration of Ramaḍān and the two festivals more than any previous ruler, and it was he who accomplished, in topography and ceremony, the integration of Fustat into the Fatimid ritual city.

Al-ʿAzīz died in Bilbays on 28 Ramaḍān 386/996;[89] his heir apparent was declared imam the next day and entered Cairo, behind his father's coffin, wearing a plain wide robe with wide sleeves (*durrāʿa*), a turban with gems, carrying a lance (*rumḥ*), and girded with a sword. For al-Ḥākim, as for his father and grandfather, the palace was the center of his court. He held an audience in the *īwān* hall of the palace on the last day of the month, seated on a gold throne, and because his accession coincided with the Festival of Fast Breaking (*ʿīd al-fiṭr*), the celebration of the festival was incorporated into the ceremonial events that marked the accession of the new caliph. In the three days since al-ʿAzīz had died, the young caliph had returned to Cairo, held an audience, and installed the highest ranking officials of his state. The primary location for the ritual celebration of the festival was the *muṣallā*, which now became as important a site as the palace for the reconstitution of the state under the new caliph.

The Kutāma Berbers, still the most powerful faction of the Fatimid army, boycotted al-Ḥākim's first audience in the palace, and gathered instead at the *muṣallā* to demand that Ibn ʿAmmār be entrusted with the leadership of the government.[90] Shortly after, they went again to the *muṣallā* to receive their rations.[91] On the first of Shawwāl, Ibn ʿAmmār ordered the chief qadi, Muḥammad b. al-Nu'mān, who had performed the funeral prayer over al-ʿAzīz, to lead the festival prayer and declare the mission (*iqāmat al-daʿwa*) in the name of the new caliph at the *muṣallā*.[92] The grief-stricken qadi, now wearing one of the late caliph's gilded swords, ascended the minbar, kissed the spot where al-ʿAzīz would have sat, and wept. The congregation burst into tears. After delivering the sermon (*khuṭba*), he again lamented the late caliph.[93] Walking between two rows of soldiers (almost certainly Kutāma), he returned to the palace from the *muṣallā*, following the same route that al-ʿAzīz himself had used to help forge the Ismaʿili ritual city and thus established ceremonially the continuity between the caliphate of al-ʿAzīz and the young al-Ḥākim. However, Ibn al-Nuʿmān was also asserting a particular configuration of power in the Fatimid state. Al-ʿAzīz had brought in Turkish slave soldiers, whose skills in archery were necessary to his campaigns in Syria, and these soldiers quickly began to contest the privileged position of the Kutāma Berbers in the Fatimid state. Both Ibn al-Nuʿmān and Ibn ʿAmmār were associated with the Berber factions, who had been the mainstay of Fatimid power in North Africa and Egypt.

When Ibn al-Nu'mān returned to the palace, he saw a gold throne set up in the Iwan, with a gold banquet table (*simāṭ*) in front of it. Al-Ḥākim came out of his private chambers on a light-colored horse and sat at the banquet table while those in his service ate.[94] Earlier that day, he had appeared on a dark horse, girded with a sword, attended by his eunuch Barjawān, while Ibn 'Ammār had issued orders on the new caliph's behalf. The young caliph was clearly a pawn in an intense power struggle between Ibn 'Ammār and Barjawān. Now, however, he sat by himself. At the banquet, al-Ḥākim was presented as the sole head of the Fatimid political and religious order, the authority who would balance the loyalties and interests of competing factions, after the prayer in which his name was pronounced in the sermon for the first time.

Al-Ḥākim did not lead a Friday prayer during Ramaḍān until two years later, in 388/998,[95] after which Friday prayers were held consistently in more than one mosque.[96] At the same time that the urban landscape was changing, Fatimid ceremonial was being elaborated. Since festival prayers took place at the *muṣallā* instead of a mosque,[97] they did not serve to integrate the mosques of Cairo fully into the ritual city. Al-Ḥākim began the elaboration of the practices associated with Friday prayer that would ultimately help to integrate new mosques into the ritual city. In 388/998, a he sat under a dome (*qubba*) while he gave the sermon in the Friday prayer,[98] following the practice established by al-Mu'izz, who delivered a sermon while sitting concealed by banners under a dome during festival prayer at the *muṣallā* in 362/973.[99] The evidence suggests that the Fatimids borrowed freely from the highly developed festival prayers when elaborating or introducing new rituals.

The ritual city had been firmly established in Cairo, but it was only under al-Ḥākim that Fustat was fully integrated. Where al-'Azīz had laid out banquets to incorporate ritual practices into an Isma'ili context, al-Ḥākim began a building program that integrated Fustat topographically into the ritual city. In 393/1002–3, he built a new mosque at Rāshida, on the outskirts of Fustat.[100] The Rāshida mosque was built on the site of a Jacobite church surrounded by Jewish and Christian graves. The mosque was completed in Ramaḍān 395/1005, and al-Maqrīzī's account implies that al-Ḥākim led Friday prayer there.[101] The mosque must have been of considerable importance to the caliph, and several sources mention that it was known at the time as the Congregational Mosque of al-Ḥākim (*al-jāmiʿ al-ḥākimī*).[102] In 398/1008, al-Ḥākim led prayer and preached the sermon there. In 401/1010–11, the mosque was torn down, apparently because the prayer niche (*miḥrāb*) was not properly aligned with the direction of Mecca (*qibla*).[103] The prayer niche was recalculated, the mosque rebuilt, and in Ramaḍān 403/1014, the caliph led Friday prayer there again.

In the same year that he first built the Rāshida mosque, al-Ḥākim began his most important construction activity by allocating forty thousand dinars to finish the mosque his father's wazir had started. The mosque came to be known by its new patron, al-Ḥākim, and was part of a cluster of structures and spaces that, from the time of al-ʿAzīz, concentrated ritual and ceremonial activity in the northern sector of the city. Now, al-Ḥākim added to the existing monument in ways that claimed the mosque, and the space it occupied, as his own. As Irene Bierman has demonstrated, al-Ḥākim's completion of the mosque outside of Bāb al-Futūḥ (as it is called in contemporary sources) marked the first time that "visually prominent writing" is displayed on the exterior of a Fatimid monument.[104] The elaboration of what Bierman calls "Officially Sponsored Writing" is clearly analogous to the elaboration of ceremonial.[105] Both point to a more complex understanding by al-Ḥākim of the ritual city and its possible uses in communicating his perceptions of his own religious and political authority. Both the exterior and interior inscriptions of this mosque were highly charged ideologically and must be understood in the context of the new uses of urban space that were being explored by the caliph.[106]

The north and west minaret inscriptions, dating to 393/1002–3, establish a clear association between this new mosque and the prayer of the rightly guided (Q. 9:18 and 24:36), who must be understood as the Fatimid imams, the direct descendants of ʿAlī and Fāṭima. The exterior inscriptions repeat the standard Fatimid foundation inscription several times, combining it with verses that invoke blessings for the Prophet and his family and praise God's benevolence in providing a light for humanity (i.e., the imam).[107] They also exhort the Believers to pray and pay alms, acts that are connected in Ismaʿili allegorical interpretation with the Ismaʿili mission (*daʿwa*) and the imam of the age. In the *Pillars of Islam*, the value of prayers in various mosques was established. Thus, praying in the Mosque in Mecca is worth one hundred thousand prayers; at the Mosque of the Prophet in Medina, ten thousand; in Jerusalem, one thousand; down to a man praying alone in his house, counting for one.[108] The *Allegorical Interpretation of the Pillars* interprets this hierarchy in terms of the ranks of the mission (*daʿwa*). In the external world (*ẓāhir*), says al-Qāḍī al-Nuʿmān, mosques are the houses (*buyūt*) in which people gather for prayer. These mosques are ordered in ranks (*ṭabaqāt*), the highest being the Mosque of Mecca, which is the paradigm of the Master of the Age (*ṣāḥib al-zamān*), whether he be a prophet or an imam. The descending order of mosques and their paradigms follows the ranks of the mission. The Qur'anic prooftexts offered by al-Qāḍī al-Nuʿmān are 24:36–37 and 9:18, the same verses that appear in inscriptions on bands of the north and west minarets of the Mosque of al-Ḥākim.[109]

Al-Ḥākim made two related claims in this unusual inscriptional program. He asserted the place of this mosque in the hierarchy of mosques that was established in both the *Pillars of Islam* and the *Allegorical Interpretation of the Pillars,* and he reiterated the link between his mosque and the Ismaʿili mission (*daʿwa*). Only two years later, in 395/1005, al-Ḥākim established the House of Wisdom (*dār al-ḥikma*) in the Western Palace. The House of Wisdom had a large library and served as a school where a wide variety of subjects, including theology, philosophy, medicine, astronomy, and even Sunni law were taught. It was also the training academy for Ismaʿili missionaries (*duʿāt*). The lectures (*majālis*) were aimed at both Ismaʿilis and non-Ismaʿilis.[110] Al-Ḥākim thus continued the tradition begun by his father establishing direct links between ritual centers and the palace, the heart of the missionary movement.

In addition to creating an important display of the Qur'anic verses, al-Ḥākim's titles were made especially prominent.[111] The visual prominence of the caliph's titulature in the foundation inscriptions constituted a powerful assertion of his legitimacy in particular. The other mosques in Mecca, Medina, and Jerusalem alluded to by the Qur'anic inscription were a part of the Fatimid empire. The caliph's name was pronounced in the *khuṭba* every Friday in those mosques. Through the complicated allusions of the allegorical interpretation (*ta'wīl*), which created an equivalence between the Mosque of Mecca and the Fatimid imam as the Master of the Age (*ṣāḥib al-zamān*), al-Ḥākim asserted pride of place to his own mosque. One can carry the reasoning a step further: the esoteric paradigm for prayer is the Isma'ili mission (*da'wa*). It was thus possible to argue that praying in the new mosque was actually the equivalent of praying in the Mosque of Mecca. Al-Ḥākim, the caliph who came to power as a boy of eleven under the guidance of tutors, now, as a man of eighteen, claimed not only the mosque, but also the empire as his own.

Through both construction and ceremony, al-Ḥākim articulated his claims to the empire as a whole while integrating Fustat into the Isma'ili ritual city. By the year 396/1006, he was hosting banquets every night and leading prayer on three Fridays during Ramaḍān. Although the accounts do not tell us precisely where he led prayer, the evidence strongly suggests that the locations were the Azhar Mosque, the relatively new Rāshida Mosque, and the Mosque outside of Bāb al-Futūḥ.[112] But al-Ḥākim's claims in this enlarged ritual city were articulated in the face of several open challenges to the caliph's authority in the years between 393/1002–3 and 401/1010–1011.[113] In 395/1004, a coalition of Arab and Berber tribes led by Abū Rakwa revolted in the name of a pretender of the Umayyad house. Abū Rakwa's rebellion included a siege of Alexandria and had considerable economic and political consequences in Egypt, causing food shortages in Cairo. Al-Ḥākim enacted a number of harsh measures to preserve order and, at the same time, enforced the sumptuary laws against the Jews and Christians, ordered the cursing of the Companions of the Prophet, forbade people to appear in the streets after sunset to conduct business, prohibited the consumption of garden mallow (*mulūkhiyya*) and fish without scales, and ordered the destruction of several churches.[114] In the aftermath of the revolt, which was successfully quelled by 397/1007, the caliph reversed some of his harsher edicts. He prohibited the cursing of the Companions of the Prophet and ordered the inscribed curses to be erased.[115] This seems to have inaugurated a period of greater tolerance of Sunni practices, and in Rajab 399/1009, the caliph proclaimed that people could begin and end their fast by the sighting of the moon, rather than by the customary calculations of the Isma'ilis, if they wished. He declared that muezzins would include the formula "Come to good works" in the call to prayer but announced that no one who omitted it would be punished. Every Muslim was enjoined to act in accordance with his own judgement in matters of religion.[116] These measures seem to have been less a part of a systematic program than a response to the vicissitudes of governance in light of the recent challenge by a rebel who had evoked considerable sympathy from the non-Isma'ili masses of the empire. Indeed, only five months later, al-Ḥākim reversed these policies.[117]

The Fatimids faced a different kind of challenge in 401/1010, when the Jarrāḥid Mufarrij revolted in Palestine. In 403/1012, he declared the 'Alid sharīf of Mecca as caliph.[118] The sharīf, Abu'l-Futūḥ, received the oath of allegiance (*bay'a*) in Mecca and then again in Ramla, where his new followers kissed the ground before him and addressed him as "commander of the faithful" (*amīr al-mu'minīn*). He delivered the Friday sermon (*khuṭba*) in his own name and gave himself the title Al-Rāshid li-dīn allāh (the rightly guided in God's religion). He was recognized in both the Hijaz and Palestine as the caliph.[119] Al-Ḥākim finally crushed the revolt only by bribing the sharīf's supporters. While the rebellion of Abū Rakwa had been a potentially devastating military and political challenge, it did not have the same charge as the rebellion of the Jarrāḥids. Whatever the merit of Abū Rakwa's claims of Umayyad lineage and its implications for the Abbasid caliphate, he could make no legitimate claim to the imamate. The sharīf of Mecca, however, was not only a descendant of the Prophet, but also an 'Alid. He could thus claim some of the same privileges of lineage (*nasab*) as the Fatimid caliph himself. Furthermore, the sharīf controlled Mecca, the destination for Muslim pilgrims and the sacred city that all Muslims face when they pray. Long before the eleventh century, it was a well-established ambition among political and religious leaders in the Islamic world to claim Mecca as part of their territory and to mark that claim by announcing their name in the Friday sermon. The sharīf's claims to the Hijaz and Palestine thus constituted not only a stinging political insult, but also a challenge to al-Ḥākim's spiritual authority.

Al-Ḥākim's response to this challenge to his authority was written, quite literally, on the face of Cairo. At the same time as the Jarrāḥid revolt, al-Ḥākim added bastions (*arkān*) to the corner towers of the Mosque of al-Ḥākim,[120] completely concealing the original exterior inscriptions. The interior inscriptions are organized around the related themes of unbelief, on the one hand, and true belief, on the other. The verses in the central aisle, dome, and left bays (Q. 48:1–22, 3:1–17, 6:1–17, 7:1–22, 8:1–13) revolve around the themes introduced in the sura Victory (*al-fatḥ*): God has provided a Messenger or a Book to show the true path to men and women; it has been rejected by the unbelievers, sinners, and hypocrites; the omnipotent God has visited the unbelievers with affliction and chastisement from which there can be no escape save God himself. The inscriptions on the right side of the mosque seem at first glance to be somewhat disjointed, but in fact they reiterate the same theme as those in the left bays. The *qibla* bay contains the first five verses of the Fātiḥa and Q. 2:255-56 (Throne Verse and following verse).

The entire inscriptional program of the mosque's interior is really an elaborate commentary on the pious invocation "Guide us in the straight path, the path of those whom you have blessed, not of those against whom you are wrathful, nor of those who have gone astray." The Throne Verse, a classic Qur'anic statement of God's omnipotence and omniscience, appears twice. The bays on the right side (Q. 36:1–25, 2:255–86, 2:1–20, 4:1–12) reiterate exhortations to follow God's envoys, warnings that the idols of the unbelievers cannot protect them against God, assertions that God protects the believers, and admonitions to believers to expend their wealth in God's way.[121] If Jonathan Bloom's dating of the interior inscriptions to between 401/1010 and 403/1012 is correct, then this program should also be understood in terms of the challenges to political and spiritual authority of both Abū Rakwa and the Jarrāḥids.[122]

The new exterior inscriptions on the west salient frieze, done sometime between 401/1010 and 403/1012–13, have a very different tone from the original inscriptions. These later inscriptions can be read as a commentary on the original verses carved on the minarets in light of the catastrophic developments of the first few years of the eleventh century. The sharīf of Mecca was most probably the real audience for the inscriptions on the new salients. The rebels had, indeed, "taken a mosque in opposition and unbelief" (Q. 9:107).[123] The Jarrāḥids and their pretender-caliph had effectively turned the most venerated mosques of Islam into mosques of "opposition and unbelief." They could be likened to the hypocrites (*munāfiqūn*) whose attempt to establish a mosque during the Prophet's lifetime had occasioned the revelation.[124] Even more important are the verses that follow, Q. 9:108–9:

> Never stand [to pray] there. A place of worship which was founded upon duty [to God] from the first day is worthier for you to stand in; therein are men who love to purify themselves.

> God loves the purifiers. Is he who founded his building upon duty to God and His good pleasure better; or he who founded his building on the brink of a crumbling, overhanging precipice so that it toppled with him into the fire of hell? God guides not wrongdoing people.

While not included in the inscription, no one could fail to think of these verses when reading Q. 9:107. The mosque completed by al-Ḥākim was surely a "place of worship founded upon duty to Allah." Moreover, in the internal logic of the allegorical interpretation (*ta'wīl*), it had already been demonstrated to be the equivalent of the Mosque of Mecca.[125]

The completed mosque was furnished at a cost of five thousand dinars in 403/1012.[126] As in earlier years, in 403/1012 al-Ḥākim led Friday prayer during Ramaḍān at three mosques. The location of the mosques, however, indicates that construction of the ritual city was taking a new direction. There was no prayer that year at the Azhar Mosque. Instead, the caliph led prayer at the newly completed Mosque of al-Ḥākim, the Rāshida Mosque, and the Mosque of ʿAmr.[127] Both the Rāshida Mosque and the Mosque of ʿAmr were in Fustat, not Cairo, and 403/1012 marked the first year that a Fatimid caliph led prayer at the Mosque of ʿAmr. The descriptions of the processions to these two mosques are notable for their emphasis on the activities of the people rather than on the caliph himself. When he went to the Rāshida Mosque and the Mosque of ʿAmr, the common people walked at his stirrup, "coming between him and his entourage [*mawkib*]."[128] This may have represented an attempt to increase the accessibility of the caliph to the common people, perhaps related to the unsettling political events of recent years.[129] This was certainly not the only mechanism available for the local population who wanted to get the caliph's ear. Since the early years of his reign, al-Ḥākim had dealt with petitions in the palace, and his chamberlain had been ordered not to prevent any petitioner access to him.[130] He had also decreed that no one be kept from approaching him when he went on his nightly excursions.[131] Al-Ḥākim's contradictory edicts concerning the religious practices of the local population already indicated an intense concern with the religious and communal life of the population. Now, caliphal processions in Fustat on these Fridays became communal events as well.

In Cairo, however, there is no report that al-Ḥākim took petitions, as he did in Fustat. The Mosque of al-Ḥākim was furnished with custom-made *dabīqī* linen drapes,[132] silver lamps and chandeliers, and carpets. He gave permission to the jurists (*fuqahā'*) who usually spent the night at the Azhar Mosque to go to the new mosque, and people walked back and forth between the two mosques unimpeded by the palace guard or the nightwatchmen.[133] On Friday, al-Ḥākim led prayer there. The Azhar Mosque was incorporated into the observance only by the jurists. Their unimpeded communication between the two mosques of Cairo linked them to each other, as al-Ḥākim's processions to the two mosques in Fustat linked them to the court. With the addition of the Mosque of ʿAmr, the center of communal and ritual life for the people of Fustat, and the Rāshida Mosque to his itinerary during Ramaḍān, al-Ḥākim integrated Cairo and Fustat into a single ritual city, forty years after the Fatimid conquest of Egypt.

This was also the year in which al-Ḥākim appeared again in festival procession. After his processions to the three mosques during Ramaḍān, he led prayer at the *muṣallā* on the Festival of Fast Breaking. But the procession was remarkably austere. He "went without anything that was usually displayed on that day—i.e., decorations, horses led by hand [*janā'ib*]." He had ten horses with saddles and bridles ornamented in silver, but there were no gold decorations at all. His white parasol (*miẓalla*) had no gold threads, and his costume was plain white without borders or gold threads. He wore no gem in his turban, and the minbar was not furnished with mats of any kind.[134] On the Sacrificial Festival, al-Ḥākim led the prayer, but his nephew, ʿAbd al-Raḥīm Ibn Ilyās, performed the sacrifices on his behalf, while the muezzins recited the formula "God is most great," as they would have in the caliph's presence. In spite of his personal austerity, al-Ḥākim sent magnificent costumes and gems to the qadi Mālik b. Saʿīd al-Fāriqī, who assisted in the sacrifices, and had him paraded on a horse with an inlaid saddle.[135]

The integration of the ritual city was reinforced the following year, when al-Ḥākim led Friday prayer in all four congregational mosques of the two cities: the Azhar Mosque, the Mosque of al-Ḥākim, the Mosque of ʿAmr, and the Rāshida Mosque.[136] There was never another year in which a Fatimid caliph led prayer in all four mosques, but the caliph had a powerful incentive. In 404/1013–14, al-Ḥākim made ʿAbd al-Raḥīm Ibn Ilyās his heir (*walī ʿahd*). The appointment was announced in a proclamation read first in the palace and then in the mosques of Fustat and Cairo, Alexandria, and Ifriqiyya. ʿAbd al-Raḥīm's name was written on banners, coinage, and inscribed textiles (*ṭirāz*).[137] Al-Ḥākim's designation of an heir other than his son was a highly questionable innovation. The reasons for this problematic designation of ʿAbd al-Raḥīm as his successor are still obscure. In a treatise composed by a missionary of al-Ḥākim, father-to-son succession was espoused as a central principle of Ismaʿilism.[138] The year after his appointment, the heir went three times to the Mosque of al-Ḥākim and once to the Azhar Mosque to lead Friday prayer in al-Ḥākim's absence.[139] These Ramaḍān processions were as important as the titles and other insignia of sovereignty that al-Ḥākim had bestowed upon his new heir, since the political and religious authority that ʿAbd al-Raḥīm would inherit were now imprinted in the map of the ritual city.

The ritual city was perhaps the only sign of the caliph's authority that did not suffer due to his increasing asceticism. In Rajab 403/1013, a proclamation was read forbidding people to kiss either the ground before al-Ḥākim or his stirrup and hand during processions. They were commanded to cease imitating the behavior of the polytheists (*ahl al-shirk*, i.e., the Byzantines) in bending toward the ground. The form of greeting should now be simply, "Peace to the Commander of the Faithful, and God's mercy and blessings upon him." They should not, either in speech or in writing, ask God to pray for him. The only formula they should use in offering supplications (*duʿā'*) should be "The peace of God, his favors, and continual blessings upon the Commander of the Faithful." On Friday, the preacher (*khaṭīb*) should say only "O God, bless Muḥammad your Chosen One and grant peace to the Commander of the Faithful ʿAlī your well-beloved. O God, give peace to the Commanders of the Faithful the forebears of the Commander of the Faithful. O God, give your most excellent peace to your servant and deputy (*khalīfa*)." He also prohibited the beating of drums or sounding of trumpets around the palace.[140] He wore sandals instead of shoes and a towel on his head instead of a turban during his nightly excursion.[141] However, he continued to provide generously for the mosques of the city. He sent 814 copies of the Qur'an to the Ibn Ṭūlūn Mosque and seven chests containing 1,290 Qur'ans to the Mosque of ʿAmr. When a census revealed that nearly eight hundred mosques had no revenue, he allocated 9,220 dirhems each month to provide for them.[142] This should serve to remind us that, however tempting it may be to emphasize the erratic character of al-Ḥākim's decrees and behavior, the evidence as a whole points to an overriding concern with urban and communal life that persisted throughout his reign. To be sure, that concern was sometimes expressed in brutally harsh and repressive edicts; but it was just as likely to be expressed in tolerant and lenient measures that permitted the population to observe the full range of its diverse religious practices. What mattered to al-Ḥākim was communal life in an urban landscape that he had come to understand as a single ritual city.[143]

Immediately upon al-Ḥākim's death in 411/1021, the ritual city was instrumental in establishing a smooth succession in traditional Isma'ili terms. At the time al-Ḥākim disappeared, his heir apparent was 'Abd al-Raḥīm Ibn Ilyās, who had been appointed in 404/1013–14. But al-Ḥākim's sister, Sitt al-mulk (who was implicated in the caliph's death), wanted to secure the throne for al-Ḥākim's son, Abu'l-Ḥasan 'Alī.[144] Her efforts were made somewhat easier by the fact that 'Abd al-Raḥīm was serving as governor of Damascus. Sitt al-mulk concealed her brother's death for several weeks while she orchestrated Abu'l-Ḥasan's succession. She arranged for the commanders of the army and for other high-ranking officials of the state to take the oath of allegiance (*bay'a*) in private. In view of the role that the city had come to play as an expression of political and religious ideas, it is not surprising that Sitt al-mulk waited nearly two months, until the Sacrificial Festival, to make her brother's death public and to announce the accession of the new caliph. In 403/1012, some months before he was declared as heir, 'Abd al-Raḥīm Ibn Ilyās had performed the sacrifices on behalf of al-Ḥākim. This had been the first public indication of 'Abd al-Raḥīm's special relationship to the caliph, and now Sitt al-mulk refuted the apparent significance of the earlier Sacrificial Festival by publicly proclaiming Abu'l-Ḥasan as the imam al-Ẓāhir on the same festival. The festival prayer at the *muṣallā* was led by the chief qadi in the name of the deceased al-Ḥākim, but al-Ẓāhir did not receive the oath of allegiance (*bay'a*) until after the qadi had returned to the palace.[145] This sequence of events evoked the accession of al-Ḥākim, when the chief qadi had returned to the palace along the same route after leading prayer, enacting on the city's map the transmission of authority from the deceased imam to his successor.

Al-Ẓāhir, who matured when the fully integrated ritual city

was well established, added still another procession to the growing repertoire of Fatimid ceremonial. In 415/1024, he went in procession on the first of Ramaḍān to Masjid Tibr.[146] The first of Ramaḍān in that year fell on Thursday, but the preparations for the procession began on Tuesday night. The Kutāma, Turks, and the rest of the troops were ordered to collect arms from the treasury and to stand around the palace awaiting further instructions. They waited until dawn and were then informed that the caliph would ride on the next day. Anyone who still did not have arms was ordered to get them. After this long wait, the Kutāma complained that they were hungry and requested bread. At the end of the day, Kutāma foot soldiers distributed arms to them. On Thursday, al-Ẓāhir rode in procession with his troops, wearing a "round" robe of *dabīqī* linen with gold threads and a matching turban (*qamīṣ mudayyar mudhahhab dabīqī wa-ʿimāma mithlahu*) and seated under a parasol with gold threads (*miẓalla mudhahhaba*) carried by the Ṣaqlabī eunuch Muẓaffar.[147] Behind him, a Kutāma dignitary carried his lance (*rumḥ*), while regiments of Turks, Kutāma, Qayṣariyya, ʿAbīd, Bāṭiliyya, Daylam, and others marched in front of him. The high officials of the state (*rijāl al-dawla*) rode behind him to Masjid Tibr and returned.

During Ramaḍān of the same year, al-Ẓāhir rode in procession on two Fridays to the Azhar Mosque and the Mosque of al-Ḥākim.[148] The chief qadi Ibn Abi'l-ʿAwwām and his boon-companion Ibrāhīm ascended the minbar with him and lowered an unpatterned white curtain (*musmaṭ bayāḍ*) that covered the dome to conceal him.[149] Incense burners containing ambergris were set before him. He delivered the sermon, and the qadi raised the curtain, he descended, prayed, and returned to the palace.[150]

On the Festival of Fast Breaking, al-Ẓāhir's procession included his troops, elephants and giraffes, gilded banners, and drums. All of the commanders of the Turkish regiments and the eunuchs, who were now among the most privileged soldiers in the Fatimid army, bore arms.[151] Al-Ẓāhir wore a silk robe with a matching turban, held a staff in his hand, and wore a sword. The Ṣaqlabī eunuch Muẓaffar carried a parasol with gold borders (or threads) over his head, the lance was carried, and black slaves paraded before him wearing costumes with gold threads.[152] The caliph led prayer and then ascended the minbar. The chief qadi Ibn Abi'l-ʿAwwām was summoned and ascended the minbar.[153] The other officials who were summoned and ascended the minbar were the boon-companion Ibrāhīm, Shams al-mulk, ʿAlī b. Masʿūd Ibn Abi'l-Ḥusayn Zayn al-mulk, ʿAlī b. al-Faḍl, and ʿAbd Allāh b. al-Ḥājib. The former governor of Sicily, Tāj al-dawla Ibn Abi'l-Ḥusayn was summoned but did not attend.[154] When the banners were fastened to conceal him, he delivered the sermon and descended, returning to the palace, where the banquet was laid out. Unlike his predecessor, al-Ẓāhir did not actually appear at the banquet; he observed the proceedings from a belvedere (*manẓara*) overlooking the audience hall. In addition, all of al-Ẓāhir's eunuch commanders held banquets at their own residences; people attended them after leaving the palace banquet.[155]

The description of the Sacrificial Festival in 415/1025 is nearly identical, with the addition of the ritual slaughtering of sacrificial animals.[156] The most significant difference is the absence of the chief qadi Ibn Abi' l-ʿAwwām and the pronounced role of the chief missionary (*dāʿī*) Qāsim b. ʿAbd al-ʿAzīz b. al-Nuʿmān. He summoned the officials who ascended the minbar with the caliph. This time, the former governor of Sicily was excluded, and the Ṣaqlabī eunuch Muẓaffar (the bearer of the parasol), as well as one Ḥasan b. Rajā' b. Abi'l-Ḥusayn and a cousin of ʿAbd Allāh b. al-Ḥājib were included. After the sacrifices following prayer, the caliph slaughtered additional animals at the palace. The scribe of the chief qadi came to distribute the meat to high ranking officials, but the black slave troops (*ʿabīd*) seized the meat and later plundered the banquet attended by the officials of the state, the caliph's family, and the Kutāma. Al-Musabbiḥī recounts that they attacked the palace, shouting, "Hunger! Hunger! We have more right to our master's banquet," as they were beaten back by the caliph's Ṣaqlabī bodyguard. A riot ensued, and the chief qadi's scribe was not able to make the proper distributions of meat until the following day, when thirteen additional she-camels were slaughtered.[157]

Although the evidence is scant, we can look at 414–15/1024–25 as a sort of snapshot of Fatimid politics and its relationship to the ritual city and Fatimid ceremonial. These were the years in which Sitt al-mulk died and the caliph was caught in a power struggle between a number of high-ranking officials who successfully isolated him in the palace. In fact, the procession on the first day of Ramaḍān was likely the invention of one of these administrators, one who clearly understood the political uses of ceremonial. The procession should not be read as an assertion of the caliph's independence. Instead, it is probably best interpreted as an expression of his isolation. Masjid Tibr was the destination of the caliph's ordinary excursions, probably insignificant pleasure outings.[158] It does not appear that the procession on the first day of Ramaḍān incorporated Masjid Tibr into the ritual city. No prayer was performed there, and it was not part of procession routes for later caliphs.

Processions were now used explicitly to balance the interests of competing factions. The prominence of the Kutāma in processions, for example, is a noteworthy feature of the processions of 415/1025. The position of the Kutāma declined steadily during the reigns of al-ʿAzīz, al-Ḥākim, and al-Ẓāhir. They never recovered from al-ʿAzīz's introduction of large numbers of Turkish troops into the Fatimid army. Despite their loss of actual power and position, they clearly retained a certain prestige. One of the markers of power during the reign of al-Ẓāhir was control of the Office of the Kutāma (*dīwān al-kutāmiyīn*), and appointment to or dismissal from that post signaled the rise and fall of the most highly placed officials at the court.[159] However, the eunuch Miʿḍād, who took over the Office of the Kutāma after Shams al-mulk's dismissal, was not among the dignitaries summoned to ascend the minbar, nor was any other representative of the Kutāma.

The ceremonies of 415/1025 showed the caliph at the head of the elaborate system of patronage that stood at the heart of Fatimid administration. The distributions of meat on the Sacrificial Festival were a part of the caliph's patronage of the state officials (*arbāb al-rusūm*, lit. "the men of designated portions") who served him. These men sponsored their own networks of patronage and the meat they received would have been re-distributed among their own supporters. The palace food riot staged by the black slaves and other troops was a protest not only against the caliph, but also against the rioters' own patrons, who had failed to protect their interests.

As the heads of this elaborate network of patronage, the caliphs had kept competing interests in check. Now, their role became increasingly symbolic. The real powers of the state lay behind the caliphate. The increasing factionalization of the army, the diminishing power of the caliph, and the gradual emergence of a symbolic Fatimid caliphate were all marked by the organization of the processions during Ramaḍān 415/1024 and the multiplication of insignia of sovereignty. The procession to the festival prayer in 415/1024 is the first report in which the staff (*qaḍīb*), lance (*rumḥ*), sword (*sayf*) and parasol (*miẓalla*) are all mentioned together. The number of officials who ascended the minbar with the caliph appears to have increased at least twofold.[160] Coming as they do at what appears to be the nadir of al-Ẓāhir's power, these developments signify not power but, rather, the illusion of power. In the years following al-Ẓāhir's caliphate, the militarization of the Fatimid state and the continued loss of power by the Fatimid caliph, the multiplication of insignia, the ostentation of costuming, and the elaboration of ceremonial would increase as the real powers of the state manipulated these visual symbols of caliphal authority. These men would also leave their own very visible mark on the ritual city that the early Fatimid caliphs had constructed and that their successors would reinterpret.

THE RESTORATION OF AL-ĀMIR AND THE REINTERPRETATION OF THE RITUAL CITY

After the description of the celebration of Ramaḍān and the festivals in 415/1025, a full century passes before there is any mention again of processions or banquets on either Ramaḍān or the festivals in the chronicles. Because of the general sparsity of information on these one hundred years, it is risky to advance a general theory of the development of Fatimid ceremonial in this period. Even so, there is evidence of dramatic change in the observance of festivals during the years when the wazir Badr al-Jamālī (fl. 466–87/1073–94) and his son al-Afḍal (fl. 487–515/1094–1121) were the virtual rulers of the Fatimid empire. Al-Afḍal was following Badr's example when he observed the festival by standing under the arch of the gate of his residence in Cairo to await the beginning of the prayer. Even after al-Afḍal had boldly built a new residence in Fustat called "Seat of the Kingdom" (*dār al-mulk*), he still came to Cairo early on the morning of the festival. When it was time to pray, he would enter the Iwan of the palace through the Festival Gate (*bāb al-ʿīd*), traditionally the caliph's exit to the *muṣallā*, where the chief qadi would lead him in prayer. Al-Afḍal would sit on a platform until the sermon was finished and then would enter the caliph's audience hall (*majlis*), pay homage in private, and receive a robe of honor (*khilʿa*) before returning to his residence in Fustat.[161] The elaborate processions to the *muṣallā* in which the caliph himself led his community in prayer seem to have been abandoned. These urban processions, which had come to signify the political and religious authority of the caliph, could not serve the purposes of al-Afḍal. Clearly, the city of Cairo was too closely identified with the authority of the caliph. Al-Afḍal had failed in his attempt to establish Fustat as a viable rival to Cairo for even temporal administration. Cairo was still the seat of the Fatimid caliphate, and her symbolic value was too important to ignore or transform. The only solution for al-Afḍal may have been to suppress one of the caliph's most powerful expressions of his political authority, urban processions.

When the caliph al-Āmir was restored to power in 515/1121 upon the death of al-Afḍal, it had been some time since the caliph had properly celebrated the festivals.[162] The new wazir, al-Ma'mūn, disapproved of the extent to which caliphal prerogatives had been usurped, and both he and the caliph's eunuchs complained about the insufficient celebration of the festival. They advised the caliph to sit in the belvedere (*manẓara*) between the Gold Gate (*bāb al-dhahab*) and the River Gate (*bāb al-baḥr*) to watch a military parade. At the time of prayer, the wazir headed a procession of amirs and soldiers who passed beneath the belvedere. The caliph's gaze "filled them with *baraka*."[163] Al-Ma'mūn intended to restore the caliph as the symbolic head of the state while asserting his own position, just as the eunuchs wished to reassert their lost prestige. But al-Ma'mūn was restoring "the customs that had existed before the days of Badr and al-Afḍal" in a very different kind of state. The army was an important and visible branch of state in the first century of Fatimid rule; in the second century, it was the state—and the restored caliphal ceremonies for Ramaḍān and the festivals, as well as for non-Islamic celebrations, reflected this new character.

The observance of the Festival of Fast Breaking in 515/1121 was complicated by the fact that the wazir al-Afḍal had died on that day. This presented a delicate problem for al-Āmir, who faced the potential wrath of the deceased wazir's sons and the troops they patronized. How was he to combine the requirements of mourning with the festival? The state had been reconstituted more than once through the celebration of festivals, particularly through processions to the *muṣallā*. But al-Āmir now had to assert his power by reestablishing prerogatives that had been abandoned.[164]

Platters for the festival had been carried during the night to the caliph; they were on gold trays covered with linen cloths with gold threads. At daybreak, stuffed dates and other delicacies, along with a variety of spices and perfumes, were brought. The caliph ordered al-Afḍal's surviving brother to bring the deceased's son to the banquet, but the boy's mother—fearing for his life—refused to let the boy go. Finally, the boy was brought to the caliph, who embraced him, kissing him on the forehead, and seated him on his right. The muezzins chanted "God is most great" while the caliph pronounced an invocation, took a date and ate part of it and passed it on to al-Afḍal's brother. He did the same with another and gave it to al-Afḍal's son. Each of the recipients stood, kissed the ground and then everyone present took a date from the caliph's hand and stood. They all broke their fast in this manner, after which food was distributed to the amirs who were waiting outside the hall in the vestibule.

The caliph and his eunuchs, who had restored him to power, then publicly mourned the fallen wazir. The chief qadi, chief missionary, and amirs were brought before the caliph, who was sitting before the curtain that concealed the coffin of al-Afḍal. When they saw that he was in mourning dress, they tore their garments, threw off their turbans, and wept. The caliph made a show of breaking the fast again with a date so that the assembly saw him, and then he signaled to al-Afḍal's brother to speak on his behalf. He said, "The Commander of the Faithful returns your greeting. You have seen what he has done and how he comports himself. The calamity that has befallen him with respect to his wazir, the director (*mudabbir*) of his state (*dawla*) and the state of his father [al-Mustanṣir], has not kept him from fulfilling his obligations today. He has broken the fast in your presence, and orders you to do the same." The caliph ran his hand over the platters and began to distribute food himself. As soon as he presented food to al-Afḍal's brother and the missionary, the rest of the assembly began to eat. Al-Afḍal's brother then took the missionary's hand and brought it to the caliph, who handed over the sermon. The missionary kissed it, put it on his head, and brought it to his chest.[165] The amirs went to the *muṣallā*, where the missionary led the prayer, ascended the minbar, and delivered the sermon.[166]

The symbolism of the shared meal is clear: the family of the deceased wazir al-Afḍal, by accepting food from the hand of the caliph himself, relinquished any claim to a grievance concerning al-Afḍal's death; the caliph, on the other hand, by sharing his table with the murdered wazir's son and brother, assured them of their own safety. The other recipients of food were both witnesses to this "transaction" and its beneficiaries. The particular character of the meal is further emphasized by the fact that the caliph "broke" his fast again publicly in front of the large assembly. This time, al-Afḍal's brother, having taken his place in the caliph's fold, spoke on the ruler's behalf, a signal to the assembly that the family of the wazir had been reconciled to the caliph. Thus in the private banquet, the state was reconstituted; in the public banquet, this fact was announced. But this symbolic giving and receiving of safety (*amān*) through food was layered onto a ritual that had other meanings. All those involved were fulfilling a personal religious obligation, as well as negotiating a political compromise. Unlike other Fatimid banquets, the actual breaking of the fast was extremely austere. It hearkened back to the days of the Prophet himself, who had traditionally broken his fast with a date or raisins. It was, perhaps, the very austere nature of the meal that made it possible to accomplish the other, political aim. Of course, banquets and shared meals alone did not guarantee the safety of their participants. The wazir al-Ma'mūn al-Baṭā'iḥī and his brother both fell victim to a banquet intrigue during Ramaḍān of 519/1125.[167] Whether to reconcile competing interests or permanently to silence troublesome or recalcitrant officials, banquets were intensely political affairs.

By the following year, caliphal ceremonies once again included elaborate banquets and public processions. In 516/1122,[168] expenditures on the banquets for the twenty-nine nights of Ramaḍān, exclusive of the caliph's private banquets and the portions for the reciters (*qurrā'*) and "wakeners" (*muṣaḥḥirūn*, i.e., those who awakened people for the predawn meal during Ramaḍān), totaled 16,436 dinars.[169] In 517/1123, similar preparations for the banquets and the processions to the mosques were made.[170] The caliph rested on the first Friday of the month, then rode to the Mosque of al-Ḥākim on the second, the Azhar Mosque on the third, and the Mosque of 'Amr on the fourth. The director of the treasury (*ṣāḥib bayt al-māl*) supervised the furnishing of each mosque. Designated servants carried special carpets, wrapped in *dabīqī* linen cloths. Three square mattresses (*ṭarraḥa*) of white *sāmān* or *dabīqī* linen, embroidered in red, were stacked in the prayer niche (*miḥrāb*). Curtains with red silk embroidered inscriptions hung to the left and right of the prayer niche. The curtain on the right contained the phrase "In the name of God, the Merciful, the Compassionate" (*basmala*), sura 1, and sura 62; the one on the left, the phrase, "In the name of God, the Merciful, the Compassionate," sura 1, and sura 63. The chief qadi had perfumed the top of the minbar three times with tripled incense (*nadd muthallath*).[171]

The caliph's procession began at the palace. From the time he mounted his horse until the time he reached the prayer enclosure (*maqṣūra*) at the designated mosque, there was a continuous recitation of the Qur'an.[172] He wore the same costume for all three processions: white silk robes with gold threads, a turban, and a *ṭaylasān*.[173] The parasol and the customary insignia were carried as he rode to the mosque, which he entered from the preacher's door (*bāb al-khiṭāba*, i.e., a private entrance leading directly to the prayer enclosure). His prayer enclosure was guarded on the outside by chamberlains and the commander of the army (*isfahsalār*), and on the inside by his personal guard (*ṣibyān al-khāṣṣ*). The caliph renewed his ritual ablution (*wuḍū'*) if necessary. When the call to prayer was pronounced, the chief qadi entered the prayer enclosure and greeted the caliph, saying: "Peace be upon the Commander of the Faithful, the prophetic descendant, the judge, and God's mercy and blessings; to prayer, may God have mercy on you, (*al-salām ʿalā amīr al-mu'minīn al-sharīf al-qāḍī wa-raḥmatullāh wa-barakātuh, al-ṣalāta yarḥamuka allāh*)."[174] After this formal greeting, the caliph, surrounded by his eunuchs and followed by the wazir, walked out. He ascended the minbar and sat under the perfumed dome; then the wazir, who was waiting at the bottom of the minbar, went up to kiss the caliph's hands and feet in full view of the congregation.[175] He fastened the curtains that hung from the dome around the caliph and descended.[176]

The caliph delivered a short sermon (*khuṭba*), reading from a text brought from the chancery. Ibn al-Ṭuwayr describes the sermon in his only first-person account in the chronicles:

> I heard [the caliph] give the sermon once in the Azhar, when he read, "O my Lord, dispose me that I may be thankful for your blessing with which you have blessed me and my father . . . (Q. 46:15)." Then he pronounced the blessing on his father and grandfather, that is, Muḥammad and ʿAlī and delivered an eloquent sermon in which he mentioned those of his ancestors that preceded him. When he got to himself, he said, while I was listening, "O God I am your servant [*ʿabd*] and the son of your

> servant, possessing for myself neither harm nor benefit [*lā amlaku li-nafsī ḍarran wa-lā nafaʿan*]."

Ibn al-Ṭuwayr continues describing the sermon in a general vein. The caliph pronounced prayers (*daʿwāt*), and supplications for the wazir (if there was one), for the aid and unity of the armies, victory for the troops, and the destruction and subjugation of dissidents and infidels. He finished with the admonition "Mention God in your prayers" (*udhkurū allāh bi-dhikrikum*). Whoever had fastened the curtains around the caliph in the dome unfastened them. If there was a wazir of the sword, he fastened it; if there was no wazir of the sword, then the chief qadi fastened and unfastened the curtains, while the chief chamberlain (*ṣāḥib al-bāb*) stood at the bottom of the minbar.

The caliph descended from the minbar and sat on the three mats (*ṭarrāḥa*) in the prayer niche to act as imam for prayer. The congregation was arrayed behind him according to rank: the wazir and chief qadi formed the first row (*ṣaff*), then the *muḥannak* eunuchs and the amirs of the collar (*al-umarā' al-muṭawwaqūn*), then the high-ranking men of the civilian and military bureaucracies (i.e., the "men of the pen and the sword").The muezzins stood with their backs to the prayer enclosure. The wazir repeated what he heard to the qadi, the qadi repeated it to the muezzins and the muezzins announced it to the rest of the congregation. The imam recited what was on the right curtain in the first prayer cycle (*rakʿa*) and what was on the left in the second prayer cycle.[177] After completing the prayer, the caliph returned to the palace, while the wazir rode behind him and drums were beat.

The prayer on the second Friday was the same as the first, but on the third Friday, when he rode to the Mosque of ʿAmr, the population decorated the streets on which the procession advanced. The people of Cairo decorated from the gate of the palace to the Ibn Ṭūlūn Mosque; the people of Fustat decorated from the Ibn Ṭūlūn Mosque to the Mosque of ʿAmr. The prefect of Fustat supervised the members of each occupational group, who spent three days and nights selecting their choicest goods and drapes. On that Friday, the caliph went on the Great Road (*al-shāriʿ al-aʿẓam*), passing by a local mosque (*masjid*) and the *dār al-anmāṭ* until he reached the Mosque of ʿAmr.[178] After the prayer, he returned to Cairo along the same route and distributed a dinar to the officials of each mosque he passed.

In its final form, accounts of the procession to mosques during Ramaḍān provide evidence for a profound reinterpretation of the ritual city. In the early Fatimid period, these processions linked the major ritual centers to the palace, expressing the Isma'ili system in which the imam stood at the center of all devotions. The processional links between palace and mosque reinforced the notion of the mosque as the seat of the missionary movement (*majlis al-da'wa*) and of prayer as the call (*da'wa*) of the imam of the time. Even when Fustat was integrated into the ritual city, it was still understood as an incorporation into an essentially Isma'ili map. As Cairo changed, the ritual city came to be reinterpreted, and the character of ritual unity changed. Cairo was not only a map on which the political and religious authority of the caliph was imprinted. It was also a growing urban center. By the time of al-Mustanṣir (r. 427–87/1036–94), the city was even more deeply inscribed in the political vocabulary of the dynasty. Major urban processions were announced to the provinces in letters from the chancery (*dīwān al-inshā'*).[179] These literary creations yield little specific information about the organization of the processions; instead, they emphasize the political and religious authority of the caliph as it was expressed through the procession. Although they contain no information, for example, about actual procession routes, they assume the "urbanness" of the processions by alluding to the splendid decorations of the streets.

From 466/1074 to 519/1125, Badr, al-Afḍal, and al-Ma'mūn sponsored construction that transformed Cairo from a royal enclave into an emerging urban center in its own right.[180] Badr al-Jamālī expanded and rebuilt the walls of Cairo in cut stone. This brought the Mosque of al-Ḥākim, Cairo's most prominent ceremonial site, inside the city walls. The population of the city was also changing. Badr allowed the Armenian Christian regiments who had accompanied him to establish their own quarters within the city.[181] Other regiments were given permission to establish their own quarters in the twelfth century. The Maṣāmida, a regiment formed during the reign of al-Mustanṣir, built their quarter just outside of Bāb Zuwayla only during the wazirate of al-Ma'mūn. Jewish and Christian notables now lived in Cairo. Cairo could no longer be the closed city it had been at the start of the Fatimid period. It now had something it had not had before: a civilian population.

Al-Ma'mūn's energetic building program reflected this change in the character of the population. He conceived of Cairo both as an official administrative center and as a potential economic center. Fustat, even when it had been the administrative center of the Abbasids, had never derived its primary income from state revenue; its economy was based on commerce. Al-Ma'mūn tried to capture some of this economic activity for the caliph's city. He built a new mint within Cairo and a warehouse (*dār al-wakāla*) for merchants coming from Syria and Iraq.[182] Al-Ma'mūn drew the general population closer to Cairo in another way: he rebuilt and repopulated the largely abandoned district of al-Qaṭā'i', reconstructing the ruins between the Mausoleum of al-Sayyida al-Nafīsa and Bāb Zuwayla.[183] He established five new parks in Fustat, renovated the caliph's pleasure pavilions along the Nile, and sponsored the construction of a number of mausolea for 'Alid saints in both Cairo and Fustat.[184]

Al-Ma'mūn's transformation of the urban landscape was accompanied by another reinterpretation of the ritual city. By this time, Fatimid processions seemed to obscure boundaries rather than to mark them. Even in the late Fatimid period, Cairo and Fustat remained separate cities, perceived as such by their residents. The processions defined the relationship of the two cities and their residents in a new way. Moreover, the procession to the Mosque of 'Amr actually obscured the boundary between the two cities: the decoration of the population of Cairo extended beyond Bāb Zuwayla to the Ibn Ṭūlūn Mosque, while the decoration of the population of Fustat began there and extended to the Mosque of 'Amr. This is precisely the area that was undergoing a profound demographic change in the 1120s, as al-Ma'mūn pursued his vigorous policy of construction and repopulation. The decoration of the procession route (found also in Nile and New Year's processions) was an urban experience par excellence. It took three days and nights, required constant supervision, and necessitated cooperation among various occupations. And, significantly, it happened in the marketplace, where Jews, Christians, and Muslims mingled. It would not be surprising to find that all three groups participated in the decoration of the streets.

The reinterpretation of the ritual city also took place through the creation of a powerful ritual language that was both broad enough to appeal to the diverse populations of Cairo and Fustat and rich enough to be invested with meaning on many different levels. He did not simply restore "the customs that had existed before the days of Badr and al-Afḍal." He created out of the landscape, court ceremonies, and popular religious practices of the population of Fustat a ritual *lingua franca.* In the early twelfth century, the Fatimid state was still Isma'ili, but it had already been rent by one serious schism and would soon face another. Many of the caliph's staunchest allies and supporters were Sunnis. The Fatimid imam was Isma'ili, but neither his capital city of Cairo nor the neighboring city of Fustat was. Ritual unity had to be expressed in a broadly Islamic, not specifically Isma'ili or even Shi'i, context. In the ritual city of the twelfth century, the ritual *lingua franca* was best expressed in the banquets and distributions of the two festivals.

In 516/1122, the Festival of Fast Breaking (*'īd al-fiṭr*) was celebrated with two banquets, one at dawn in the Iwan before the festival prayer and another in the Gold Hall (*qā'at al-dhahab*) on returning from the *muṣallā.*[185] The caliph attended both of these banquets in person, although he might be concealed behind either a curtain or a grillwork screen (*shubbāk*).[186] The first banquet was set up in the Iwan the night before the festival, and the fast was broken as soon as the dawn prayer was completed.[187] Although there is no information in Ibn al-Ṭuwayr's account about exactly who attended this first banquet, we can take Ibn al-Ma'mūn's guest list as representative: the wazir, his sons and brothers, the amirs and their lieutenants, and representatives of the provinces.[188] They were all seated according to rank. In al-Ma'mūn's time, the festivities included a parade of horses through the Iwan while the fanfare (*rahajiyya*) was played. The trainers brought their mounts in from the Daylam Gate (the palace gate closest to the stables), approached and kissed the ground, and then led the horses around the hall, displaying their heavily ornamented saddles. The caliph's eunuchs led the horses designated to carry the parasol (*dawābb al-miẓalla*) up to the grillwork loge in which the caliph sat.[189] More than one thousand horses were presented in this way, in addition to mules (*bighāl*) and other mounts.[190] The fanfare ceased after the parade of horses was over. Then the Qur'an readers began to recite "verses appropriate to the occasion."[191]

The caliph's meal (*fiṭra*) was carried in while the Qur'an readers were reciting, and the caliph broke his fast by saying, "God is most great," and eating a date. He gave one to the wazir, who did the same. The caliph then began to sample the varieties of food that had been brought, passing the food on to his wazir, who placed it in his sleeve.[192] The caliph also honored the wazir's sons and brothers by presenting them personally with food, which they accepted, kissed, and placed in their sleeves. Both Ibn al-Ma'mūn and Ibn al-Ṭuwayr report that no one was compelled to break his fast. This seems remarkable until it is placed in the context of late Fatimid history. During the second century of Fatimid rule in Egypt, the army was composed primarily of Turkic soldiers, many of whom were Sunni. Even the high-ranking officials of state, including the wazir, were not necessarily Isma'ilis. If the caliph were to effect any unity through ceremonial, if he were to assert himself as a political head, it would have to be in a broadly Islamic, not a specifically Isma'ili or even Shī'ī, context. Ironically, the tension created by this religious diversity was most easily resolved in this ritual setting.

The ceremonial setting in which the ritual was being observed allowed for surprising flexibility. That flexibility was vested in the symbolic activity that characterized these ceremonies. In this particular case, it meant that whoever did not hold the opinion that the Isma'ili calculation of the date of the festival (*'īd*) was the proper one, was required only to make a gesture (*awma'a*) as if he were eating and to place the food in his sleeve. Ibn al-Ma'mūn relates, in fact, that everyone who was present made the same gesture and placed the food in his sleeve to derive its *baraka*. The significant act was receiving the food, making a symbolic gesture, and placing it in the sleeve, not actually ingesting the food to break the fast. A symbolic gesture had superseded the act of breaking the fast as the central activity of the banquet.[193] Furthermore, people were encouraged to take food from the caliph's banquet and redistribute it outside the palace. Al-Ma'mūn announced, "No one who takes anything from this place is blameworthy; indeed, he will acquire nobility and distinction." He filled his own sleeve after kissing whatever he had taken from the platter, and the others followed suit.[194]

This first banquet was followed by the procession to the *muṣallā* and the festival prayer. Preparations were also made along the procession route. In what seems to be a twelfth-century version of the practice introduced by al-'Azīz in 380/990, the troops lined the route from the gate of the palace to the *muṣallā*.[195] It is impossible to know whether the benches built by al-'Azīz still remained, but his original intent seems to have been transformed. The physical link between palace and *muṣallā* with a specifically Isma'ili meaning was replaced by a continuum of soldiers, almost certainly non-Isma'ilis. It reflected the realities of the late Fatimid military state. Moreover, neither Ibn al-Ma'mūn or Ibn al-Ṭuwayr mentions the continuous reciting of the formula "God is most great" (*takbīr*). The liturgical link was lost. The Isma'ili ritual city, so carefully constructed in the early years of the dynasty, was being reinterpreted. Cairo remained a ritual city, to be sure, but it was no longer to be understood necessarily in Isma'ili terms.

When it was time for the prayer, the caliph emerged from his palace in costume with a banner,[196] a turban with a jewel,[197] and the staff in his hand.[198] Al-Ma'mūn approached him alone, kissed the ground, and took both the sword (*sayf*) and lance (*rumḥ*) while a fanfare was played.[199] The parasol had been opened to the caliph's right as he exited from the Festival Gate. The entourage proceeded to the *muṣallā*, passing through the rows of soldiers that lined the procession route. The caliph was surrounded by his personal bodyguard, and he and the wazir were followed by heavily armed soldiers. As the entourage reached the gate of the *muṣallā*, the chamberlains dismounted and the wazir al-Ma'mūn rode past the caliph and saluted.[200] Only the wazir entered the *muṣallā* mounted, but he dismounted at the second gate inside and waited for the caliph. When the caliph entered, the wazir took the bridle of the caliph's horse in his hand and led him to the last vestibule, where the caliph dismounted and walked to the prayer niche as the muezzins were pronouncing, "God is most great.[201] The *muṣallā* had been covered with special carpets and draperies. Curtains hung on the sides of the prayer niche, and mats or carpets were stacked there.[202] Banners (*liwā'*) hung from the minbar, the steps were carpeted, and pillows were stacked at the top. The dome had been perfumed and was guarded by the qadi. The chief missionary sat in the vestibule with the Isma'ilis,[203] the amirs, descendants of the Prophet (*ashrāf*), dignitaries (*shuyūkh*), and the witnesses.

The caliph began to pray; the wazir and the qadi were standing behind him,[204] arrayed to his right and left. They relayed the phrase "God is most great" to the muezzins who stood by their side; they, in turn, relayed it to another group of muezzins who were leading men and women in prayer outside the *muṣallā*. The prayer itself was almost identical to those described in earlier years. The caliph recited the greeting (*salām*) after the prayer and then ascended the minbar.[205] At the top of the minbar, he gestured to the wazir, who kissed the ground and ascended, saluted again, and stood on the top step.[206] The wazir summoned the chief qadi, who approached and kissed each step until he reached the third one,[207] where he stopped and took out the booklet from his sleeve,[208] kissed it and touched it to his head, and then read its contents outloud. In al-Āmir's time, it named the festival, as well as its customs, and contained invocations for the state (*dawla*).[209] According to Ibn al-Ṭuwayr, it contained a list (*thabat*) of the officials who were summoned formally to ascend the minbar.[210] As in former times, the caliph was concealed by the banners hanging from the minbar. After the prayer ended, the entourage returned to the palace.

As was the custom in late Fatimid times,[211] the caliph visited the tombs of his ancestors when he returned to the palace. The wazir left from the Festival Gate with the amirs, went to the Gold Gate, and entered the Gold Hall. There he supervised the distribution of a large number of platters and portions to his own entourage to be taken to his residence and to numerous high-ranking officials of the state. These distributions by the wazir were particularly characteristic of the late Fatimid period. Then the caliph entered the Gold Hall. A silver table called "The Round" (*al-mudawwara*) had been set up in front of the throne (*sarīr al-mulk*) and extended from there to the door of the hall opposite known as *al-muḥawwal*.[212] The table was covered with a rich variety of foods and delicacies, including two large sugar castles that had been set up at each end of the banquet.[213]

Ibn al-Ma'mūn actually reports two identical banquets at this time, apparently to accommodate the large number of people who attended in al-Ma'mūn's day. At the second banquet, the caliph invested the wazir al-Ma'mūn with a robe of honor (*khilʿa*) during the meal. This was a *khilʿa* in the original sense of the word: an outer garment that the caliph took off and gave to the wazir.[214] According to the description of Ibn al-Ma'mūn, during the second banquet, the director of the royal wardrobe (*mutawallī khizānat al-kiswa al-khāṣṣ*) brought a complete outfit (*badla*) to the caliph.[215] The caliph took off the robes that he had been wearing, donned the outfit, and then gave his robes to the wazir.[216] Although investitures with robes of honor were common in the earlier Fatimid period, distributions of clothing to dignitaries do not seem to have been a feature of early Fatimid banquets. Nor can we know if, or how much, food was actually carried away from the banquet and distributed to the general population. In the time of Ibn al-Ma'mūn and Ibn al-Ṭuwayr, a great portion of the food laid out during the banquet seems to have been destined for the populations of Cairo and Fustat.[217] Ibn al-Ma'mūn remarks more than once that those attending the banquets were encouraged to carry away food and redistribute, or even sell, it. But food was not the only thing distributed on the festival. Distributions of costumes (*kiswa*) were so abundant during the reign of al-Āmir that the festival was known commonly as the Festival of Gala Costumes (*ʿīd al-ḥulal*).[218]

The celebration of the Sacrificial Festival was similar in most respects to the Festival of Fast Breaking. The festival was usually celebrated for three days, corresponding to the *ayyām al-tashrīq* of the pilgrimage.[219] The caliph would sacrifice at both the *muṣallā* and the ritual slaughterground (*manḥar*). Ibn al-Ṭuwayr described the actual sacrifice. The caliph, wazir, and other dignitaries would stand on a platform, surrounded by the *muḥannak* eunuchs. A servant led one animal to the platform and the chief qadi, who held the end of the spear, placed the tip on the animal's throat. Then the caliph pierced the animal's throat. This was repeated until all the animals had been sacrificed.[220]

Ibn al-Ṭuwayr records that on the first day there were 31 young camels and a grown she-camel; on the second day, 27 camels; on the third day, 23 camels.[221] Ibn al-Ma'mūn, writing in 515/1121 and 516/1122, reports a greater variety of sacrificial victims. In 515/1121, a total of 2,561 head were sacrificed. Of these, 117 she-camels, 24 head of cattle, and 20 water buffalo (a total of 161) were sacrificed by the caliph in three locations—the *muṣallā*, the *manḥar*, and the Sābāṭ Gate.[222] The remaining 2,400 sacrifices were slaughtered by butchers. In addition to these sacrifices, 107 costumes were distributed to the amirs of the collar (*al-umarā' al-muṭawwaqūn*) and the *muḥannak* eunuchs, the *kātib al-dast*,[223] the director of the chamberlains (*mutawallī ḥajabat al-bāb*) and other court functionaries. The expenditures for banquets, exclusive of those for the palace residents and the cost of the sugar castles, exceeded thirteen hundred dinars.

Ibn al-Ma'mūn gives more precise details for the festival in 516/1122 when 1,946 animals were sacrificed. He tells us who received the meat. A total of 113 camels were sacrificed by the caliph himself at the *muṣallā* and al-Manākh,[224] for the wazir and his entourage and those who attended the prayer. Every day, as alms for the poor, a she-camel was sacrificed; on the third day of the festival, a camel was slaughtered for the poor in the Qarāfa cemetery. The remainder of the sacrifices, carried out at the Sābāṭ Gate, were for distribution in the palace, the wazir's residence, and to the entourage of the caliph and wazir; they included 12 camels, 18 head of cattle, 15 water buffalo and 1,800 rams. There were distributions every day at the Sābāṭ Gate, as well as alms for the poor from the scrap meat from the camels and the cattle.

The list of recipients of Ibn al-Ṭuwayr is somewhat different. According to his account, most of the sacrifices of slaughtered camels went to the court officials and dignitaries (*arbāb al-rusūm*) to confer the caliph's blessing (*li'l-tabarruk*); the chief qadi and chief missionary distributed portions to students in the House of Wisdom, to the professors in the congregational mosques of Cairo, and to the leaders of the Isma'ilis (*nuqabā' al-mu'minīn*), also "for blessing."[225] In addition, the first animal slaughtered on the first day of the festival was sent to the king and missionary of the Yemen.[226] There is no mention at all of alms to the poor, although we might assume that these were always a part of any major distribution. Certainly, the absence of any mention of it in the text cannot be taken as proof that such distributions to the poor were discontinued.

The distributions from the time of Ibn al-Ṭuwayr are intended for an entirely different group of recipients than those from the time of the wazir al-Ma'mūn. In al-Ma'mūn's day, the sacrifices reached vast numbers of people: officials of state as well as large numbers of the poor. The distribution points in Cairo ensured that they would reach large numbers of people, and when a camel was slaughtered in the Qarāfa cemetery, it was clearly intended for the poor of Fustat. But distributions in the time of Ibn al-Ṭuwayr were limited in number and scope. They were made chiefly by the qadi and missionary, not by the wazir, and they went mostly to the Isma'ili community. This may be due to something of a resurgence of official Isma'ilism during the last years of the Fatimid caliphate. The overt Isma'ili content of festivals had been practically stripped away from Fatimid rituals after the reign of al-Mustanṣir. Al-Ma'mūn cast a wide ceremonial net, attempting to appeal to as broad an audience as possible. But the Ṭayyibī schism after the accession of al-Ḥāfiẓ inspired a more explicit expression of Isma'ilism in the capital. The designation of the first sacrificial animal for the king and missionary of the Yemen must have been a direct response to the rise of the Ṭayyibī sect.[227] This may help to account for what seems to be the reappearance of the distributions to a specifically Isma'ili audience. Nonetheless, the distributions to Isma'ili students and professors do not necessarily mean the imposition of specifically Isma'ili ritual practices on the population as a whole. The distribution of sacrifices for the festival was essentially individual and personal; it was analogous to the head of a family sacrificing and distributing the meat to his own children. In a very real sense, the Isma'ilis in the Fatimid state were the imam's children, and at the end of the Fatimid period, the family was quite small.

The distributions of such large quantities of food and clothing and their redistribution among the population were part of the creation of the ritual *lingua franca* that deliberately emphasized those aspects of ritual that could be conceived of as broadly Islamic, of a language that was, in fact, urban. Al-Ma'mūn responded to the political demands of his time by reinterpreting the ritual city and by integrating the ritual life of the court into the flourishing local religious tradition. At this time the Fatimids began to borrow explicitly from the religious practices of the general population. The cult of saints, so deeply embedded in the religious consciousness of Egyptians of all religious affiliations, organized many of the local religious practices. On Festivals, ordinary people visited saints' tombs, where they donned new clothing, prayed, and held banquets. Fustat itself had a long tradition of festival celebrations transcending the boundaries of religion. The Christian festivals of Epiphany, the Festival of the Cross, and Nawruz were celebrated by the entire population. Other festivals, like the celebration of the inundation of the Nile, had always been urban and communal events. Differences in religion and the integrity of religious communities were not necessarily compromised by the common public celebration of festivals. There was, of course, periodic resistance to these common celebrations. But the Fatimid caliphs were never successful at halting these practices; they were too tightly woven into the social fabric of Fustat.

Al-Ma'mūn's ritual *lingua franca* was informed by much the same spirit as the communal celebrations of the populations of Fustat. He patronized the construction of monuments to 'Alid saints, increased dramatically the material aspects of festivals to allow for redistribution, and deemphasized the explicitly Isma'ili aspects of particular ceremonies and rituals. The creation of the ritual *lingua franca* allowed for a multiplicity of meanings to be expressed in the ritual city. Even the official celebration of the Day of Ghadīr Khumm, the Shiʿi festival that commemorates the Prophet's designation of ʿAlī as his heir (*waṣī*), was divested of its ideological content and celebrated in the same fashion as the two festivals. While we might think that Ismaʿilism was no longer an issue, this is not the case. Ismaʿilism became just one of the multiple meanings that could be expressed in the ritual city.

CHAPTER 4

Politics, Power, and Administration: The New Year's Ceremony

New Year's Eve came more than once a year for medieval Egyptians. The Night of the Decree (*laylat al-qadr*), on which the Qur'an is said to have been revealed to the Prophet, was regarded in Muslim popular tradition as a New Year.[1] The Coptic Nawruz, falling on the first day of Tūt, was celebrated by the Muslim and Christian populations alike, but it was at the sufferance of the ruler. In 363/973–74, al-Muʿizz prohibited public festivities on Nawruz. His prohibition was disregarded the following year, when three days of festivities provoked the caliph to arrest and publicly humiliate the offending celebrants.[2] But the New Year's Days that really mattered for the government were the ones that marked the beginning of two fiscal years. One was the rise of the Nile, marking the start of the year for the land tax (*kharāj*); the other was the first of Muḥarram, the beginning of the Muslim lunar calendar. But the first day of Muḥarram did not, as far as we can tell, occasion great public festivities. The big celebrations for medieval Muslims were the Festival of Fast Breaking and the Sacrificial Festival.

In spite of evidence to the contrary, historians from the fourteenth century to the present have consistently regarded the New Year's procession on the first day of Muḥarram as a part of Fatimid court ceremonial from the beginning of the dynasty's hegemony in Egypt. We can trace the error to the Mamluk historian Ibn Taghrī Birdī (d. 874/1470), who attributed the introduction of the New Year's procession to the caliph al-Muʿizz.[3] The only report of an audience for New Year's greetings in early Fatimid times is during the reign of the caliph al-Ḥākim in 390/999,[4] and the first mention of a procession for the New Year appears in the year 517/1123, when al-Ma'mūn al-Baṭā'iḥī was the wazir for the caliph al-Āmir. The procession seems to have been added to an established custom of high dignitaries attending audiences given by the caliph and the wazir to offer greetings for the New Year.[5]

New Year's ceremonies in the wazir al-Ma'mūn's time provided primarily a formal setting for the distribution of the newly minted gold and silver coins struck at the Cairo mint (*dār al-ḍarb*).[6] The caliph distributed coins to his entourage, brothers and wives, relatives, female servants and the high- and low-ranking eunuchs (*al-ʿawālī wa'l-adwān*). Then, the wazir received the coins designated for him, his children and brothers, the amirs and official guests, and the troops. Al-Ma'mūn redistributed these coins according to official registers designating the recipients and amounts during an early morning banquet at his residence. After the distributions, the wazir's insignia and outfit for the procession were brought to his residence.

When the caliph mounted his horse, the wazir al-Ma'mūn was summoned. As the caliph left from the Gold Gate, the parasol was opened while a fanfare was played and the cortege was organized. The unmounted horses led by hand (*janā'ib*) and the ranks of soldiers were arrayed to the caliph's right and left. The cavalry and the infantry wore their distinctive uniforms and carried parade arms. The caliph left Cairo from Bāb al-Futūḥ and reentered the city through Bāb al-Naṣr.[7] The merchants of both Cairo and Fustat had decorated the procession route with their goods in order to obtain the blessing (*baraka*) conferred by the caliph's glancing upon their wares. The gates of the quarter of the regiment of the black slaves (*al-ʿabīd*), which was right outside of the city walls, had been decorated with drapes and curtains. After the caliph reentered the city, alms (*ṣadaqāt*) were given to the poor and pensions (*rusūm*) were distributed to the high-ranking officials who resided in Cairo.[8]

The Qur'an reciters were arrayed along the vestibule (*dihlīz*) from the door to the caliph's wardrobe (*khizānat al-kiswa al-khāṣṣ*). The caliph changed from his processional costume there, and he went to visit the palace mausoleum. Both the caliph and the wazir then held audiences and banquets where the annual pensions were distributed. The functionaries of the ministries attended and presented their annual reports, detailing the resources and expenditures for the year, including various goods that were destined for the cities of Mecca and Medina and for the storehouses on the frontiers. Finally, the accounts of revenues and of the *ṭirāz* were presented. Thus, although the procession was a significant element in the festivities, the day was devoted primarily to a highly formalized accounting in the palace of the various branches of the government.

The basic structure of Fatimid administration was established and its first major reforms occurred early in the history of the dynasty.[9] Right after the conquest of Egypt, Jawhar continued the administrative practices of the defunct Ikhshidid state. This system of administration, and particularly of tax collection, was highly decentralized until al-Muʿizz arrived in Egypt. He appointed Yaʿqūb ibn Killis and one ʿAslūj ibn Ḥasan as directors of tax collection and financial affairs.[10] They were responsible for consolidating the collection of taxes in the administrative complex (*dār al-imāra*), adjacent to the Ibn Ṭūlūn Mosque, which was also the site of the court for the redress of grievances (*maẓālim*). The tax revenues, especially from the delta textile towns of Tinnīs and Damietta, were increased. Al-Muʿizz also instituted monetary reforms. Just before the conquest of Egypt, the Ikhshidid state had suffered a monetary crisis and its coinage was seriously debased. Jawhar minted new gold coins (Muʿizzī dinars) of a high intrinsic quality, withdrew the debased coinage from circulation, and collected taxes only in the new Muʿizzī dinars.[11] The high degree of fineness of Fatimid coins was sustained throughout the Fatimid period, even during the economic crises of the reign of al-Mustanṣir.[12]

One of the reasons that the Fatimids were able to sustain the intrinsic quality of their coins was a plentiful supply of gold. When al-Muʿizz came to Egypt in 361/972, he brought one hundred camels carrying gold bars shaped like millstones. But the Fatimids also had access to the gold mines of Upper Egypt, which they exploited until the costs of production outstripped the yield.[13] Both the mines and the pharaonic tombs, which had been a major source of gold for the Tulunids, began to dry up in the eleventh and twelfth centuries. By the time Saladin came to power in the late twelfth century, the dwindling supplies of gold resulted in debased gold coinage.[14]

The high standard of Fatimid coinage did not, however, guarantee its prestige.The authority of the Fatimid caliph was challenged by the coins struck by the Nizārīs at Alamūt in the name of Nizār, the dispossessed son of al-Mustanṣir. In addition, the extraordinary fineness of the gold Fatimid dinars inspired the Crusaders to mint imitation dinars, which damaged the prestige of the

Fatimid coins.[15] The Crusaders imitated the external appearance of the gold coins of al-Mustanṣir and al-Āmir, but they did not maintain their intrinsic quality. These substandard dinars flooded the Mediterranean, causing a loss of confidence in Fatimid currency. In addition, the loss of Syria to the Crusaders meant the loss of the Syrian mints. In response, the Fatimids launched an investigation into minting, and in Shawwāl 516/December 1122, a mint was built for the first time in Cairo.[16] *Al-dār al-āmiriyya*,[17] located near the Azhar, served as a mint, treasury, and exchange.[18]

The establishment of a new mint also had administrative implications. Since the minting and inscription of coins (*sikka*) was a caliphal prerogative, the administration of the mint was under the supervision of the caliph's officials. In Egypt, the mints had originally been supervised by the chief qadi, who sent his representatives to open and close the mint, attend the refining of metals, and check the fineness of the alloys.[19] Part of al-Āmir's reform, however, included the appointment of the *mushārif dār al-ḍarb*, a new official in the civilian administration who would supervise the mint. He took over most of the supervisory functions that had previously been fulfilled by the chief qadi, including that of auditing the mint's accounts.[20] One of the primary responsibilities of the supervisor of the mint and of the qadi was to ensure the integrity of the coinage and to prevent theft of the gold.

Maintaining the integrity of Fatimid coins was important for the security of Egypt's place in the international trading community. However, the fineness of coinage was also important because it asserted the caliph's symbolic position at the head of Fatimid administration. Both the banquet, where the new coins were distributed to the highest ranking military and civilian officials of the state, and the procession that began and ended at the palace provided an elaborate showcase for the new administrative machinery of the state. Foremost among the changes following the restructuring of the Fatimid bureaucracy under Badr al-Jamālī and al-Afḍal was the reassertion of the caliph's position in the state. Al-Ma'mūn's restoration of the caliphal celebrations of the festivals was one component of this change; the minting of new coins by the caliph was another. The critical position of the wazir, however, remained unchanged. It was he, not the caliph, who actually distributed the coins in a banquet at his residence. The significant difference now was the fiction that he was acting on behalf of the caliph.

This is not to say that al-Ma'mūn lacked power. On the contrary, only someone as powerful as al-Ma'mūn could have accomplished the restoration of the caliph al-Āmir. Unlike al-Afḍal, who displayed frank independence, the new wazir chose to exercise his power in more subtle ways. He restored the caliphal prerogatives that had been usurped like the celebration of the festivals, the processions during Ramaḍān, the minting and inscription of coins (*sikka*), and the inscription of textiles (*ṭirāz*), and then he associated himself so closely with the caliph that he derived benefit from them, as well. But al-Ma'mūn's primary ceremonial accomplishment was the creation of the ritual *lingua franca* that operated as an urban language in twelfth-century Cairo and Fustat. His rich urban language grew out of an elaboration of the ceremonies for the festivals, and the procession for the New Year served as part of that process. Although the documentation for the New Year's procession under al-Ma'mūn is sparse, he seems also to have exploited the landscape of the ritual city to express the reconstitution of the Fatimid administration. The procession route went through the northern part of the city, passing by the Mosque of al-Ḥākim and the *muṣallā*. The distribution of the newly minted coins may well have been modeled on the distributions at the banquets for Ramaḍān and the festivals, where food and clothing were given in addition to money. The ritual city was once again the center Fatimid administration.

THE MODEL PROCESSION: IBN AL-ṬUWAYR'S DESCRIPTION OF THE NEW YEAR

By the time of Ibn al-Ṭuwayr, the New Year's procession had become so elaborate that he regarded it as the model Fatimid procession, and he described the processions for both the first of Ramaḍān and the Opening of the Canal at the inundation of the Nile in terms of the New Year celebrations. His exceptionally rich text is the only other description of a New Year's procession in the Fatimid sources, and it dates in all probability from the last three decades of Fatimid rule. There was no doubt now that Cairo was the seat of administration, but another set of issues seems to have emerged. At that time, the primary concern was not the reassertion of caliphal prerogatives but the complex negotiation of power between caliph, wazir, and army upon which the administration of the state depended.

The celebration of the New Year actually began in the final ten days of Dhu'l-ḥijja, the last month of the Muslim calendar, when insignia, arms, clothing, and other ceremonial objects were brought out of the palace treasuries in preparation for the procession.[21] On 29 Dhu'l-ḥijja, two reviews were held at the palace. The first took place in the morning, when the caliph sat in the grilled loge (*shubbāk*) in the Iwan to review the horses and arms that would be used in the procession on the next day. He sent a messenger (*ṣāḥib al-risāla*) to summon the wazir.[22] As soon as the messenger returned, the caliph left his quarters in the palace on horseback and rode to the grilled loge, which was covered with a curtain. The majordomo (*zimām al-qaṣr*) stood on his right and the director of the treasury (*ṣāḥib bayt al-māl*) stood on his left.[23]

The wazir rode from his residence with an entourage of amirs, who dismounted upon reaching the gate of the palace. But the wazir entered the Festival Gate (*bāb al-ʿīd*) on horseback and proceeded to the first door in the long vestibule (*dihlīz*), where he usually dismounted. He walked along with the retinue of pages, sons and relatives whom he had chosen to accompany him.[24] A large, iron chair had been set up for the wazir beneath the grilled loge; when he reached it, he sat down with his feet touching the ground. When the wazir was seated, the majordomo and the director of the treasury lifted the curtain, and the caliph appeared seated on a magnificent throne. The wazir stood, saluted him and paid homage by gesturing toward the ground three times.[25]

After the wazir sat down again, the Qur'an reciters recited verses for a period of about half an hour. Then the amirs saluted and began to present the horses and mules selected from the caliph's stables.[26] These mounts were led by their grooms "like brides."[27] The end of the review was signaled by more recitations by the Qur'an reciters. The curtain was lowered, and the wazir rose and went behind it to kiss the caliph's hands and feet. Then he left, mounting up again at his customary place in the vestibule, and returned to his residence with an escort of amirs.

The second review took place after the noon prayer to select the caliph's costume for the procession. The wazir was not present at this private review, which included the caliph's entire outfit, i.e., his costume, the parasol, standards and banners, and his sword and lance. The costume that the caliph chose was white, devoid of ornamentation (*al-bayāḍ ghayr al-muwashshaḥ*), and matched to his turban and parasol. The turban (*mandīl*) was given to the *muḥannak* eunuch known as the winder of the noble crown (*shādd al-tāj al-sharīf*). He was also entrusted with the gem called "the Unique" (*al-yatīma*).[28] After the caliph's costume was selected and arranged, the various cloths used as banners and standards were attached to their poles. The first was the parasol (*miẓalla*), which matched the caliph's costume.[29] Then the two "standards of praise" (*liwā'ay al-ḥamd*), made of white silk embroidered in gold, were attached to two long lances.[30] Like the parasol, they were not displayed until the procession began. After that, twenty-one banners of embroidered silk on backgrounds of different colors, each with three inscribed bands (*ṭirāz*), were attached to lances. Two lances with crescents of solid gold (*dhahab ṣāmiṭa*), each with a red or yellow brocade lion, were also brought out. The mouths of the lions were round disks, which the wind entered to puff up the figure. The caliph's sword (*al-sayf al-khāṣṣ*), ornamented in gold and inlaid with jewels was brought out; it was in a sheath embroidered in gold, so that only the hilt was visible.[31] Finally, the caliph's lance and shield were brought out.[32]

Before dawn on the first day of Muḥarram, the high-ranking "masters of the pen and the sword" assembled at the parade ground between the two palaces.[33] The wazir's escort of amirs went to his residence to ride to the Eastern Palace with him. Unlike the day of the review, he was not summoned on New Year's Day itself, because his attendance at the procession was an obligatory service. This seems to be a clear change from the time of al-Ma'mūn; he was summoned for the caliph's procession on the New Year. In the years between Ibn al-Ma'mūn's account and Ibn al-Ṭuwayr's account, the procession had become a part of the regular ceremonial calendar. The insignia with which the wazir had been honored were carried in front of him: ten silver staffs and ten litters.[34] The wazir also received two standards on long lances, which were carried immediately in front of him,[35] and in addition to these, he received ten banners (*bunūd*), which were larger than the standards (*liwā'*) and made of embroidered *dabīqī* linen in various colors. Their lances were dressed with tube-shaped decorations (*anābīb*) and had pomegranates and crescents at their heads. The wazir was preceded by his sons and brothers and by amirs, both mounted and on foot. They all wore splendid costumes and each of them wore the tail of his turban down, without wrapping it under his chin (*kull minhum murkhā al-dhu'āba bi-lā ḥanak*).[36] The wazir himself wrapped his turban under his chin (*bi'l-ḥanak*) and wore a gilded sword. When he reached the palace, his entourage dismounted at the gate while he entered on horseback and proceeded to his customary dismounting station. He walked the rest of the length of the colonnade to the audience hall, accompanied by his sons, brothers, and servants. The wazir sat in the small structure (*maqṭa'*) that was for his use during audiences. When the wazir and the amirs had taken their places, the caliph's horse was brought to the door of the audience hall.

The next stage in the preparations for the procession was the assemblage of the caliph's insignia and his entourage. After the caliph mounted his horse from a chair (*kursī*), the three main insignia, the parasol, sword, and inkstand, were brought out and given to their porters. The porter unfurled the parasol with the assistance of four Ṣaqlabī eunuchs, and he placed it firmly in the stirrup of his horse, holding the pole with a bar over his head. Next, the sword was given to its bearer, who lowered the tail (*dhu'āba*) of his turban upon accepting it and remained thus as long as he carried it.[37] Finally, the inkstand was brought out and given to its porter, a *muḥannak* eunuch, who placed it between himself and the pommel of the saddle. These three insignia would be carried closest to the caliph during the procession.[38] After the insignia were assembled, the wazir left his place and stood alongside the caliph's horse.[39] The master of the audience hall (*ṣāḥib al-majlis*) raised the curtain and the caliph, preceded by his *muḥannak* eunuchs, emerged, revealing the costume chosen for the day. His turban was wrapped under his chin, and the tail hung down on the left (*wa-huwwa muḥannak murkhā al-dhu'āba mimmā yalī jānib al-aysar*); he wore the Maghribī sword and carried the staff (*qaḍīb al-mulk*) in his hand.

A designated group then saluted the wazir, his family, the qadi,[40] and the amirs. The wazir left after the amirs had filed out one by one; he mounted his horse in the vestibule (*dihlīz*), rode to the gate of the palace, and waited for the caliph. The caliph was surrounded by his *muḥannak* eunuchs. When he became visible as he neared the palace gate, a special trumpet, known as *al-gharbīya* (or: *al-gharība*) was sounded. The regular trumpets were then sounded as the parasol was opened at the moment the caliph appeared at the gate. The caliph waited just as long as it took for his *muḥannak* eunuchs and the other dignitaries in his entourage to mount up. The porter of the parasol rode at his left, keeping the caliph under the parasol's shade. The commanders of the caliph's

Sons & troops of amirs, elite soldiers
Lowest ranking amirs
Amirs of the silver staff
Amirs of the collar
Muḥannak eunuchs

Prefect of Cairo

Standards of praise

Standards of Praise

Porter of Inkstand & entourage
Porter of Sword & entourage

Wazir's escort

Flywhisks Flywhisks
parasol

Commander **CALIPH** Commander

Rikābiyya

Commander Commander
Commander Commander

Rikābiyya

Chief chamberlain
(Ṣāḥib al-bāb)

Rikābiyya
10 men with swords in brocade sheaths
Men of the small arms

WAZIR + entourage

500 Men of Coats of Mail

Drums
Cymbals
Flutes

Porter of Lance and shield
500 archers from fleet

Maṣāmida
Rayḥaniyya
Juyūshiyya
Faranjiyya
Wazīriyya

(4000 infantry)

Two elite guards (ṣibyān al-khāṣṣ) carrying banners with lions
21 Rikābiyya carrying banners with Fatimid slogans

Āmiriyya
Ḥāfiẓiyya
Ḥujariyya al-kibār
Ḥujariyya al-ṣighār
Afḍaliyya
Juyūshiyya
Atrāk al-mustanaʿīn
Daylam
Akrād
Ghuzz

(3000 cavalry)

Commander of armies
(Isfahsalār)

ORGANIZATION OF THE NEW YEAR'S PROCESSION

mounted escort (*ṣibyān al-rikāb*, lit. "men of the stirrup") then surrounded the caliph, displacing the *muḥannak* eunuchs who had previously guarded him.[41]

Once the caliph had emerged, the entire procession (*mawkib*) was organized. The sons and soldiers of the amirs headed the procession, along with mixed groups of elite soldiers. They were followed, in ascending order of rank, by the low-ranking amirs (*adwān al-umarā'*), the amirs of the silver staff,[42] and then the amirs of the collar.[43] The *muḥannak* eunuchs followed the amirs, then came two bearers of the "standards of praise" (*liwā'ay al-ḥamd*), one on each side. Behind them, the escort that had accompanied the wazir from his residence to the palace rode on the right. On the left, the bearers of the inkstand and the sword rode, each accompanied by ten or twenty other men.

The next large segment of the cortege consisted of the caliph and his entourage. He was surrounded by his mounted escort (*ṣibyān al-rikāb*), who carried swords, clubs, ceremonial maces, and iron clubs.[44] They wore layered turbans (*al-manādīl al-ṭabaqiyyāt*), swords, and sashes and carried their arms unsheathed. They were arrayed on each side of the caliph "like two extended wings."[45] Directly in front of the caliph's horse, there was an empty space; near the head of his mount, two Ṣaqlabī eunuchs carried flywhisks.[46] The commanders of the mounted escort surrounded the caliph's horse: two at the bit, two at the neck, and two at the stirrups. The commander at the caliph's right stirrup was the "commander of commanders" (*muqaddam al-muqaddamīn*); he held the caliph's whip and executed the caliph's commands during the course of the procession. Just behind the caliph, another group of the mounted escort (*ṣibyān al-rikāb*) guarded him from the rear. Behind them, ten men carried swords in red and yellow brocade sheaths with thick tassels.[47] They were followed by three hundred men bearing small arms (*ṣibyān al-silāḥ al-ṣaghīr*), a corps of high-ranking black slaves, each carrying two lances with polished gold spearheads and a silver-studded shield.[48]

Following the caliph and his large entourage was the wazir with his own entourage of approximately five hundred men wearing coats of mail (*ṣibyān al-zarad*).[49] The wazir, like the caliph, also had an empty space in front of him, but it was smaller than that of the caliph. The wazir was careful not to lose sight of the caliph.[50] After the wazir marched men playing drums, cymbals, and flutes.[51] The bearer of the lance and the shield (*ḥāmil al-rumḥ wa'l-daraqa*) came next, followed by five hundred archers. The rest of the procession consisted almost entirely of various regiments, in two large groups. The first group of Maṣāmida,[52] Rayḥāniyya,[53] Juyūshiyya,[54] Franks, and Wazīriyya,[55] numbered more than four thousand. Behind these regiments, two of the caliph's elite bodyguards (*ṣibyān al-khāṣṣ*) carried lances with crescents of solid gold (*dhahab ṣāmiṭa*) and the red and yellow "puffed up" brocade lions. Twenty-one of the mounted escort (*ṣibyān al-rikāb*) followed them, carrying fine banners (*rāyāt liṭāf*) of different colors, embroidered with silk in contrasting colors and bearing the Fatimid slogan, "Assistance from God and near Victory" (*naṣr min allāh wa-fatḥ qarīb*). They were attached to lances and each had three *ṭirāz* bands. Behind these banners came about three thousand cavalry from the Āmiriyya and Ḥāfiẓiyya regiments, the older and younger palace cadets (*al-ḥujariyya al-kibār* and *al-ṣighār*),[56] and the Afḍaliyya, Juyūshiyya, Turks, Daylamites, Kurds, and Ghuzz regiments.[57]

The cortege followed one of two procession routes, known as the "long" and "short" routes. The long procession route left Bāb al-Naṣr, passed the reservoir of 'Izz al-mulk,[58] turned in the direction of Bāb al-Futūḥ and reentered the city from there. The short procession route left from Bāb al-Naṣr, turned immediately left, and went along the wall to Bāb al-Futūḥ.[59] The people of the city were told which of the two routes would be followed; once the announcement had been made, there was no change in the itinerary, clearly so that the people could decorate the streets.

The procession stopped at the Aqmar Mosque, where the cortege opened up so that the wazir could move forward in order to escort the caliph into the palace. As the wazir passed the caliph, he bowed his head emphatically.[60] The caliph responded with a slight gesture, a high honor reserved only for a wazir of the sword. The wazir entered the palace, followed by the caliph. The *muḥannak* eunuchs then resumed their positions around the caliph, and the wazir attended the caliph as he dismounted. The caliph retired to his apartments after the wazir, the *muḥannak* eunuchs, and the amirs had paid homage to him. Then, the wazir returned to his residence, where his escort paid homage and dispersed. When they returned to their homes they found the gift for the New Year (*al-ghurra*) that had been brought to them. A total of 3,000 newly minted dinars inscribed with the date of the new year were distributed. Of these, the wazir received 360 dinars, 360 *rubāʿīs*, and 360 *qīrāṭs* (i.e., one of each for every day of the lunar year). His sons and brothers received 50 of each; the high-ranking men of the sword and the pen received gifts ranging from 10 to 1 of each.

THE NEGOTIATION OF POWER IN THE NEW YEAR'S PROCESSION

The procession cortege was composed of several blocks, each organized internally according to the ranks of the troops relative to one another, but positioned as a *whole* in terms of proximity to the caliph. These blocks were linked by insignia of sovereignty. Each block was composed of a group of troops of different origins whose place in the empire was powerfully communicated by their position within the cortege. Here, as on other ceremonial occasions, rank could be construed in more than one way. What mattered in the procession was rank relative to the caliph, and this was expressed by proximity to the caliph more than absolute position in the cortege. Thus, in the first block at the head of the cortege were five groups in the following order: sons of amirs and various elite troops; "lesser" amirs (*adwān al-umarā'*); amirs of the silver staff (*arbāb al-quḍub al-fiḍḍa*); amirs of the collar (*arbāb al-aṭwāq*); *muḥannak* eunuchs. These troops were organized in ascending order of rank relative to the caliph, with his own *muḥannak* eunuchs the closest to him. Their order in the procession replicates precisely the ranks of amirs and eunuchs listed by al-Qalqashandī in his discussion of the Fatimid army.[61] Just after them, the two Standards of Praise were carried. This block was followed by the inkstand and the sword. The inkstand was carried by a eunuch,[62] the sword by a high-ranking amir.[63] These were the first of the insignia of sovereignty to appear in the procession.

The caliph and his entourage came after the amirs. This was, naturally, the most elaborately organized part of the procession. The caliph was surrounded by a bodyguard composed of the commanders of the mounted escort, the guard that carried unsheathed ceremonial arms.[64] The most important of the insignia, the parasol (*miẓalla*), was carried over the caliph's head by a high-ranking amir. Although the parasol, as was discussed in chapter 2, clearly symbolized the palace, the personal guard in processions did not replicate the organization of an audience. For one thing, the personnel was different. The mounted escort (*ṣibyān al-rikāb* or *al-rikābiyya*), according to Ibn al-Ṭuwayr, occupied the positions held by the *muḥannak* eunuchs in the palace, who seem to have enjoyed the prerogative of greatest proximity to the caliph only inside the palace. The *muḥannak*s relinquished their privileged positions to the commanders of the mounted escort at the moment that the caliph exited the gate of the palace and the parasol was opened, and they resumed those positions only when the caliph reentered the palace gate.

The wazir and his entourage headed another section of the procession. The relative positions of the caliph and the wazir expressed the tension in late Fatimid Egypt between the theoretical subordination of the wazir and the political realities that conferred the powers of governance upon him. From the time of the Jamālī regime, wazirs of the Fatimid state were almost exclusively military men. The actual power they wielded within the Fatimid state was unrivaled by any of the later caliphs and was so great that the wazir al-Afḍal did not even attempt to disguise his independence. When al-Ma'mūn al-Baṭā'iḥī became wazir to al-Āmir and "restored" him to power, he did this largely through the reinstitution of ceremonial prerogatives that al-Afḍal had usurped, a result it seems of both al-Ma'mūn's plan for Fatimid government and the maneuvering of the caliph's eunuchs. Thus, from the time of al-Ma'mūn on, the conventions of the hierarchy that placed the caliph at the top were carefully preserved in ceremony, if not in the actual operation of the government.

The tension created by this situation must have been enormous. Late Fatimid administrative hierarchy, to the extent that we can reconstruct it, placed the wazir at the head of both the civilian and the military bureaucracies. The wazir, who was a "man of the sword," had much broader powers and prerogatives within the civilian administration than a "man of the pen." He blurred the boundaries among civil, religious, and military authority. The wazir, for example, was addressed by the title "judge of judges" (*qāḍī al-quḍāt*) although he exercised no judicial functions.[65] He occupied a crucial position as the person responsible for executing the caliph's commands,[66] and he often spoke for the caliph. Theoretically, his authority was derived from the caliph, but his ability to act in the political arena was not a function of his investiture by the caliph; it was clearly constituted in large part by the loyalty he could command from his own troops and from various factions of the army that supported him. Since the army was often in conflict with the caliph and his government, the constitution of the wazir's political power often placed him at odds with the theoretical source of his authority.

The wazir's position relative to both the caliph and the troops in the procession negotiated the tension inherent in his office. His high rank relative to other men who served the state was expressed by the empty space before him in the procession; his subordinate position relative to the caliph, by the fact that this space was smaller than the one before the caliph. The wazir and his entourage were linked to the caliph by the ten soldiers carrying swords in red and yellow brocade sheaths. The colors red and yellow were associated directly with the caliph and also appeared in the banners with the lions further along in the procession. Men playing drums, cymbals, and flutes were interposed between the wazir and the troops, and the troops walked behind the caliph's lance and shield, and his banners. Whereas the wazir had the caliph in his line of vision, the troops would have been able to see only the wazir and, perhaps, the caliph's insignia. Furthermore, the troops that were placed closer to the wazir were the lesser ranking regiments of the infantry, those who were walking behind the caliph's lance and shield that were carried by a porter from the regular army.[67] The more highly valued cavalry, on the other hand, were further away from the wazir and rode behind the caliphal banners carried by members of the caliph's elite troops: the porters of the red and yellow lion banners were from the caliph's elite guard (*ṣibyān al-khāṣṣ*), while the porters of the banners with the Fatimid slogan were from the caliph's mounted escort (*ṣibyān al-rikāb*).

The procession route also expressed the ambiguous relationships of power in the Fatimid state. From one point of view, the procession claimed the northern part of the city as the caliph's. The route took the elaborate cortege past the wazir's residence (*dār al-wizāra al-kubrā*) that al-Afḍal had abandoned, reintegrating it into the landscape of the caliphal city. In this way, the Fatimid caliph symbolically laid claim to a territory, his own city, which, like the rest of the empire, was no longer really his. While the fiction could be maintained as the caliph rode out of his city, it could not be as easily sustained when he returned to the palace through Bāb al-Futūḥ, the official entryway to the city. Upon his return, the cortege stopped at the Aqmar Mosque, the only place besides the palace where a salute occurred. That mosque, which had been built by the wazir al-Ma'mūn, never became a site for Friday prayer or for any other ritual of the court. It was, however, the only mosque in Cairo oriented to the street plan and was replete with Isma'ili symbolism. Here, the wazir both saluted the caliph and changed his position in the procession to escort the caliph into the palace, articulating a complicated compromise between men who understood fully the realities of their relative positions. The caliph needed the wazir to enter his palace, just as he depended upon him to assure order in his state.

The interests of the caliph and the wazir did not conflict entirely. Both had an interest in preventing a breakdown of order among a fractious army, and both knew that the loyalties of the troops could fluctuate wildly according to their perception of their self-interest. The Fatimid army in the twelfth century was as diverse in its loyalties as it was in its ethnic and racial composition. Remnants of personal troops of various commanders, wazirs, and caliphs—or their descendants—were powerful constituents and rivals. Nonetheless, the procession asserted that these were all the caliph's troops, and it cast the shadow of the palace over the quarters of the soldiers living in the northern part of Cairo.

The northern part of Cairo was home to the powerful Juyūshiyya and Rayḥāniyya regiments, both composed primarily of black slave troops (*'abīd).* The black slave troops had always been an important element in the Fatimid army.[68] Although they were primarily infantry, they served in both the elite guard (*ṣibyān al-khāṣṣ*) and the eunuch corps.[69] During the reign of al-Ḥākim, the black slave troops became the mainstay of the caliphate. They are said to have been responsible for the plunder of Fustat in 410/1020, and they emerged as the primary rivals to the Turkish troops for power in the Fatimid state.[70] Under al-Mustanṣir, the black infantry became even more important, and their rivalry with the Turks erupted into civil war in 454/1062.[71] They lost ground under Badr al-Jamālī and al-Afḍal, but persisted into the late Fatimid period as the major infantry force of the Fatimid army.[72]

Equally important, al-Afḍal had established a new regiment, the *ṣibyān al-ḥujar* or *al-ḥujariyya*, most probably around the year 501/1106, in response to the poor showing of the Fatimid army against the Crusaders in Palestine.[73] They were housed in barracks (*ḥujar*, hence their name) built near Bāb al-Naṣr and the "Seat of the Wazirate" (*dār al-wizāra*).[74] Although barracks existed in the early Fatimid period, they had not been used primarily to train a standing army. They had, instead, been used to train military administrators. The Ḥujariyya of al-Afḍal, on the other hand, were meant to be a well-trained, easily mobilized regiment.[75] Furthermore, according to William Hamblin, they seem to have been used by al-Afḍal to limit the broad powers of the eunuchs who were so closely associated with the caliph. By the late Fatimid period, however, Ibn al-Ṭuwayr considered them to be part of caliph's personal guard.[76]

Much of the energy of the wazir and the caliph was devoted to maintaining a careful balance among these highly competitive regiments who seem, in fact, to have been the primary audience for the procession. The route of the procession and the organization of the cortege communicated to these troops that it was the caliph whom they served. Although wazirs were powerful, the caliphs were not without resources. The Juyūshiyya and Rayḥāniyya regiments had both allied themselves with the caliph al-Ḥāfiẓ in 542/1146 when he defeated the wazir Riḍwān.[77] The Ḥujariyya were, at this time, part of the caliph's personal guard. These troops paraded through their own quarters behind the caliph, linked to the caliph by the insignia of sovereignty that were dispersed throughout the cortege.

The different segments of the cortege itself were tied together with the insignia of sovereignty. High-ranking amirs and eunuchs at the head of the procession were linked with the caliph's entourage by the inkstand and sword; the wazir following directly behind was linked to him visually; the infantry and cavalry following him were linked by the caliph's lance and shield. The dispersal of the insignia of sovereignty throughout the procession provided cohesion and continuity within the cortege itself. Both the procession route and the organization of the cortege reclaimed the northern part of the city for the caliph, just as they asserted the caliph as the head of both the administration and the army. This was all in contradiction to the actual situation of the army and the administration as they had been restructured by the Juyūshī regime. The New Year's procession symbolically reclaimed a territory that no longer really belonged to the caliph. The wazir and the caliph were complicitous in creating the fiction that kept the caliph at both the center and the head of the Fatimid state.

CHAPTER 5

The Urban River

THE HIGHWAYMAN OF EGYPT: AGRICULTURE AND IRRIGATION

"Egypt is the gift of the river," said Herodotus. Medieval Egyptians also knew this to be true. The narrow strip that supplied Egypt with food could be cultivated only because of the annual flooding of the Nile. It is no exaggeration to say that everything depended on the inundation: food, prices, the economy and, therefore, the kingdom in general. The absolute dependence of the country on the Nile was expressed not only in administrative structure, but also in the long history of Nile cults.[1] But the Nile was not an unequivocal blessing, and the river could be impetuous: too little water and there was famine, too much and there was mass destruction. It is easy to understand, then, why al-Qāḍī al-Fāḍil, writing of the Nile in the twelfth century, said, "It is the only [real] highwayman in Egypt, both desired and dreaded."[2]

Reports of a low Nile, or failure to increase, often inspired panic in the population. At the beginning of the increase (*ziyāda*), ancient custom had been for the guardian of the Nilometer (*qayyās*) to announce daily the level of the Nile. The practice was abolished by al-Muʿizz, however, and the historian al-Maqrīzī (d. 845/1442) thought it one of the most sensible policies enacted:

> In that month [i.e., Shawwāl 362/973] al-Muʿizz prohibited proclaiming the increase of the Nile [*ziyādat al-nīl*] or writing about it to anyone other than himself or Jawhar. He permitted this proclamation only when the Nile had reached its plenitude, that is, when it reached 16 cubits and the canal was cut. Note well the utility of this policy: if, at a given moment, the Nile stops rising or rises [too] little, the people worry and tell themselves there will be a lack of water. They then hoard grain, refusing to sell in anticipation of rising prices. Those who have money make [a great] effort to store cereal, whether anticipating high prices, or for storing provisions for their family. This

> brings on short supply and if it happens that the Nile does rise, the price of commodities becomes unstable; if it does not rise, there is famine and drought.[3]

But the population feared equally the destruction caused by too great an increase. Al-Maqrīzī recounts that when the people learned the water had reached sixteen cubits, they would say, "We take refuge in God from a finger in twenty [cubits]," that is, from the water reaching a height of twenty cubits, because of the massive flooding that would ensue.[4] Aside from its destructive powers, too great an increase could be taken as an omen of ill-fortune. In 543/1149, the water rose to a remarkable nineteen cubits and reached the first street outside of Cairo. When the caliph al-Ḥāfiẓ heard that the water had reached the city gate,[5] he shut himself up in grief. One of his intimate courtiers asked him the cause of his grief, and he showed him a book in which it was written,"When the water arrives at the New Gate, ʿAbd al-Majīd (i.e., al-Ḥāfiẓ) will die." True to the prophecy, al-Ḥāfiẓ fell ill and died less than a year later.[6]

While "winter" crops required only the flood waters, the "summer" crops required heavy waterings by artificial irrigation.[7] An elaborate system of irrigation canals carried water to the land.[8] According to the medieval authors, the winter crops did not require more than the flooding of the Nile.[9] In Egypt, rural taxes depended both on the type of crop and on the height of the Nile flood.[10] The ruler did not have the right to impose the tax on cultivated land (*kharāj*) until the Nile had reached plenitude, usually at a height of 16 cubits.[11] After the water had receded, the agent (*dalīl*) surveyed the land, distinguishing between cultivable and noncultivable land and indicating the amount of cultivation that was appropriate to the level of the flood. Thus an elaborate administrative structure existed to exploit the water of the Nile, and foremost among the government's responsibilities was maintaining irrigation canals. These canals were closed off by dirt dams that were opened when the water had reached the appropriate height. The opening or "cutting" (*kasr*) of the dams of major irrigation canals occurred in the context of a formal ceremony.

THE CEREMONY TO CUT THE CANAL

In his short history of the ceremony,[12] Omar Toussoun postulated that a ceremony to cut the canal had existed even before the Arab conquest of Egypt, but that its location had been at ʿAyn Shams (Heliopolis). The Fatimids, he said, moved the ceremony from ʿAyn Shams to Cairo when they conquered Egypt. His primary evidence for this reconstruction is the passage in al-Muqaddasī describing the ruler's attendance at the cutting of the canal at ʿAyn Shams.[13] Such a ceremony had probably existed for some time at ʿAyn Shams, which had been Egypt's primary city for centuries before the foundation of Fustat, and all evidence points to an early Christian celebration at that location. But the existence of a ceremony at one location certainly does not preclude other locations for similar, or identical, ceremonies at the time of the inundation. Danielle Bonneau reports Nile ceremonies in the Greco-Roman period in numerous locations and at numerous times throughout the year.[14] Limiting their Nile ceremonies to a single time in the calendar did not require the Arab rulers of Egypt to limit them to a single place. It seems more likely that a ceremony to cut the canal took place at both the ʿAyn Shams and the Fustat locations. Such ceremonies took place all along the canal and at various points along the Nile itself. Another canal, Khalīj al-dhikr, built by Kāfūr al-Ikhshīdī, was opened before the main canal, a practice that persisted until the reign of the Mamluk Sultan Qalā'ūn in 724/1323–24.[15] After the Fatimid conquest, the canal that came to be known as the Canal of Cairo was cut,[16] and later the wazir al-Ma'mūn al-Baṭā'iḥī initiated an opening of the Abu'l-Munajjā Canal, which had been built by al-Afḍal in 506/1112.[17]

The Canal of Cairo dates in legend back to the time of Abraham.[18] When Abraham sent Hagar and Ismaʿil to Mecca, she appealed to the king Toutis for aid, informing him that she was in a barren place and imploring him for water. He ordered the canal to be dug and sent her wheat (*ḥinṭa*) by boat, thus revitalizing the Hijaz. Work on the canal was continued by Andromanos, some four centuries before the advent of Muḥammad. The first redigging of the Islamic period dates, according to the historian Ibn ʿAbd al-Ḥakam, to the days of the caliph ʿUmar. The canal was redug immediately after the conquest of Egypt by ʿAmr b. al-ʿĀṣ and was used to transport provisions to the Hijaz.[19] In honor of the caliph, the canal was named "the Canal of the Commander of the Faithful" (*khalīj amīr al-mu'minīn*).[20] The canal functioned until 101/723, when it silted up due to neglect; its new outlet became Timsah, approximately halfway between Cairo and Qulzum.[21] It was a navigable waterway when the Fatimids conquered Egypt.[22]

At the time of the establishment of Cairo, the mouth of the Canal of Cairo was located at the Quarter of the Seven Reservoirs (*khaṭṭ al-sabaʿ siqāyāt*), on the outskirts of Fustat. Al-Quḍāʿī says that on the canal there was a bridge (*qanṭara*) at al-Ḥamrā' al-Qaṣwī built in the year 69/688–89 by the son of ʿAmr b. al-ʿĀṣ.[23] In 318/930 and again in 331/942–43, the bridge was lengthened, probably to extend it to the receding Nile. During the Fatimid period, the caliph al-ʿAzīz rebuilt it. Another historian, Ibn ʿAbd al-Ẓāhir, says that no trace of this aqueduct remained in his day but that its location was behind the Quarter of the Seven Reservoirs. This bridge was the location of the dam that was opened until after the year 500/1106–7.[24] The evidence suggests that opening the canal at Fustat was an established practice when the Fatimids conquered Egypt and founded Cairo. Fustat was the administrative center of the two cities and, indeed, of the Fatimid empire. It was also the commercial heart of the two cities, and foremost among its attractions were the warehouses along the shore of the Nile.[25] A new ruler who wanted to display his sovereignty to the subject population would have no better way than to parade to Fustat. The meaning of the ceremony of the cutting of the canal, at least in the Arab period, was tied to the administrative responsibilities of the government in maintaining the elaborate system of irrigation canals, thereby ensuring the prosperity of the land.[26] By attending the cutting of the canal, a new ruler would make himself visible to the population and assure the continuity of responsible administration after a change of dynasty.

When al-Muʿizz arrived in Cairo from North Africa, he rode to cut the Canal of the Qanṭara in Dhu'l-Qaʿda 362/973. This seems to be not the Canal of Cairo, which later Fatimid caliphs opened at the time of the inundation, but rather the Banī Wā'il Canal.[27] He rode along the shore to Banī Wā'il in a grand procession. The dignitaries of state rode behind him, and Abū Jaʿfar Aḥmad b. Naṣr rode with him and informed him of the places he was passing. The common people (*al-raʿiyya*) pronounced prayers for him. Then, the caliph turned toward Birkat al-Ḥabash and proceeded on to the desert (*al-ṣaḥrā'*) along the trench (*khandaq*).[28] He passed by the graves of Kāfūr al-Ikhshīdī and ʿAbd Allāh b. Aḥmad b. Ṭabāṭabā al-Ḥusaynī, and then returned to the palace.

In 363/974, al-Maqrīzī reports simply that al-Muʿizz went to cut the canal (*fatḥ al-khalīj* or *kasr al-khalīj*).[29] There are two separate accounts of processions by al-ʿAzīz to cut the canal. One contains the important details that he rode with a parasol (*miẓalla*) and wore an outer garment of brocade with gold threads (*qamīṣ dībāj muthaqqal*) and a turban ornamented with a jewel (*tāj muraṣṣaʿ bi'l-jawhar*).[30] The other, for the year 383/993, simply states that he went to cut the canal.[31] There is also a dated report from the reign of al-Ḥākim in 404/1013–14, when he opened the canal on the seventeenth day of the Coptic month Misra (corresponding to al-Muḥarram) at a height of fourteen cubits and eight fingers.[32] In spite of the scarcity of details, there is no doubt that the caliph went annually to open the canal. Al-Maqrīzī says specifically that al-Musabbiḥī mentioned processions of al-ʿAzīz, al-Ḥākim, and al-Ẓāhir for every year.[33] Al-Musabbiḥī also reported the popular gathering of Christians and Muslims in Muḥarram 415/1024, on the third day following the opening, at the Church of al-Maqs, where they set up tents next to the bridge (*qanṭara*) for eating, drinking, and merriment. The festivities continued until the caliph al-Ẓāhir sailed in a boat (*markab*) to al-Maqs. He spent some time there and then returned to his palace.[34]

There are no other accounts of ceremonies at the inundation by Egyptian historians before the twelfth century, although the Persian traveler Nasir-i Khusrau offers a dramatic account of al-Mustanṣir's Nile procession in 438–39/1047.[35] He describes a large tent of Rūmī brocade, and two other pavilions.[36] For the preceding three days, drums had been beaten and trumpets sounded in the stables to accustom the mounts to the noise. On the day of the procession, when the caliph mounted his horse, there were ten thousand horses in the cortege with gold saddles and collars and bridles inlaid with precious stones. All of the fabrics were custom-made seamless Rūmī brocade or *būqalamūn*.[37] The ruler's name was embroidered along the borders of the saddle cloths (i.e., *ṭirāz*). Each horse was covered with a coat of mail or other armor. Helmets were affixed to the pommel of the saddle, and other arms were affixed to the saddle itself. A large number of camels carried richly ornamented litters, and mules paraded with packsaddles, inlaid with gold and gems, and coverings adorned with pearls. There were ten thousand men to lead the horses and they advanced by groups of one hundred, preceded by men sounding trumpets and beating drums, while companies of soldiers marched behind them. They led the horses, followed by the camels and mules, to the head of the canal.

The ruler was a great distance behind the soldiers and horses. Nasir-i Khusrau described him as a beautiful young man with a shaved head, mounted on a mule of which the saddle and bridle were of the utmost simplicity, without any gold or silver ornaments (as opposed to the elaborate ornamentation of the parade horses). He wore a wide white robe (*durrāʿa*) made of *dabīqī* linen that was valued at ten thousand dinars.[38] His turban consisted of a length of white fabric wrapped around his head, and he carried a whip in his hand. Three hundred Daylamī soldiers marched in front of him on foot. They wore costumes of Rūmī brocade, bound at the waist by belts. The sleeves of their robes were wide, in the Egyptian style and they carried short pikes and axes. All of the troops were on foot, marching in companies and detachments. The bearer of the parasol, who rode alongside of the caliph, wore a turban of cloth with gold threads and ornamented with precious gems, costing ten thousand Maghrebi dinars. The parasol itself was covered with precious stones and pearls. To the right and left, eunuchs carried incense burners with ambergris and aloe. As the caliph passed by the people, they prostrated themselves and called out benedictions.[39] The caliph was followed by the wazir, the chief qadi, and scholars and high functionaries of the state. He proceeded to the head of the canal and waited under the pavilion for a short while. Then, he threw a spear at the dam. This was the signal for the workmen to rush forward and attack the dam with pickaxes, hoes, and shovels until it gave way.

This description is as significant for what it does not tell us as for what it does tell. There is no mention of the pleasure palace overlooking the canal (*manẓara*) or of the route of the procession, nor is there any information about the order (*tartīb*) of the procession itself. It was written primarily to convey an impression of the young caliph and therefore contains the details that would catch the traveler's eye. Most important, however, is the fact that this description, like those of Ibn Zūlāq and al-Musabbiḥī, contains absolutely no mention of a ceremony to perfume the Nilometer (*takhlīq al-miqyās*).

LATE FATIMID NILE CEREMONIES

In the late Fatimid period, there were two distinct ceremonies at the time of the inundation, at two different locations. The first was the perfuming of the Nilometer (*takhlīq al-miqyās*), which took place when the Nile reached the sixteenth cubit. The second, following the perfuming by one to three days, was the procession to cut the canal (*fatḥ al-khalīj* or *kasr al-khalīj*). The ceremony to perfume the Nilometer was a late introduction, probably dating no earlier than the wazirate of al-Ma'mūn. I shall return to the dating and details of this ceremony later. The late procession to cut the canal resembles the earlier ceremony in many respects but, like most other late Fatimid ceremonies, was considerably more elaborate. Both Ibn al-Ma'mūn and Ibn al-Ṭuwayr describe the twelfth-century ceremony to cut the canal. Ibn al-Ma'mūn's accounts of the ceremony in the years 516/1122, 517/1123, and 518/1124 are more elaborate than Ibn al-Ṭuwayr's.[40] Many of the details of the ceremonies described by the two later historians are similar, some are even identical. The ceremony was located at the pleasure pavilion known as *manẓarat al-sukkara*, in the area of al-Marīs on the west bank of the canal.[41]

It was also customary to erect large tents on the west bank of the canal by *manẓarat al-sukkara*, from which the caliph and his entourage observed the cutting of the dam. When the Nile reached sixteen cubits, Ibn al-Ma'mūn reports for the year 516/1122, the tents were taken out. The royal treasuries contained numerous smaller tents and several magnificent and complicated creations. The largest and most elaborate of these comprised four vestibules (*dahālīz*) and four halls (*qāʿa*), in addition to the main hall. The center pole (*ʿamūd*) of the large hall reached a height of fifty cubits.[42] It had been manufactured over a period of nine years during the wazirate of al-Afḍal, and when it was finally set up, a number of people were injured and two died. Henceforth, it was known as *al-qātūl*, "The Killer."[43] Only the large hall was erected along with the four vestibules and perhaps one of the pavilions (*surādiq*). Ibn al-Ṭuwayr remarks that the highest ranking officials (*arbāb al-rutab*) set up tents just north of "The Killer."[44] Their proximity to the caliph's tent depended on their rank.[45] Both "The Killer" and the *manẓarat al-sukkara* were covered with elaborate carpets and wall hangings and supplied with a variety of richly ornamented trays. In Ibn al-Ṭuwayr's time, the center pole of the tent was wrapped in white, red, or yellow brocade (*dībāj*) from top to bottom. The throne (*sarīr al-mulk*) was set up next to the center pole and covered in *qurqūbī* silk.[46] In 517/1123, lustre trays (*al-ṣawānī al-dhahab*) filled with human and animal figurines were brought in addition to the wall hangings and carpets. There were elephants, giraffes, lions, and other beasts made of gold, silver, and amber, all ornamented with pearls, sapphires, and chrysolite. One elephant figurine in particular had a body of "kneaded" amber, silver tusks, and two large gems with a nielloed gold nail for its eyes; there was a seat (*sarīr*) carved of *ʿūd* (an odoriferous wood) with silver and gold cushions, mounted by figures of men wearing helmets and carrying shields and unsheathed swords of silver in their hands. One figurine of a lion carved out of *ʿūd* had ruby eyes. In addition to the figurines and the textiles, various fruits and flowers were sent to *manẓarat al-sukkara*, at a cost of some one hundred dinars.[47]

The preparations for the procession proper began in one of the halls of the palace. Although not specifically designated, it must have been either the Gold Hall (*qāʿat al-dhahab*) or the Iwan, the two sites of major audiences. All of the costumes, mounts, and insignia of sovereignty were brought out of the treasuries and assembled there. The caliph emerged wearing the costume reserved for festivals (*ziyy al-khilāfa*); it was made of *ṭamīm* brocade.[48] His turban (*mandīl*) was wound in the style called "the Arab winding" (*al-shadda al-ʿarabiyya*) or "the winding of reverence" (*shaddat al-waqqār*), and it was ornamented with sapphires, emeralds, and the jewel (*al-jawhar*) that adorned the top of the turban. As soon as it was donned, the banners were flown and all talking ceased.[49] Neither relatives nor intimates of the caliph were permitted to greet him except by kissing the ground at a distance; only the wazir was permitted to approach.[50]

The officers of the treasuries, carrying his inlaid sword (*sayf*) and lance (*rumḥ*), marched in front of him, followed by the Ṣaqlabī eunuchs,[51] carrying flywhisks (*midhābb*) with gold poles. The caliph walked on silk carpets between two columns of men organized by rank (*al-ṣaffayn al-murattabayn*). As the caliph passed by, the men in the columns kissed the ground until he reached the hall (*majlis khilāfatih*) and ascended the brocade-covered throne (*kursī*) from which he would mount his horse. The trainers and stable attendants (*al-rawwād wa-azimmat al-iṣṭabalāt*) lined up the horses for the parasol (*khiyal al-miẓalla*) after the silk blankets and *dabīqī* linen cloths with gold threads (*al-shiqaq al-dabīqī al-mudhahhaba*) were removed from the saddles. The rest of the objects that he had chosen were brought.[52] The Qur'an reciters began to read as soon as the caliph mounted his horse. At this time, the officers of the mounted escort (*muqaddamī al-rikāb*, lit. "officers of the stirrup"), and the trainers replaced the *muḥannak* eunuchs at his stirrups and bridle.[53] The clients and relatives of the caliph (*al-mawālī wa'l-aqārib*) returned to their designated places.[54]

The caliph summoned the wazir, using all of his titles; the wazir approached, kissing first the ground and then the caliph's stirrup. The caliph bestowed the great honor upon him of kissing his hand, which was empty because the staff (*qaḍīb al-mulk*) was not carried on this festival.[55] After the wazir finished paying homage,[56] he took the sword from the Amir Iftikhār al-Dawla, one of the highest ranking *muḥannak* eunuchs serving as superintendant of the royal wardrobe (*aḥad al-umarā' al-ustādhīn al-mumayyazīn al-muḥannakīn mutawallī khizānat al-kiswa al-khāṣṣ*). The wazir then gave the sword to his brother, who carried it in the procession. He lowered the tail of his turban and wore a gold belt (*minṭaqa*) while carrying the sword, as a sign of honor and respect.[57] The lowered tail of the turban and the gold belt were associated only with the most important insignia of sovereignty. Neither the bearer of the lance (*rumḥ*) nor the bearer of the shield (*daraqa*) lowered the tail of his turban or wore a belt.[58]

The wazir and his sons were summoned to come to the door of the Gold Hall (*qā'at al-dhahab*). Then the caliph exited from the hall to the first vestibule (*dihlīz*) and was met by the ten commanders of his mounted escort who rode on his right and left (*jamā'atu ṣibyān rikābihi al-'asharatu al-muqaddamīn arbāb al-maymana wa'l-maysara*). They were followed by the "young men of letters" (*ṣibyān al-rasā'il*) and the "young men of homage" (*ṣibyān al-salām*), wearing turbans of fine linen with borders (*al-manādīl al-shurūb al-mu'allama*) and fulled *dabīqī* linen sashes at their waists (*bi-awṣātihim al-'irāḍ al-dabīqī al-maqṣūra*), who summoned various officials while the procession was being organized. These young men each had a specific duty to perform, and it appears that they carried orders from the caliph to other members of the procession. There were no black slaves among this group, which was composed entirely of *muwalladūn* (sons of Turkish and other soldiers who married into the local population)[59] as well as the sons of dignitaries.

Another group surrounding the caliph wore long, sleeved garments that were open in front (*al-qanābīz al-mufarraja*) and fastened with sashes (*manādīl*) made of Sūsī linen.[60] They carried from the royal treasury (*al-silāḥ al-khāṣṣ*) the arms that were used only when the caliph went out in procession. The caliph emerged from the Gold Gate (*bāb al-dhahab*) while the *gharbīya* trumpet and the regular trumpets (*abwāq al-salām*) were being sounded. The parasol was unfurled and the caliph began the procession while the Qur'an was being recited. The cortege assembled in order. The chief chamberlain and his assistants organized the front part of the procession, and the master of the audience hall organized the rear of the cortege. Each person's place was designated in chits (*madārīj*) that had been written and distributed before the procession. The chief chamberlain (*mutawallī al-bāb*) and his assistants were in front of the caliph, and the master of the audience hall followed behind.[61] The troops formed "two forbidding fortresses" (*ḥisnayn māniʿayn*) of cavalry and infantry, crowded together in battle lines and carrying gilded weapons. Each regiment was led by its commander (*zimām*). There was no space between them for any passerby. The stores and houses and gates of all the quarters had been decorated with various types of brocade, *dabīqī* linen drapes, and different kinds of arms.

The procession continued until it reached the tents that had been set up; then the caliph stopped the cortege and summoned the wazir along with some of his own escort (*muqaddamī rikābihi*, lit. "officers of his stirrup"). The wazir passed by alone and gestured as if kissing the ground before the caliph,[62] and the caliph returned the greeting with his sleeve.[63] After these greetings were exchanged, the wazir's entourage regrouped on foot at his stirrup. The caliph resumed his procession after the wazir assumed a new place at the head of the cortege. Everyone who was given the honor of attending the caliph's stirrup now dismounted according to rank, with the bearers of the sword and lance and the "young men of homage" (*ṣibyān al-salām*) being the last to dismount.[64] As a sign of particular distinction, each of these officials was summoned by all of his titles and kissed the ground. They formed a cordon around the caliph as he entered the heavily guarded tent.

The wazir dismounted at the third vestibule (*dihlīz*), approached the caliph, and took the bit of his horse from the trainer.[65] He then led it across the tents, which were decorated with human and animal forms and covered with *jahramīya* and Andalusian carpets.[66] When he reached the large hall (*al-qāʿa al-kubrā*), the caliph dismounted onto the throne. He seated the wazir on the chair (*kursī*) that had been prepared for him.[67] Arms bearers (*al-mustakhdamūn ḥamlat al-silāḥ*) surrounded the caliph so that no one could see him.[68] The amirs, guests, and chamberlains then lined up in rows while the entire Qur'an was recited (*khatama al-qur'ān*).[69] The poets were presented according to ranks,[70] and when the last of them had finished paying homage, servants and trainers (*rawwāḍ*) brought back the mounts.

The caliph mounted up while the wazir held the bit. The men at his stirrup were on foot. The entire cortege was organized again, and now the Qur'an reciters took the place of the fanfare (*rahajiyya*). The caliph left the hall (*qā'a*) and exited from the vestibules of the southern door of the tent (*wa-ṣa'ada min al-qā'a allatī fī dahālīz al-bāb al-qiblī minhā fa-kharaja minhu*). The amirs and guests kissed the ground as the caliph left. Then the caliph, his wazir, his sons and brothers, his companions, and entourage, all went up to the *manẓarat al-sukkara*.

The caliph's brother greeted him with an elaborate salute and kissed the ground. The caliph sat down, with the wazir on his right and his brother on his left.[71] One of the windows (*ṭāqāt*) of the pavilion was opened. As soon as the people saw the caliph, they kissed the ground and then continued to look toward him. The workmen (*mustakhdamūn*) were standing on the dam, and when the wazir gave the order to break it, they kissed the ground and yielded their places to workers from the royal gardens (*al-basāṭīn al-sulṭāniyya*).[72] These workers then opened the dam with pickaxes (*ma'āwil*).[73] While the dam was being broken, the Qur'an and the formula "God is most great" (*takbīr*) were being recited on the west side of the canal (where the caliph was), and the fanfare (*al-rahaj wa'l-la'b*) was played on the east side.[74] After the dam was opened and the water leveled off in the canal, Nile boats (*'ushariyyāt*) were launched.[75] Ibn al-Ma'mūn says simply that they were embellished with gold and silver and decorated with inscribed curtains, while their captains and crew wore beautiful costumes.[76] Ibn al-Ṭuwayr describes some of these boats. A group of boats was then launched "as if they were servants before the gold boat" (*al-'ushārī al-dhahabī*), the Nile boat that was used by the caliph when he went to perfume the Nilometer.[77] Then the six large royal boats were launched:[78] the gold (i.e., the caliph's private boat), silver,[79] red, yellow, lapis lazuli (*lāzuwardī*), and Sicilian (*ṣiqillī*).[80] The cabins were covered with multicolored *dabīqī* linen curtains, and "on the heads and necks there were crescents and pearl necklaces." These Nile boats were used only for the personal entourage of the caliph at the time of the inundation.[81]

After the Nile boats were launched, the windows were closed and the caliph retired to a chamber (*maqṣūra*) that had been prepared for him in the pavilion. A number of officials then received robes of honor.[82] First, the prefect of Fustat was summoned from the east shore of the canal (*al-barr al-sharqī*) and invested with a complete costume, consisting of a turban and robe with gold threads, and two additional robes of *ʿattābī* silk and siglaton.[83] He did not actually enter the pavilion, but after receiving his robe of honor, he kissed the ground beneath the pavilion and crossed the canal to resume his place. Next, the superintendants of the gardens and their supervisors were summoned and received complete costumes with *ʿattābī* silk and siglaton robes. The head of the Office of the Fleet (*mutawallī dīwān al-ʿamā'ir*) and the naval officers (*muqaddamī al-ru'asā'*) received the same type of costume.[84]

A banquet was then laid out in the tents and the pavilion. Platters were set upon tables at the west door of the tent. The wazir ordered his brother to cross the canal to sit at the head of the banquet; the wazir's brother was accompanied by the chief chamberlain (*mutawallī ḥajabat al-bāb*), his deputies (*nuwwāb*), and the rest of the chamberlains. The amirs and guests, summoned by cupbearers (*suqāt*) from their tents,[85] took their assigned places at the banquet. They were followed by the troops, according to rank. After the banquet for the amirs was finished, the wazir's brother returned to the pavilion, and the chief chamberlain stayed behind to host the banquet of the purchased and black slaves and the rest of the infantry (*al-ʿabīd wa'l-mustakhdamīn min al-rājil wa'l-sūdān*).

Ibn al-Ṭuwayr,[86] indicates that there a separate banquet, for the chief qadi and his notary witnesses, was held in a white *dabīqī* linen tent. The chief steward (*ṣāḥib al-mā'ida*) and his servants carried trays from the palace,[87] containing one hundred collections of wide bowls (*ṭayāfīr*) covered by silk round pieces, on top of which were mats (*ṭarrāḥāt*) scented with a light musk (*misk fātiḥ*).[88] The wazir received his customary amount in addition to three trays (*ṣawānī*) of figurines; his sons and brothers also received trays of figurines. But, out of respect for religious law, the banquet trays that were carried to the chief qadi and his witnesses had no figurines (*min ghayr tamāthīl tawqīran li'l-sharʿ*)[89]. Each amir also received food and a tray of figurines, much of which ultimately reached the people.

Ibn al-Ma'mūn does not mention a separate banquet for the chief qadi and his witnesses, however he describes the caliph's banquet in the pavilion. The caliph's brother sat on his left and the wazir on his right, after each had paid homage. The wazir's sons and brothers, the head of the chancery (*kātib al-dast*) and his son, and the highest-ranking eunuchs (*al-ʿawālī al-khāṣṣ al-mustakhdamūn fi'l-khidam al-kibār*) attended. We know that other high-ranking officials did not attend the banquet, for Ibn al-Ma'mūn says that each of the officials who did not attend the banquet received something from it as a token of the day. This included the chief qadi and his witnesses as well as the chief missionary (*dāʿī*) and his cousin, who had the distinction of remaining the entire day in the hall of the large tent where the throne was set up. When the caliph's banquet was over, each person attending kissed the ground and left, taking what was left over "for honor and blessing" (*al-sharaf wa'l-baraka*).[90] In addition, Ibn al-Ma'mūn describes in another place lists (*ithbātāt*) designating the distributions of gold, silver, and trays of food including grilled sheep and sweets to members of the caliph's entourage and other lower-ranking officials. After the banquet was over, the noon prayer was performed.

The caliph changed his costume, donning a complete silk outfit (*badla*) with the "winding of majesty" turban (*shaddat al-waqqār*) and the jewel. The caliph then had the commander of his private wardrobe (*muqaddam khizānat al-kiswa al-khāṣṣ*) send another costume to the wazir. It was carried by one of the caliph's eunuchs. This costume, a complete silk outfit with a white turban wound in the *al-dāniyya* fashion, rather than the *al-ʿarabiyya*, is identified by Ibn al-Ma'mūn as one of the outfits worn to the Friday prayers.[91] This can only mean a costume worn by the caliph on one of the three Fridays he led prayer during Ramaḍān. It is, perhaps, identical with the costume worn by the caliph to the Azhar, a complete processional silk costume, with a white turban and a cowl (*ṭaylasān*).[92] After the wazir thanked the caliph, he was ordered to accompany the caliph's brother to one of the Nile boats (*ʿushāriyyāt*). The door of the pavilion that let onto the shore of the canal was opened for them, and a processional Nile boat (*ʿushārī mawkibiyya*) was brought. The caliph's brother sailed with his entourage and the wazir remained on the shore paying homage to him, while the rest of the Nile boats were launched.

The wazir returned to the pavilion, where the caliph chose a horse and mounted it. The officers of his mounted escort (*muqad-*

damū al-rikāb) surrounded him and the Qur'an reciters recited the Fātiḥa as he left, pavilion and entered the southern door of the tent.[93] The caliph crossed through the main hall (*qāʿa*) by his throne, where the highest-ranking scribes (*shuyūkh al-kuttāb*) and the amirs (*ʿawālī*), the qadi, and the missionary were permitted to greet him, after which they exited into a garden.[94] The caliph was with his cavalry and amirs, and he left the garden after distributing portions. Then the fanfare returned, and the cortege was organized as it had been initially. In the account of Ibn al-Ma'mūn, the caliph then proceeded to the dam (*sadd*) at Birkat al-Ḥabash, which was cut in his presence. This is reminiscent of the procession of al-Muʿizz in 362/973 to cut the dam at the Banī Wā'il canal, and it may indicate that even in the twelfth century, the Fatimids presided over the cutting of more than one dam. On the other hand, the accounts of Ibn al-Ṭuwayr and Ibn ʿAbd al-Ẓāhir indicate that the caliph returned directly to the palace along the west bank of the canal, crossed it, and then entered the palace through Bāb al-Qanṭara.

PERFUMING THE NILOMETER

The official charged with monitoring the rise of the Nile, in keeping with the policy inaugurated by al-Muʿizz, reported to the caliph privately on a daily basis. This official was traditionally called by the name *cum* title Ibn Abi'l-Raddād. While ordinary residents of Cairo and Fustat might watch the river and guess at the level of the water, control over definitive information remained with the caliph and Ibn Abi'l-Raddād. Although the level of the water was supposed to be announced officially only after a certain point, the preparations for the ceremonies to cut the canal and to perfume the Nilometer constituted a sort of public announcement that there would be plenitude.

There is no description of a ceremony to perfume the Nilometer, however, until the year 517/1123.[95] At the beginning of inundation of the Nile, al-Ma'mūn ordered servants to stay overnight in the Pearl Pavilion (*manẓarat al-lu'lu'*) to guard it. When the Nile reached fifteen cubits, he ordered tents taken out; when it approached plenitude, the caliph moved at night from his palace to the Pearl Pavilion with his entourage, while the wazir al-Ma'mūn moved to the Gold House (*dār al-dhahab*), both of which were on the eastern shore of the canal.[96] The costumes (*kiswa*) were also brought. Unlike the costumes for the two festivals, this was limited to the caliph, his brothers, four of his female servants, the wazir and his sons, and Ibn Abi'l-Raddād.[97]

When the Nile reached plenitude, the caliph and the wazir rode to the arsenal (*ṣināʿa*) in Fustat.[98] Although Ibn al-Ma'mūn does not provide details of the procession to the arsenal, Ibn al-Ṭuwayr, in his undated account, describes the route in detail. The caliph left Cairo from Bāb Zuwayla, proceeded to the end of the Garden of ʿAbbās (*bustān ʿabbās*), and then turned at the Mosque of Ibn Ṭūlūn toward the great bridge, which he followed until he reached the Nile shore in Fustat. From there, he went along the Khashshābīn until he reached Dār al-Fāḍil,[99] next to *bāb al-ṣāgha*, the market hall (*qaysāriyya*) of the goldsmiths.[100] The vestibule (*dihlīz*) was lined with benches (*maṣāṭib*) that were covered with ʿAbbadānī mats.[101] The caliph crossed, followed by the wazir and came out on the other side, heading toward the customs house and then to the Suyūriyyīn.[102] They then went to the *manāzil al-ʿizz* (Dwellings of Glory) and from there to Seat of the Kingdom (*dār al-mulk*).[103] The wazir dismounted at the door of Seat of the Kingdom and entered before the caliph. Then the caliph and the wazir boarded a Nile boat (*ʿushārī*) from Seat of the Kingdom. The Nile boats had been decorated with multicolored *dabīqī* linen curtains.[104] The caliph boarded the boat along with three or four of the *muḥannak* eunuchs; then the rest of the caliph's personal retinue (*khawāṣṣ*) boarded the boat. The caliph sat inside his cabin, and the wazir stood outside the door. When everyone had boarded the boat, it set sail for the Nilometer.

The wazir and the eunuchs entered the well (*fisqiyya*), followed by the caliph. Then the caliph and the wazir each prayed separately. The caliph mixed the saffron and musk perfume himself and handed it to the director of the treasury (*ṣāḥib bayt al-māl*), who then gave it to Ibn Abi'l-Raddād. The latter threw himself into the well, still wearing his undershirt (*ghilāla*) and turban. He hung from the column by his legs and his left hand and perfumed the column with his right hand while the Qur'an reciters recited verses. The caliph left immediately in his Nile boat, either going back to Seat of the Kingdom and then to Cairo or sailing to al-Maqs.

Following the perfuming, Ibn Abi'l-Raddād received a robe of honor at the palace.[105] In 517/1123, Ibn Abi'l-Raddād received a "golden" outfit (*badla*) with a robe (*thawb*) made of a linen and silk weave.[106] He received a *ṭaylasān muqawwar*.[107] In Ibn al-Ṭuwayr's day, he was also entrusted with four pouches, each containing five hundred dirhems. Ibn Abi'l-Raddād paraded through the city, wearing his robe of honor, riding one of the five mounts given to him and accompanied by four mules, which carried the pouches. The *abwāq* trumpets were blown in front of him, while the large drum (*ṭabl*) was beaten behind him, in the same manner as was done for the amirs. Whenever he passed a gate used by the caliph to enter or exit the palace, Ibn Abi'l-Raddād dismounted, kissed the gate, and mounted again. This was the standard practice of everyone who was invested with a robe of honor, from the amirs of the collar (*al-umarā' al-muṭawwaqūn*) to those of lower rank, of both the civil and military bureaucracies. Ibn Abi'l-Raddād then left Cairo from Bāb Zuwayla and headed toward Fustat on the Great Road (*al-shāriʿ al-aʿẓam*), passing by the Mosque of ʿAbd Allāh and Dār al-Anmāṭ to the Mosque of ʿAmr and on to the bank of the river, where he crossed to the Nilometer.

Ibn al-Ṭuwayr and Ibn al-Ma'mūn give nearly identical accounts of the overnight stay in the Nilometer.[108] Ten qintars of bread (*khubz*), ten grilled lambs, ten vessels of confections, and ten candles were brought from the palace kitchens. The Qur'an reciters and the professors of the Friday mosques of Cairo and Fustat attended.[109] The candles were lit during the last part of the night while the Qur'an was recited continuously.

DATING THE NILOMETER CEREMONY

The ceremony to perfume the Nilometer presents several problems in dating. None of the earlier chroniclers mentions a procession to perfume the Nilometer; indeed, there is no mention of any ceremony at all at the Rawda Nilometer until the year 517/1123. Does this silence indicate a real absence of the ceremony, or does it merely reflect a gap in the sources? Ibn Zūlāq makes no mention of any ceremony at the Nilometer. Al- Musabbiḥī, a thorough and competent chronicler, records the processions of the caliphs al-ʿAzīz, al-Ḥākim, and al-Ẓāhir to the opening of the canal (*fatḥ al-khalīj*) for every year. There are also several instances when Ibn Abi'l-Raddād (the guardian of the Nilometer and, in the later period, the official charged with the actual perfuming of the column), was invested with a robe of honor at the time of the inundation.[110] Both of these historians provide descriptions of every other procession and ceremony, so it is unlikely that they would fail to mention the perfuming of the Nilometer, had the ceremony been in existence during their lifetimes. Moreover, its close association in both time and place with the cutting of the canal makes it all the more unlikely that they would have recorded one of the two ceremonies so carefully, while failing to mention the other. The traveler Nasir-i Khusrau, who provides a dramatic description of al-Mustanṣir's procession to the canal, makes no mention at all of perfuming the Nilometer.

What, then, of the possibility that the later historians are responsible for omitting the references? This, too, is unlikely. Neither Ibn Taghrī Birdī nor al-Qalqashandī reports on early ceremonies; their discussions of Fatimid institutions and ceremonial are based almost entirely on the lost history of Ibn al-Ṭuwayr. On the other hand, al-Maqrīzī, a scrupulous anthologizer, draws on sources dating from every period of Fatimid history. Had early descriptions of Nilometer ceremonies been available to him, it is safe to assume that he would transmit them in his characteristically accurate and complete fashion.

If we are on relatively safe ground in presuming that there was no ceremony to perfume the Nilometer up to around 441/1049 (the concluding date of Nasir-i Khusrau's sojourn in Cairo), we are on less-certain terrain in trying to establish when the ceremony was introduced. There are no accounts of Nilometer ceremonies during the wazirates of Badr al-Jamālī or his son al-Afḍal, but this is consistent with the general absence of data on ceremonial during the later years of al-Mustanṣir's caliphate. I do not presume that all ceremonies simply ceased during this period when Badr al-Jamālī and al-Afḍal were the virtual rulers of the Fatimid state. In describing several ceremonies that were of an essentially religious character (such as the processions on the two festivals) or honored the Fatimid family (such as birthdays [*mawlid*]), Ibn al-Ma'mūn remarks that al-Afḍal cut off these practices and that the wazir al-Ma'mūn reinstituted them. I do not think that we should assume that the Nile ceremonies, which had such a long history and could easily have been separated from the person of the Fatimid imam, were among the ceremonies abandoned by al-Afḍal. Because Ibn al-Ma'mūn does not remark that the ceremony to cut the canal was reinstituted, as he does when discussing the other ceremonies abandoned by al-Afḍal, I am inclined to think that the opening of the canal continued as usual under al-Afḍal. But since the perfuming of the Nilometer is also discussed without any mention of its being either reinstituted or newly introduced, it seems plausible that the ceremony was in existence prior to 516/1122.[111]

When was the ceremony actually introduced? The answer may lie in the history of the Nilometer itself.[112] It was constructed originally in 247/861 by the Abbasid caliph al-Mutawwakil. The upkeep and repair of the Nilometer was the sole responsibility of the government. In 266/879, Ibn Ṭūlūn appropriated one thousand dinars for repairs.[113] Nasir-i Khusrau reported an annual stipend for Ibn Abi'l-Raddād to maintain the Nilometer. During the Fatimid period, there were two major additions and renovations at the Nilometer. In 415/1024, al-Ẓāhir built a stone wall around the Nilometer, and in 485/1092, al-Mustanṣir built a mosque on the west side of the Nilometer. Regrettably, the sources provide almost no data at all on this mosque. There is a lacuna in the text of al-Maqrīzī's *Khiṭaṭ* and Ibn Duqmāq's terse statement provides only the date of construction. Neither source mentions why this mosque was built by al-Mustanṣir and Badr al-Jamālī just two years before the aged caliph's death. There was not a low Nile, nor had there been any low Niles in recent years. A few years earlier, however, the Nile had reached a height of eighteen cubits, four fingers, producing a devastating flood that caused massive destruction.[114]

The inscriptions on the mosque of the Nilometer hint at a hidden agenda for the construction of this new mosque.[115] The foundation inscription is dated Rajab 485/August 1092, about the time when the rise of the Nile would have begun. The three other inscriptions are Q. 11:90, 9:18, and 61:13. The three verses and the attribution to al-Mustanṣir and Badr are repeated in the wall of the peristyle of the Nilometer to the right of the entrance.[116] Was the mosque, along with its inscriptions, a response to an event reported by Ibn Taghrī Birdī in Rabīʿ I of the same year? On Tuesday in the middle of that month, the astronomers sighted a conjunction of Saturn and Mars in Cancer, regarded as a particularly unlucky conjunction.[117] Perhaps this ominous conjunction inspired the construction of the mosque. The memory of the long drought of 457–64/1065–72 lingered, and the memory of the devastating flood of 481/1088 was fresh. Was the mosque at the Nilometer, started just as the increase was beginning and inscribed with verses on the theme of repentance, meant to have an amuletic charm against the dangerous conjunction?

We cannot establish a direct relationship between this conjunction and the building of the mosque or between the mosque and the introduction of the ceremony to perfume the Nilometer. But the circumstantial evidence warrants the speculation that building the mosque was an attempt to ward off potential harm, and, perhaps, that the ceremony to perfume the Nilometer was also a response to it. The evidence points toward dating the ceremony to sometime after the construction of the mosque. It seems to have been introduced between 485/1092 and 516/1122. Whatever the date of its introduction, we know that, from at least 516/1122 on, the Nilometer was the site of important ceremonial activity. By the Ayyubid period, it had become something of a ritual center, displacing the *muṣallā* as the traditional place for the prayer for rain (*al-istisqā'*). If instituting a ceremony to perfume the Nilometer was not the result of a changed attitude about the Nilometer, perhaps it was a factor in the new and different significance that the place acquired in later years.

THE URBAN RIVER

Although there is an unbroken history of Nile ceremonies from the Pharaonic period to the time of the building of the High Dam at Aswan, we cannot assume that the ceremonies meant the same thing throughout their long and varied history. Danielle Bonneau's work demonstrates that even the emergence of a cult of the Nile was only one of many developments. In the Arab period, these ceremonies, which differed considerably from the Nile ceremonies of Roman Egypt, seem to have been statements about the responsibility of the government to maintain the elaborate system of canals that irrigation agriculture required.

The procession to cut the canal in Fatimid times continued established practices while acknowledging that the Fatimid ruler was now responsible for maintaining the canals that were essential to Egyptian irrigation and agriculture. It was, in part, an attempt to establish legitimacy through public and formal assumption of administrative responsibilities. However, the flooding of the Nile marked more than just the beginning of an agricultural season. The inundation occurred at the end of the busy seafaring season and therefore coincided with the influx of imports and foreign merchants into the markets of Fustat as well as the collection of large amounts of tax revenue at the customs house of the port.[118] Whether intentionally or not, the ceremonies at the inundation symbolized, on some level, the river as part of the complex network of trade and commerce in which the Fatimids and their subjects were so active. However, the ceremonies also reminded the population that participation in trade was not shared on equal terms between the government, one of the largest consumers in the country, and the merchants. The marketplace through which the caliph's procession advanced was a place where many social boundaries were obscured, but those boundaries did not fall away altogether. The rank-conscious and highly stratified procession reminded the residents of Fustat of one of the fundamental asymmetries in their society. The imperial administration had easy access to commercial networks, but merchants did not have comparable access to networks of power within the government.[119]

As with the New Year's procession to which it was compared by Ibn al-Ṭuwayr, the procession to cut the canal displayed the full apparatus of Fatimid military and civilian administration. There was, however, one notable absence: not a single provincial official is mentioned as having attended. The late Fatimid inundation ceremonies seem to have more to do directly with urban experience than with agriculture. They were tied not to the Nile, but to the canal; not to rural agriculture, but to the particular urban settings of Cairo and Fustat. The preparations for the ceremonies required the mass relocation of the caliph and court officials from the palace to the pleasure pavilions arrayed along the canal from Cairo to Fustat.[120] The ceremonies themselves involved carefully orchestrated processions through the streets, markets, and granaries of Fustat.

Like other late Fatimid ceremonies, the inundation processions had urban meanings. Many practices associated with the rise of the Nile resemble the celebration of the Coptic Nawruz, and the ceremonies provided a sanctioned and festive setting for the common popular practices of Cairo and Fustat's diverse population. Similar to the New Year's procession, the inundation processions also created a link between the two cities of Cairo and Fustat. In this case, however, the unifying thoroughfare was not the Great Road but the canal, which became a navigable waterway linking Fustat and Cairo only during the inundation season. As with the Ramaḍān and festival processions, the inundation processions established connections among the palace, the river, the canal, and the marketplaces. Even the building of the mosque at the Nilometer did not go unnoticed. It, too, was integrated into the ritual city when the Fatimids began to perfume the Nilometer. As they had constructed the ritual city in topography and ceremony, the Fatimids also integrated the Nile into the urban landscape, transforming the highwayman of Egypt into an urban river.

CHAPTER 6

Ceremonial as Polemic

Among the ceremonies that were unique to the Fatimids, and that were not continued in some fashion after the fall of the dynasty, was the celebration of the Festival of Ghadīr. Unlike other Fatimid celebrations, which were indigenous to Egypt (like the festivities at the inundation of the Nile) or were broadly Islamic (like the celebrations of Ramaḍān, the two festivals, and the Islamic New Year), the Festival of Ghadīr had a specifically Shiʿi origin. Nonetheless, the festival underwent changes similar in character to those of other Fatimid ceremonies. At the beginning of the Fatimid period, the Festival of Ghadīr, like the observance of the ʿĀshūra fast commemorating the death of Ḥusayn, was primarily a popular celebration. By the twelfth century, the celebration of the Festival of Ghadīr was orchestrated by the government and modeled on the celebrations of the two festivals; in spite of its Shiʿi origins, it became a part of the ritual *lingua franca* created during the reign of al-Āmir. Near the end of the Fatimid period, the Festival of Ghadīr was appropriated by the Ḥāfiẓī Fatimid imamate into its rhetorical arsenal for use against its detractors. This chapter traces the route of the Festival of Ghadīr from popular celebration, to court ritual, and finally to polemic.

THE EVENT AT GHADĪR KHUMM AND ITS IMPORTANCE IN ISMAʿILI THOUGHT

It is reported in the traditions of the Prophet's life (*ḥadīth*) that on the eighteenth day of Dhu'l-ḥijja, in the year 10/632, Muḥammad stopped at the Pool of Khumm (Ghadīr Khumm) on his return from the Farewell Pilgrimage. The heat was sweltering that day, and his followers took refuge under a grove of trees. A platform was raised for the Prophet, who wished to make a pronouncement before the large assembly dispersed. He called them together for the noon prayer, and, when it was finished, he raised ʿAlī's hand in full view of the congregation, saying: "Do you not recognize that I have a claim upon the Believers that is prior to any claim they have upon themselves?" They said, "Yes." And then he said, "Do you not recognize that I have a claim upon every Believer that is prior to any claim he has upon himself?" And they answered, "Yes." Whereupon the Prophet then said, "Whoever's master (*mawlā*) I am, ʿAlī is his master. O God, assist whomever assists him and oppose whomever opposes him." At this, ʿUmar b. al-Khaṭṭāb addressed ʿAlī, "Greetings to you, O son of Abū Ṭālib. You have become the master of every Believer, man and woman."[1]

For Shiʿis, the circumstances alleged to have taken place at Ghadīr Khumm constituted the single most important piece of evidence with which they legitimized the succession of ʿAlī b. Abī Ṭālib and his descendants. The event at Ghadīr Khumm (referred to as *waṣiyyat ʿalī*) was the proof that the Prophet had, indeed, made provisions for his succession by transferring the leadership of the community to ʿAlī and his progeny.[2] Shiʿis believe that this testament bequeathed both the Prophet's political and religious authority to ʿAlī. They also believe that ʿAlī received the unique authority to legitimately interpret revelation, Qur'an, for the community and that this authority was transmitted to the imams who came after him. The commentaries on this one event thus multiplied, and it became the central argument in the Shiʿi polemic against the Sunni doctrines of consensus and election.[3] Although it was included in the *ḥadīth* collection of Ibn Ḥanbal, most Sunni authorities ignored the event, and those Sunnis who accepted the event as an historical fact naturally rejected the Shiʿi interpretation.

The episode at Ghadīr Khumm had even more far reaching implications for the Ismaʿili Fatimids: accepting the tradition of ʿAlī's received authority (*waṣiyya*) was considered a prerequisite to the fulfillment of every other religious duty for Ismaʿilis. The public pronouncement of the *waṣiyya* of ʿAlī was tied directly to Qur'anic revelations concerning the other religious obligations (*farā'iḍ*) of prayer, alms, fasting, and pilgrimage.[4] Furthermore, ʿAlī's received authority was fundamental to the notion of *walāya* (complete submission and allegiance to the imam), a divinely imposed duty that is the first and most important of the pillars of Ismaʿilism. It is, according to Ismaʿilis, the "foundation of belief."

Ismaʿili thinkers sought authority for their assertion of the relationship among the *waṣiyya* of ʿAlī, *walāya*, and other religious duties in both Qur'an and *ḥadīth*. Al-Qāḍī al-Nuʿmān (d. 363/974) reports in his *Pillars of Islam* (*Daʿā'im al-islām*) that

Muḥammad said: God ordered the believers to pray in the Qur'an, but they did not know what prayer was or how to pray, so he commanded the Prophet Muḥammad to explain this and he informed them of all the regulations concerning prayer. In the same way, he commanded them to give alms, but they did not know what this was and the Prophet once again explained it; thus it was for fasting and pilgrimage. All this the Prophet did according to his custom (*sunna*).[5] God then imposed the duty of *walāya* on the believers.[6] Because they did not understand *walāya*, God commanded the Prophet to explain it to them, just as he had commanded him to explain the other four pillars. But Muḥammad hesitated in carrying out this last command because he feared that the people would reject him. Muḥammad's reluctance occasioned the revelation of Q. 5:67: "O Messenger, deliver that which has been sent down to you from your Lord; for if you do not, you will not have delivered his Message. God will protect you from men." After this revelation, the Prophet designated ʿAlī as the heir to his authority on the Day of Ghadīr Khumm.

On the Day of Ghadīr Khumm, God imposed *walāya* and marked the conclusion of the religious duties by revealing Q. 5:3: "Today, I have perfected for you your religion and I have completed my blessing upon you, and I have approved Islam for your religion." Ismaʿilis understood that the perfection of religion meant not only the imposition of prayer, alms, fasting, and pilgrimage, and *walāya*; it also meant the Prophet's designation of ʿAlī as his successor (*walī*).[7] If the Prophet's mission to deliver God's message would have remained unfulfilled without *walāya*, how could the religious duties of the simple believer be valid without it? If *walāya* was the perfection of religion itself, how could the true believer fail to perfect his own faith through it? Thus, al-Qāḍī al-Nuʿmān and other Ismaʿili ideologues raised the scaffolding on which all of Ismaʿili piety was constructed. Ismaʿili theologians and jurists asserted that God had commanded *walāya* of the imams, the authoritative successors to the Prophet and ʿAlī. The imam of the time stood at the center of belief.[8] Belief in the imam of the time completed, perfected, and legitimized all other religious duties.[9] The designation of ʿAlī as Muḥammad's successor at Ghadīr Khumm, the revelation of the religious obligations, and the duty of *walāya* were thus inextricably tied to one another.[10]

Walāya required absolute obedience to the imam of the time. Such obedience was, in fact, the equivalent of obedience to God.

Obedience is one: obedience to God is obedience to his messenger and to the imams. This is clear, according to al-Qāḍī al-Nuʿmān, from Q. 4:59: "O you who believe, obey God and obey his messenger and those in authority among you."[11] He elaborates extensively on this prooftext in both the *Pillars of Islam* and his manual of protocol for Ismaʿilis, *The Book of the Desired Behaviour in Following the Imams* (*Kitāb al-himma fī adab ittibāʿ al-a'imma*). In support of this interpretation, he quotes the Prophet himself as having said of the verse, "They are the imams among us, and obedience to them is obligatory."[12]

The solemn duty to obey the imam who stood at the center of belief, whose obedience was identical with the duty to obey God and the Prophet, loomed large in the minds of Ismaʿilis. Even a lifetime of prayer, alms, fasting, and pilgrimage meant nothing without recognition of and obedience to the imam. Ismaʿilis knew what they risked if they failed in that duty. The Prophet himself had warned them: "Whoever dies without acknowledging the imam of his time dies the death of an infidel."

POPULAR CELEBRATIONS OF THE FESTIVAL OF GHADĪR

Early observances of the Festival of Ghadīr (*ʿīd al-ghadīr*) were primarily popular celebrations. Little is known about Shiʿi observances of the festival until the fourth/tenth century, when the Buyid amīr Muʿizz al-dawla gave orders to decorate the city of Baghdad and to light fires at the police headquarters (*majlis al-shurṭa*).[13] The same year, the public celebration of ʿĀshūra was first reported, and the two festivals were usually associated from that time on. In Baghdad, these public festivities led inevitably to rioting between the Sunni and Shiʿi factions in the predominantly Shiʿi Karkh quarter. The Festival of Ghadīr was celebrated with official sanction in Egypt for the first time in 362/973, when a group of people from Fustat, together with the North African troops (*al-maghāriba*) gathered for invocations (*duʿā'*) on the eighteenth day of Dhu'l-ḥijja, proclaiming that Muḥammad had made ʿAlī his successor on the day of Ghadīr Khumm. This pleased the caliph al-Muʿizz greatly.[14]

Although it was the first time that the festival was celebrated in Egypt, it was not the first instance of a public, popular celebration of a Shiʿi festival. In 350/961–62, prior to the conquest of

Egypt, Shiʿi sympathizers had gone to the grave of the ʿAlid saint Kulthūm in the Qarāfa cemetery to curse the Companions of the Prophet and lament his martyred grandson Ḥusayn.[15] This public demonstration provoked a battle between the garrison and the populace (*al-raʿiyya*) and many of the residents of the Qarāfa were killed. Some ten years before the Fatimid conquest of Egypt, there was a sizable enough Shiʿi population, perhaps residing in or near the Qarāfa, to incite battles reminiscent of those in Baghdad between Sunnīs and Shiʿis at Karkh.[16]

In Baghdad, popular Shiʿi celebrations prompted a response from the Sunni population. Eight days after the Day of Ghadīr (*yawm al-ghadīr*), on the twenty-sixth day of Dhu'l-ḥijja 389/999, the people of the predominantly Sunni Baṣra quarter celebrated the day on which the Prophet is said to have entered the cave with Abū Bakr. Similarly, eight days after ʿĀshūra, they commemorated the day on which Musʿab b. al-Zubayr was killed.[17] No such counter-celebrations seem to have been held in Egypt, but there is no reason to doubt the essentially popular character of the festival.

Over the course of the next century, these popular practices in Egypt were adopted as court ceremonies. The Festival of Ghadīr was celebrated regularly during the reigns of al-ʿAzīz and al-Ḥākim. The practices must already have been well established and understood, for the court histories mention them only with the comment that the festival was celebrated "according to the custom."[18] Two accounts attributed to the historian al-Musabbiḥī (d. 420/1029) provide some clues as to what the custom was. In an undated account, perhaps from the reign of al-Ḥākim, he reports that people gathered at the Azhar along with the Qur'an reciters (*qurrā'*), jurists (*fuqahā'*), and singers (*munshidūn*).[19] They stayed for the noon prayer and then went to the palace, where portions (*jā'iza*) were distributed.[20] Some light may be shed on the dating of this account by comparing it with al-Musabbiḥī's description of ʿĀshūra for the year 396/1005. The markets were closed and the singers (*munshidūn*) went to the Azhar then into the streets for public lamentations and mourning. The next day, the judge ʿAbd al-ʿAzīz b. al-Nuʿmān called together all of the singers (*munshidūn*) who had participated and instructed them not to appropriate goods from people in their stores, nor injure them, nor engage in further public lamentation. He enjoined those who wanted to engage in lamentations to go to the outskirts of the city. But a group gathered nonetheless on Friday at the Mosque of

ʿAmr in Fustat, the heart of the Sunni city, and after the prayer went out into the streets, lamenting the martyr Ḥusayn and cursing the Companions of the Prophet. A man was arrested and executed, and an announcement was made that the same fate awaited anyone who cursed ʿA'isha and her husband.[21]

The similarities in the descriptions, the close association of Ghadīr Khumm and ʿĀshūra, and the common locations are compelling circumstantial evidence to date this Festival of Ghadīr ceremony to sometime in the 390s/1000s. But the accounts incidentally yield more important information: then, as in later times, Fustat housed a large Sunni population whom it would not pay to antagonize, a reminder that although Ismaʿilism may have been the ideology of the dominant group, it was by no means the dominant ideology. In the earliest years of Fatimid rule in Egypt, the government was still quite sensitive to the potential for serious unrest that public Shiʿi practices might provoke. The relationship between the customs followed on ʿĀshūra and Ghadīr Khumm is further attested in an account from some twenty years later, during the reign of al-Ẓāhir. In 415/1025, the people of Fustat "followed their custom" on the day of Ghadīr Khumm, put on fine clothes, and the *munshidūn* went to the palace to offer invocations and poetry. But on this occasion, no one cursed the Companions or gathered for public lamentations.[22] In these years, the only time the celebration was prohibited altogether was during the reign of al-Ḥākim in the year 399/1009,[23] the same year in which he introduced a number of repressive measures directed chiefly against Christians and Jews.

What is clear from these brief descriptions is the still largely popular character of the celebration. Since they were not yet official court ceremonies, chroniclers most likely did not think them worthy of more than a mention in passing. But gradually, changes were introduced—in location, in content, and in personnel—as the Fatimid caliphate became more firmly entrenched in Egypt. From the early celebration in 350/962 before the Fatimid conquest at the mausolea of the Qarāfa cemetery, the celebrations moved to the streets of Fustat, to the Azhar, and, finally, to the palace itself. These changes show in part how a popular celebration moved progressively closer to the Ismaʿili center of Cairo and ultimately was assimilated into the ceremonial of the court, reflecting the changes that occurred as the Ismaʿili ritual city was being constructed through topography and ceremony.

THE FESTIVAL OF GHADĪR AND THE RITUAL *LINGUA FRANCA*

By the time of al-Āmir,[24] the celebration of the Festival of Ghadīr had become an elaborate affair, modeled on the rituals of the Sacrifical Festival (*ʿīd al-naḥr*), which immediately preceded it. While still retaining many of its popular elements, the festival was now part of the cluster of court-sponsored ceremonies that began with Ramaḍān and ended with the solemn observance of ʿĀshūra. It is not surprising that the rituals and customs observed during the Sacrifical Festival became the model for the Festival of Ghadīr. Though a distinct festival, it was nonetheless an extension of the observances for the Sacrificial Festival, just as the occasion of Ghadīr Khumm itself had been an extension of the pilgrimage. The location of part of the observances shifted to the sacrifice ground (*manḥar*) north of the Festival Gate Plaza (*raḥbat bāb al-ʿīd*).[25] And, like the celebration of the Sacrificial Festival on which it was modeled, under al-Āmir the celebration of the Festival of Ghadīr had little or no explicitly Shiʿi or Ismaʿili content. It became, like Ramaḍān and the two festivals, part of the ritual *lingua franca* that characterized Fatimid ceremonial in the first half of the twelfth century.

In 516/1122–23, the "poor and wretched" along with the eunuchs of the first rank (*al-ʿawālī*) and those of lesser rank (*al-adwān*) flocked to the gate of the wazir as was their custom, seeking marriages for widows.[26] The festival, Ibn al-Ma'mūn comments, was observed by everyone, rich and poor alike. This implies that it was celebrated by Sunnis and, perhaps, non-Muslims, like other Fatimid festivals. It had retained its popular elements even as it became a court ceremony. Like the Festival of Fast Breaking and the Sacrificial Festival, the Festival of Ghadīr in the age of al-Āmir was characterized by the materialization of ceremonial. It had its own, albeit more modest, wardrobe (*kiswa*) that included costumes for the caliph and wazir, as well as 790 gold dinars and 144 pieces of clothing to be distributed to the commanders of the infantry and cavalry.[27]

The muezzins of both the Friday and daily mosques stood at the gates of the palace, which were decorated with drapes and curtains. Banquets like the ones on the first day of the Sacrificial Festival were set out in the Gold Hall (*qāʿat al-dhahab*). On the morning of the festival, the caliph made his customary sacrifices, and then the butchers slaughtered the same number of rams as on the Sacrificial Festival (*'īd al-naḥr*). The meat was distributed to those attached to the court.[28] Then the caliph sat in the belvedere (*manẓara*) and a fanfare was played.[29] The wazir and the amirs approached and greeted the caliph, and when it was time for prayer, the muezzins at the palace gates pronounced the formula "God is most great" for the festival. When the wazir entered the palace, the preacher (*khaṭīb*) had already completed the sermon and the judge Abu'l-Ḥajjāj Yūsuf b. Ayyūb led the prayer for the festival. The descendant of the Prophet (*sharīf*) Ibn Uns al-Dawla ascended the minbar and delivered a second sermon (*khuṭba*), as was customary on the festival. The wazir then went to the Royal Door (*bāb al-mulk*) in the Iwan to find the caliph seated, awaiting his arrival. The caliph bestowed upon the wazir a complete robe of honor (*khil'a*) made from the costume from the Sacrificial Festival, including a red robe (*thawb*).[30] He girded him with a sword inlaid with jewels, and when al-Ma'mūn kissed the ground, the caliph fastened a jeweled collar around the wazir's neck with his own hands. These extraordinary honors emphasized in this, as in other celebrations of the time, the high position of the wazir and his close relationship to the caliph. The costume was a *khil'a* in the most literal sense: a piece of clothing belonging to the caliph that was "cast off" and given to a person of high rank. In bestowing this gift on the wazir, the caliph was conferring his benefit (*ni'ma*) on him, and the wazir himself conferred his own benefit (*ni'ma*) after receiving the robe of honor by distributing another 2580 dinars of his own money.[31]

When the caliph exited from Royal Door (*bāb al-mulk*),[32] the Qur'an reciters met him.[33] The people now all came to pay homage to him as he exited from the Festival Gate surrounded by his sons, brothers, and his personal guard of amirs. A fanfare was played, drums were beat, and the troops lined up in rows. The caliph's son distributed portions of food at the banquet. The first and second banquets were arranged like those of the first day of the Sacrificial Festival. A third banquet (*simāṭ*) was then set up for the caliph and his relatives and companions. Afterwards, the wazir held an audience in his audience hall (*majlis*) to receive the greetings of the notables. The supervisors of the wardrobes each received 100 dinars, and the supervisor of the treasury (*bayt al-māl*) brought a box containing 5,000 dinars, which he used to "ransom" the jewelled collar and the inlaid sword from the wazir.

Al-Ma'mūn then ordered a memo to be written to the caliph to inform him of the money he had just received; the remainder was distributed to various high-ranking amirs, officials, guests, and servants.

On almost a point-by-point basis, the similarity between the celebrations of the Sacrificial Festival and the Festival of Ghadīr during the time of al-Āmir is striking. The festivities followed the path of those for the Sacrificial Festival from the belvedere (*manẓara*) above the Gold Gate (*bāb al-dhahab*) built specifically for military reviews, to the sacrificial ground (*manḥar*), where the ritual aspects of the festival were observed. The Festival of Ghadīr was in some respects an extension of the pilgrimage, since the designation of ʿAlī (*waṣiyyat ʿalī*) took place on the return from the Prophet's farewell pilgrimage. But as celebrated during the caliphate of al-Āmir, the Shiʿi aspects of the festival and its particular significance for the party of ʿAlī were deemphasized, and it was celebrated as a festival with universal Muslim appeal. Al-Ma'mūn's orchestration of the Festival of Ghadīr retained popular elements and was imbued with the ritual character of the Sacrificial Festival, but it had no explicitly Shiʿi content. Although it was a uniquely Shiʿi festival, it became part of the ritual *lingua franca* that al-Ma'mūn constructed as part of his political and religious program.

CEREMONIAL AS POLEMIC

Although the celebration of the Festival of Ghadīr was stripped of its explicitly Ismaʿili elements during the reign of al-Āmir, the festival as celebrated by the partisans of al-Ḥāfiẓ became once again a thoroughly Ismaʿili affair. The general population probably did not desist from its customary practices on the festival, but the ceremony that took place at court was stripped of all popular elements. It was a symbolic statement of official Fatimid Ismaʿili doctrine when opposition to the Ḥāfiẓī line emerged in the Yemen.

These Yemeni opponents to the Ḥāfiẓī regime asserted the imamate of al-Ṭayyib, the son of al-Āmir, whose birth had been celebrated in Cairo in 524/1130.[34] This son, Abu'l-Qāsim al-Ṭayyib, was named as heir (*walī ʿahd*) by al-Āmir a few months before the latter's death. But al-Ṭayyib was not destined to succeed his father, and Egyptian Fatimid sources took little or no notice of his disappearance after al-Āmir's death.[35] Upon the death of al-Āmir, his cousin, ʿAbd al-Majīd was proclaimed as regent with the title al-Ḥāfiẓ li-dīn allāh (the Protector of God's religion). However, al-Ḥāfiẓ claimed to be acting not as the regent of al-Ṭayyib but rather as that of an unborn future caliph whose birth had been prophesized by al-Āmir in a dream.[36] A proclamation to this effect was read on Tuesday, the fourth day of Dhu'l-qaʿda, two days after the assassination of the caliph al-Āmir, in a solemn ceremony in the Iwan, with the regent al-Ḥāfiẓ seated in the *shubbāk*, a ceremonial prerogative normally reserved to the caliph. The groundwork was already being laid for al-Ḥāfiẓ's eventual claim to the imamate.[37]

After a brief period of political intrigue, the regent al-Ḥāfiẓ appointed Abū ʿAlī Kutayfāt, the son of al-Afḍal b. Badr al-Jamālī, as wazir. Abū ʿAlī's first official act after his confirmation as wazir was to imprison al-Ḥāfiẓ. He inaugurated a persecution of the residents of the palace so intense that it was likened to "thunder and lightning" (*al-irʿād wa'l-ibrāq*) while he searched for al-Āmir's child.[38] He intended to depose the regent and kill him, it seems, in retaliation for the earlier murder of his own brothers, whom al-Āmir killed after the death of al-Afḍal.[39] But he found no child and was unable either to kill or depose al-Ḥāfiẓ.[40] So he deposed the Fatimid line altogether and had the Friday sermon (*khuṭba*) read in the name of the Expected Imam of the Twelvers.[41] However, the army revolted and deposed Kutayfāt at the beginning of 526/1131. Al-Ḥāfiẓ was released from prison and reaffirmed as regent.[42] The occasion of al-Ḥāfiẓ's release was celebrated during his reign as the Victory Festival (*ʿīd al-naṣr*).[43]

Al-Ḥāfiẓ was successful in consolidating his power, but his position as regent had become untenable. During the Twelver interlude, no heir to al-Āmir had appeared. It would be increasingly difficult to continue to act on behalf of an heir who clearly did not exist. In a bold move, al-Ḥāfiẓ declared himself the imam.[44] Ibn Muyassar reports: "He rode in the attire of the caliphs from the Festival Gate (*bāb al-ʿīd*) to the Gold Gate (*bāb al-dhahab*) . . . He ordered that the following sermon (*khuṭba*) be pronounced from the minbars: 'O God, bless the one through whom you have fortified your religion after your enemies tried to destroy it . . . our Lord and Master, the Imam of our era and of our time, ʿAbd al-Majīd Abu'l-Maymūn'."[45] This claim to the imamate was elaborated in a proclamation that Stern characterized as "the charter on which the whole Fatimid rule was based during the forty or so years which were to remain to it."[46] The remarkable assertion of this proclamation was simply that al-Āmir had transmitted the imamate to his cousin al-Ḥāfiẓ, just as Muḥammad had conferred the succession on his cousin ʿAlī at Ghadīr Khumm.[47]

In the years following the accession of al-Ḥāfiẓ, the Festival of Ghadīr was appropriated by his regime, just as the event at Ghadīr Khumm itself became a cornerstone of Ḥāfiẓī legitimacy. The celebration of the Festival of Ghadīr during the last years of Fatimid rule shows both how deeply embedded the rhetoric of Ḥāfiẓī legitimacy was and how fundamental ceremonial had become to the political idiom of the dynasty. Ibn al-Ṭuwayr's account of the celebration of the Festival of Ghadīr describes a festival with an unmistakable Ismaʿili (and Ḥāfiẓī) flavor.

The ceremony Ibn al-Ṭuwayr describes probably dates to sometime after 549/1154, either during the reign of al-Fā'iz or al-ʿĀḍid, since its most important rituals took place at the martyrium (*mashhad*) of Ḥusayn. This monument was built in 549/1154 when the wazir Ṭalā'iʿ b. Ruzzīk transferred Ḥusayn's head from Ascalon to Cairo.[48] Ṭalā'iʿ feared lest this precious relic fall into the hands of the advancing Franks, so he built a mosque outside of Bāb Zuwayla, on the southern extremity of Cairo, to house the head. But al-Fā'iz (or, more likely, some unknown adviser of the child caliph) ordered the construction of the martyrium in the palace, and the head was brought there. The political implications of the move are clear: the palace was the appropriate location for an ʿAlid relic, particularly one with the symbolic importance of the head of Ḥusayn. This new monument, in such close proximity to the Fatimid tombs, constructed topographically the association between Ḥāfiẓī historiography and the remote ʿAlid past.

Everything about the new celebration of the Festival of Ghadīr expressed its Ḥāfiẓī character. During the reign of al-Āmir, the ceremony took place on the parade ground between the palaces (*bayn al-qaṣrayn*), the sacrificial square (*manḥar*) and the Iwan of the palace, following the pattern of the Sacrificial Festival. After 549/1154, the ceremony shifted to the southern extremity of the palace, at the martyrium (*mashhad*) of Ḥusayn.[49] The ceremony itself consisted of a sermon (*khuṭba*) and a caliphal procession. But the caliph did not leave the city of Cairo, did not ride with a parasol (*miẓalla*) or the insignia, and did not make any of the customary distributions. On the day of Ghadīr Khumm, the wazir was summoned to the palace to pay homage to the caliph. He then rode mounted from his customary place in the vestibule (*dihlīz*),[50] exited, and stood facing the Gold Gate (*bāb al-dhahab*) of the palace.[51] After this, the caliph exited on horseback, stopping in the arch of the gate surrounded by his *muḥannak* eunuchs and some of the amirs of the collar, who were commanded by the wazir to pay homage to the caliph in the same manner that he did.

Like most other ceremonies, this one began with a dress parade. The costumes and outfits were paraded according to rank: first those of the caliph and his entourage, then those of the amirs of the collar, followed by those of the various regiments of the army, led by their commanders. There were more than five thousand cavalry, close to one thousand infantry archers, and nearly seven thousand foot soldiers. Next, the outfits of the wazir and his son or relatives, followed by those of the chief chamberlain (*ṣāḥib al-bāb*), his companions and the commander of the army (*isfahsalār*), and the prefects of Cairo and Fustat were paraded.

After the dress parade, the formal procession began when the caliph exited from the Gold Gate, rode to the Zuhūma Gate in the palace, and turned left to enter the passageway that led to the Daylam Gate. He was surrounded not only by his mounted personal guard (*ṣibyān al-rikāb al-khāṣṣ*), but also by a number of his *muḥannak* eunuchs. Ordinarily, when passing the tombs of his ancestors in the Saffron Tomb (*turbat al-zaʿfarān*), the caliph would pay some sort of homage. On this occasion, he passed them without paying any homage at all and proceeded to the martyrium. The chief judge and the witnesses were waiting for him in the vestibule of the Daylam Gate, where the martyrium (*mashhad*) of Ḥusayn is located, and they came out to pay homage. The judge kissed the caliph's foot, while the witnesses waited a distance of about a *qaṣaba* from the head of his mount. Then the entourage turned and entered the Iwan through this vestibule. The caliph continued around the perimeter of the palace to the Festival Gate, where he entered his grilled loge (*shubbāk*). After he was seated, the wazir paid homage to him and sat down to the left of the minbar set up for the preacher. Curtains of precious fabrics had been hung in the hall, and the "seat of the mission" (*kursī al-daʿwa*) had been set up with nine steps for the sermon. The chief judge and the witnesses, the amirs and soldiers who were Shiʿis, and the officials and notables who followed the Ismaʿili school sat beneath it.

The preacher (*khaṭīb*), dressed in a silk costume (*badla*), read the sermon (*khuṭba*) from a notebook, written in the chancery (*dīwān al-inshā'*) that contained the text of the Prophet's designation of ʿAlī as his successor (*naṣṣ al-khilāfa*). After this, the judge led two prayer cycles (*rakʿa*). When the prayer was completed, the wazir paid homage once again at the grilled loge (*shubbāk*) in which the caliph was concealed. The congregation greeted one another in the Ismaʿili fashion and dispersed. According to Ibn al-Ṭuwayr, it was a more important festival than the Sacrificial Feast, and most of the Ismaʿilis made sacrifices on it.

This late celebration of the Festival of Ghadīr expressed symbolically the Ḥāfiẓīs' continuing polemic against the Ṭayyibīs. Al-Ḥāfiẓ's assertion of a new foundation for the imamate had transformed the Festival of Ghadīr from a universal ʿAlid festival into a singularly Fatimid event. The Ḥāfiẓī interpretation of the distant ʿAlid past invested the event at Ghadīr Khumm with new meaning. And that new meaning found expression through al-Ḥāfiẓ's proclamation, in topography, and finally in ceremony.

At a time when the Fatimids had a fully developed ceremonial idiom at their disposal, a ceremony allowed the association of numerous symbols to give powerful expression to the ideology of the Ḥāfiẓī caliphate in a manner that a proclamation or polemical treatise could not. This Festival of Ghadīr was now divorced completely from the celebration of the Sacrificial Festival, with which it had come to be associated. The sermon was not that of the Sacrificial Festival, customarily delivered on the Festival of Ghadīr, but rather the actual text of the Prophet's designation of ʿAlī as his successor (*waṣiyyat ʿalī*). It was the antithesis of the celebration of the two festivals, which were played out on the whole map of Cairo and Fustat. No longer a part of the ritual *lingua franca*, the Festival of Ghadīr was now a private occasion, limited to professed Ismaʿilis of the Ḥāfiẓī persuasion.

Moreover, Cairo had long since ceased to be an exclusively Ismaʿili city. The urban map expressed such a wide range of meanings that it was now too diffuse to be used to articulate the tightly constrained argument that this dynastic polemic required. What the Ḥāfiẓī Fatimids needed was not the vast generality of the ritual *lingua franca* of twelfth-century Cairo but an Ismaʿili particularity. And it was in the palace, the immobile center, that they found it. Thus, the caliph rode in procession within the confines of the palace itself, without any of the insignia of sovereignty associated with temporal rule, and headed toward the martyrium of Ḥusayn. He passed by the tombs of his ancestors (*turbat al-zaʿfarān*), the place he visited by convention when he rode in processions outside of the palace with the parasol (*miẓalla*), without so much as a ceremonial nod. This caliphal procession around the perimeter of the palace marked definitively a boundary between the palace and the rest of the ritual city, severing the links that were so painstakingly constructed by the processions for Ramaḍān and the festivals, the New Year, and the inundation of the Nile, thereby claiming the palace, the caliph's Fatimid ancestors, and the ʿAlid past for the Ḥāfiẓī state.

CHAPTER 7

Epilogue

The Mamluk historians from whom we receive our view of the Fatimids understood ceremonial to be an integral part of the character of the dynasty, a hallmark of the Fatimid style of rule. Today, the single fact about the dynasty known by all Egyptians is that the sugar-dolls that they buy on festive occasions date back to the Fatimids. What Mamluk historians, modern scholars of the Fatimids, and even modern-day Cairenes have in common is the image of the ritual *lingua franca*, of ceremonies with broad appeal and little if any explicit Isma'ili content.

But the contemporary reality of Fatimid ceremonies as they developed over two hundred years was a different one. In the Fatimid world, these ceremonies had a multiplicity of meanings that were obscured by Mamluk historians. In all of these processions, the changing city was a map on which a multitude of relationships were drawn and redrawn. Thus, the processions on Ramaḍān and the festivals first constructed the Isma'ili ritual city and then reconfigured the Fatimids' relationship to a diverse population that did not share their political theology; the New Year's procession reclaimed the city and the state as the caliph's political domain, reconfiguring his relationship to the army; the Nile processions reconfigured the relationship of the Fatimid city to its landscape; finally, the celebration of the Festival of Ghadīr separated the dynasty from, and then reconfigured its relationship to, the 'Alid past.

Ironically, the exclusivity and particularity of the polemical Festival of Ghadīr epitomize the broadly expressive capabilities of the urban language the Fatimids constructed in Cairo and Fustat through their other ceremonies. For the Fatimids and their partisans, the ritual *lingua franca* and Isma'ili ideology coexisted and were expressed simultaneously in their urban processions. It is fitting, then, to end with the poetic epitaph that 'Umāra al-Yamanī wrote after the fall of the Fatimid dynasty.[1] In it, he juxtaposes images of the ritual *lingua franca* and the imam who stood at the center of Isma'ili belief.

I weep for the generous deeds you displayed
Time passed over them, but they did not pass away

The guest house that befriended your guests
Is today more desolate than a ruin, gone without a trace

The breaking of the fast where your generosity showed itself
Complains against the unbearable injustice of time

The robes you gave in the two seasons are faded,
The once-new cloths have become threadbare and worn.

What a festival was the day of the canal,
When you paraded your ornaments on mounts!

What pure torrents of generosity you showered
On the New Year and the Two Feasts!

The whole earth trembled on the day of Ghadīr,
While between your palaces were brandished spears

And horses paraded with adornments and cloths,
Like brides in their jewels and festive robes.

How great were the trays offered your guests,
Borne upon shoulders or on wheels.

You did not favor your own people with your generosity
Until you had spread it to the most distant community

Your stipends went to Christians and to Jews,
To resident guests and visiting envoys

How grand were the ṭirāz gifts of Tinnīs
Which you gave to the nations and people of the earth

And the favors you bestowed upon the mosques
And those who taught religious science and practice.

Perhaps the world has found a refuge in you
And through you, untied its knots

By God, may he who hates you be denied the Resurrection
May none other than your friend be spared his torments

Nor drink water on the day of thirst and heat
From the hand of the best of men, the seal of the Prophets.

May he who betrayed the Imam al-ʿĀḍid, son of ʿAlī
Not see the Paradise which God has created

My imams and guides! O treasure of mine,
To whom I offer my deeds as surety

By God, I could not give them their deserved praise
For their virtue is like a torrent, a downpour

And I would not, praise be to God, blush
To multiply my words or increase them

They are the door of salvation in this world and the next
Loving them is the foundation of faith and deed

They are the guiding light, like lanterns in darkest night
They are the rain-filled plain, when all else is dry

Imams, created out of light, whose light is
The pure essence of God's unfading light

By God, my love for them will abide ceaselessly
However long he may tarry in calling me to eternity.

NOTES

CHAPTER 1

1. See, for example, Ernst H. Kantorowicz, *The King's Two Bodies: A Study in Medieval Political Theology* (Princeton, 1957); Marc Bloch, *The Royal Touch* (London, 1973); Ralph Giesey, *The Royal Funeral Ceremony in Renaissance France* (Geneva, 1960). For the ancient world, see S. R. F. Price, *Rituals and Power: The Roman Imperial Cult in Asia Minor* (Cambridge, 1984). To these historians should be added the work of the anthropologists Clifford Geertz, Victor Turner, and Raymond Firth and the historical sociology of Norbert Elias.

2. Some important works are Peter Brown, *Society and the Holy in Late Antiquity* (Berkeley and Los Angeles, 1982); idem, *The Cult of the Saints: Its Rise and Function in Latin Christianity* (Chicago, 1981); Richard Trexler, "Florentine Religious Experience: The Sacred Image," *Studies in the Renaissance* 19 (1972): 7–41.

3. For example, Richard Trexler, *Public Life in Renaissance Florence* (New York, 1980); E. Muir, *Civic Ritual in Renaissance Venice* (Princeton, 1981); N. Z. Davis, "The Sacred and the Body Social in Sixteenth-Century Lyon," *Past and Present* 90 (1981): 40–70. For a landmark study of architecture and ceremonial in Ottoman society, see Gülru Necipoglu, *Architecture, Ceremonial, and Power: The Topkapi Palace in the Fifteenth and Sixteenth Centuries* (Cambridge, 1991).

4. Roy P. Mottahedeh, *Loyalty and Leadership in an Early Islamic Society* (Princeton, 1980).

5. Aḥmad b. ʿAlī al-Qalqashandī, *K. Ṣubḥ al-aʿshā fī ṣināʿat al-inshā*, 14 vols. (Cairo, 1913–19) (henceforth *Ṣubḥ*).

6. Taqī al-dīn al-Maqrīzī, *K. al-Mawāʿiẓ wa'l-iʿtibār bi-dhikr al-khiṭaṭ wa'l-āthār*, 2 vols. (Būlāq, 1853) (henceforth *Khiṭaṭ*).

7. Taqī al-dīn al-Maqrīzī, *K. Ittiʿāẓ al-ḥunafā bi-akhbār al-a'imma al-fāṭimiyyīn al-khulafā*, 3 vols. (Cairo, 1967–73) (henceforth *Ittiʿāẓ*).

8. Abu'l-Maḥāsin Ibn Taghrī Birdī, *Al-Nujūm al-zāhira fī mulūk miṣr wa'l-qāhira*, 12 vols. (Cairo, 1929-55) (henceforth *Nujūm*).

CHAPTER 2

1. M. b. M. al-Yamanī, *Sīrat al-ḥājib Ja'far* (Life of the chamberlain Ja'far), ed. W. Ivanow, *Bulletin of the Faculty of Arts, Cairo U.*, 4, pt. 2 (1936), Arabic section: 107–33, 125 for this incident in particular. (It has been translated by W. Ivanow in *Ismaili Tradition Concerning the Rise of the Fatimids* [Oxford, 1942]).

2. Ibid., pp. 125–26.

3. The Arabic *rasm*, for example, means "drawing," as well as "record," "inscription," "ceremony," "rate," and "fee."

4. Hilāl al-Ṣābi', *Rusūm dār al-khilāfa* (henceforth *Rusūm*) (English title page: The Etiquette, Protocol and Diplomacy of the 'Abbāsid Caliphate in Baghdād), edited by Mīkhā'īl 'Awwād (first printing, Baghdad, 1964; second printing, Beirut, 1986). The English translation by E. A. Salem, *The Rules and Regulations of the 'Abbasid Court* (Beirut, 1977) is a useful guide but is poorly annotated and at times unreliable.

5. See *EI2*, s.v. *"adab"*; G. E. von Grunebaum, *Medieval Islam* (Chicago, 1945), 250–57; Ira M. Lapidus, "Knowledge, Virtue, and Action: The Classical Muslim Conception of *Adab* and the Nature of Religious Fulfillment in Islam," in *Moral Conduct and Authority: The Place of Adab in South Asian Islam*, ed. Barbara Daly Metcalf (Berkeley and Los Angeles, 1984), pp. 38–61.

6. See 'Awwād's extensive bibliography in his edition of *Rusūm*, the most comprehensive list of sources on protocol and ceremonial that I have seen to date. It is especially useful because of its numerous references to unpublished manuscripts.

7. On the formation of social bonds of tenth- and eleventh-century Iran and Iraq, see Mottahedeh, *Loyalty and Leadership*. Evidence for the personal nature of social bonds in the medieval Mediterranean world is discussed by S. D. Goitein, "Formal Friendship in the Medieval Near East," *Proceedings of the American Philosophical Society* 115, no. 6 (1971): 484–89 and A. L. Udovitch, "Formalism and Informalism in the Social and Economic Institutions of the Medieval Islamic World," in *Individualism and Conformity in Classical Islam*, ed. Amin Banani and Speros Vryonis, Jr. (Wiesbaden, 1977), pp. 61–81.

8. On the use of the term *ceremonial idiom* see Erving Goffman, *Interaction Ritual* (New York, 1967), p. 56: "All of the tokens employed by a given social group for ceremonial purposes may be referred to as its ceremonial idiom."

9. For a discussion of this issue in a European context, see Norbert

Elias, *The Court Society* (New York, 1983), chap. 5, "Etiquette and Ceremony: Conduct and Sentiment of Human Beings as Functions of the Power Structure of Their Society," pp. 78–116 and esp. 78–104.

10. See Goffman, *Interaction Ritual*, "The Nature of Deference and Demeanor," esp. pp. 56–95.

11. The general requirements of protocol are discussed in *Rusūm* in the chapter "Qawānī al-ḥijāba wa-rusūmuhā" (The rules and regulations for the chamberlain), pp. 71–79; in [al-Jāḥiẓ?], *Kitāb al-tāj fī akhlāq al-mulūk*, ed. Ahmed Zaki Pasha (Cairo, 1914) (henceforth *Tāj*), in the chapter "Al-dukhūl ʿalā al-mulūk," pp. 7–9 and passim; in al-Qāḍī Abū Ḥanīfa b. M. al-Nuʿmān b. Muḥammad, *Kitāb al-Himma fī adab ittibāʿ al-aʾimma*, ed. M. Kāmil Ḥusayn (Cairo, n.d.) (henceforth *Himma*), in the chapter "Al-qiyām bayna yaday al-imām wa'l-julūs," pp. 109–16.

12. *Himma*, pp. 105–9; *Tāj*, pp. 7–8; *Rusūm*, p. 33.

13. *Himma*, pp. 106–7, 111; *Tāj*, p. 69; *Rusūm*, p. 32.

14. *Himma*, p. 110; *Tāj*, pp. 68–69; *Rusūm*, pp. 34–35.

15. *Himma*, pp. 111–12; *Tāj*, pp. 68, 113; *Rusūm*, p. 35.

16. *Himma*, pp. 107–8; see the story of Ibrāhīm b. al-Mahdī, whose excessive use of the perfume *ghāliyah* annoyed the Abbasid caliph al-Muʿtasim, *Rusūm*, pp. 32–33.

17. *Himma*, p. 114; *Tāj*, p. 120; *Rusūm*, p. 38. For the caveat against praising those in the caliph's disfavor, see *Himma*, pp. 114–15 and *Rusūm*, pp. 78–79. For an unexpected twist, see *Rusūm*, pp. 9–11, the story of Nāzūk's *mawkib*.

18. *Himma*, p. 113.

19. *Himma*, p. 112; *Rusūm*, pp. 35, 46–47, 52–56.

20. *Himma*, p. 112; *Rusūm*, pp. 34, 88–89, the story of Thābit b. Qurrah, who left the caliph's presence while the caliph was conversing with a Greek servant, because Thābit, unbeknownst to the caliph, understood the language and did not want to overhear a confidence.

21. See the anecdotes in *Rusūm*, pp. 76–77. Similarly, there was no possible excuse for certain violations, as in the unfortunate incident involving General Abū ʿAbd Allāh al-Bazyar, who suffered from gout. One day, he entered the palace gates with his afflicted foot upon the neck of his mount for relief. The caliph al-Ḥākim happened to be sitting in the belvedere (*manẓara*) over the gate, and the unsuspecting (and long-suffering) general paid for his mistake with his life (*Ittiʿāẓ*, vol. 2, 51).

Of course, under certain circumstances men might disregard the rules of protocol for political reasons. When Shams al-mulk, who held the office of intermediary (*wasāṭa*) under al-Ẓāhir, fell somewhat out of favor, he was taunted during a procession by a rival who intentionally broke every imaginable rule of protocol: "The younger Persian *sharīf*, who was the superintendant of the arsenal, was riding behind the caliph, talking to Shams al-mulk, bending his head and shaking his turban, and gesturing as if he were blowing his nose and flinging his snot in Shams al-mulk's face. After that, Shams al-mulk stayed at home for three days" (Al-Amīr al-Mukhtār ʿIzz al-mulk b. Aḥmad al-Musabbiḥī, *Akhbār Miṣr [Tome Quarantiène de la Chronique d'Egypte de Musabbiḥī]*, ed. A. F. Sayyid and Thierry Bianquis [Cairo, 1978], p. 18).

22. *Himma*, pp. 104, 109. See also al-Qāḍī al-Nuʿmān's *Daʿā'im al-islām wa-dhikr al-halāl wa'l-harām wa'l-qaḍāya wa'l-aḥkām* (ed. A. A. Fyzee, 2 vols. [Cairo, 1951-60]; henceforth *Daʿā'im al-islām*), where he says that standing in prayer is like standing before a ruler (pp. 158 ff.).

23. The Qur'anic verse "Obey God and obey his messenger and those in authority among you" (Q. 4:59) was the proof text for the Ismaʿili axiom that "God has made obedience of the imams incumbent upon his servants and has associated it with his obedience and the obedience of his messenger." The same verse is quoted without comment in the preface to *Tāj*. It is not quoted at all in *Rusūm*. See *Himma*, p. 38 and passim. The verse and axiom are often quoted also in *Daʿā'im al-islām* and al-Qāḍī al-Nuʿmān, *Ta'wīl al-daʿā'im*, ed. M. Ḥasan al-Aʿẓamī (Cairo, 1967–72) (henceforth *Ta'wīl al-daʿā'im)*. See the chapters on Imamate and Walaya.

24. This statement rests, in turn, on the Ismaʿili distinction between *islām* (submission) and *īmān* (faith). *Daʿā'im al-islām*, chap. 1, pp. 3–19 and *Ta'wīl al-daʿā'im*, second *majlis* of bk. 1. There, al-Qāḍī al-Nuʿmān explains *īmān* as both act and word, that is, displayed both by what one says and by what one does or believes. Here, then, is a practical application of this doctrine: one could kiss the ground before the imam, if one believed and intended it to be a glorification of God, and the act would not be reprehensible.

25. *Himma*, pp. 104–5. In spite of this argument, the subject remained, at least in certain circles, a controversial one. The caliph al-Ḥākim prohibited the people from kissing the ground before him in 403/1012–13, as well as from kissing his stirrup or his hand, and he ordered them to refrain in general from following the behavior of the infidels (*ahl al-shirk*) in bending toward the ground, which was the Byzantine custom. These customs were reinstated shortly after al-Ḥākim's prohibition (*Ittiʿāẓ*, vol. 2, 96).

Rusūm (p. 82) makes only one mention of suspicion of the custom of kissing the ground: an official disapproved of ʿAḍud al-dawla's kissing the ground before the Abbasid caliph al-Ṭā'iʿ, asking, "Is he God?" to which ʿAḍud al-dawla remarked to his secretary, "Tell him that [the caliph] is the vicegerent of God on earth."

26. *Himma*, pp. 113–114.

27. Ibid., p. 110. See *Daʿā'im al-islām*, where one will make his prostration (that is, touch his forehead and nose to the ground). This is a standard protocol in prayer (see, for example, *al-Mukhtaṣar* of al-Qudūrī, an eleventh-century manual of Ḥanafī jurisprudence, pp. 9–11).

28. *Himma*, pp. 110–11 and *Daʿā'im al-islām*, p. 161, no. 472.

29. *Himma*, p. 111.

30. *Himma*, p. 113; *Tāj*, pp. 8, 22. See Edward William Lane, *Arabic-English Lexicon*, 8 vols. (1863–93; reprint, 8 vols. in 2, Cambridge, 1984), p. 2956c.

31. *Himma*, p. 113. The same posture is described in *Tāj*, pp. 8, 22, as *muqʿin*, the posture assumed between the two prostrations of prayer. See entries for *aqʿa* in M. b. Mukarram Ibn Manẓūr (d.1312) *Lisān al-ʿArab* and M. b. M. Murtada al-Zabīdī (d. 1791), *Tāj al-ʿArūs*, both available in numerous modern editions.

32. See notes 24 and 25 above for the discussion of arguments for and against kissing the ground, and *Himma*, p. 105, bottom. In later Fatimid times, kissing the caliph's hand appears to have been regarded as a greater privilege than kissing the ground. Unlike the Abbasid authors of *Tāj* and *Rusūm*, al-Qāḍī al-Nuʿmān does not distinguish between classes in protocol. He notes in his preface that he has purposely avoided classifying acts of homage according to ranks because this would make the treatise excessively long. This incidental remark suggests that only a small part of the material concerning variations in protocol for different ranks and classes of people has reached us.

Tāj, however, specifies that if the person entering is from the higher classes he should stand neither too close nor too far, salute the king while standing upright, approach if summoned, and bend over the king's hands and kiss them. He then retreats until standing in his rank's designated place and sits if the king gestures to him to do so. If he is from the middle classes, he stops as soon as the king sees him and approaches only if summoned. Then, he advances three steps and stops, waiting for another summons. If he enters from the door immediately in front of the king, he should turn to a path to the right or left in order to approach him indirectly. If the king is silent, he departs without speaking or saluting. If the king calls him closer, he approaches a few steps with bowed head and then raises it, repeating this sequence until the king stops beckoning him. If the king addresses him, he answers in a modest voice, and when the king stops speaking, he gets up and retreats, walking backwards (*al-qahqarī*). If it is possible for him to conceal himself from the king's view, he may turn around. (*Tāj*, pp. 7–8; this etiquette for withdrawing from the ruler's presence is found also in *Rusūm*, p. 35 and *Himma*, p. 116).

Hilāl al-Ṣābi' (*Rusūm*, pp. 31–32), summarizes the ancient and contemporary protocol for entering the caliph's presence: In the past, when a wazir or amir approached, the caliph gave him his hand covered with his sleeve, honoring him with kissing it as a recognition of his high rank. The practice was changed to kissing the ground, in which the crown princes, members of the Banū Hāshim, qadis, jurists, ascetics, and Qur'an reciters (*qurrā'*) did not participate. Nor did they kiss the caliph's hand, but, rather, they saluted using the formula "*Al-salām ʿalayka amīr al-mu'minīn wa-raḥmatu'llāh wa-barākatuh.*" They had joined the others in kissing the ground by the time of al-Ṣābi', although a few remained steadfast in refraining. The middle ranks of the army and those beneath them could not kiss the ground because of their low rank.

In the manual of protocol written for the Mamluk sultan Baybars, *khidma* is discussed: "There are those who consider *al-khidma* to be kissing the ground if the king is mounted and the threshold if he is seated, and those who consider it [to be] kissing the carpet, and those who regard bending in homage (*al-inḥinā' fi'l-khidma*) to be like the *rukūʿ*, and those who consider it to be only the salute (*al-salām*) and addressing with epithets and sitting down. As for kissing the hand upon arriving or taking an oath or asking forgiveness . . . it is a sound custom which neither law nor policy prohibits" (Al-Ḥasan b. ʿAbd Allāh al-ʿAbbāsī, *Athār al-uwal fī tartīb al-duwal* [Bulaq, n.d.], p. 60).

33. This may, of course, have been true even in the early Fatimid period. Since al-Qāḍī al-Nuʿmān acknowledges in his preface to the *Himma* that he will not discuss distinctions in rank, it is likely that his general prescriptions have obscured important differences.

34. *Khiṭaṭ*, vol. 1, 386.27–29 and *Ṣubḥ*, vol. 3, 496.7–11. Note also that the pointed index finger is a prayer gesture.

35. The *maqṣūra* is an enclosed chamber near the prayer niche (*miḥrab*) reserved for the caliph. Such chambers were introduced during the period of the Rāshidūn caliphs, and they became so widely used by rulers that they were eventually associated with royal authority. For the history of the *maqṣūra*, see *EI2*, s.v. "masdjid"; on enclosures in the Tomb of the Prophet and their significance, see Shaun Elizabeth Marmon, *Eunuchs and Sacred Boundaries* (forthcoming).

36. *Khiṭaṭ*, vol. 2, 281.16 and *Ṣubḥ*, vol. 3, 506.15–16.

37. *Khiṭaṭ*, vol. 1, 389.28 and see Marius Canard, "Le Ceremonial fatimite et le cérémonial byzantin: Essai de comparison," *Byzantion* 21 (1951): 382 n. 1. The qadi also kisses the caliph's foot in front of the Mosque of Ibn Ṭulūn during the procession to the Nile, *Khiṭaṭ*, vol. 1, 477–78 and *Ṣubḥ*, vol. 3, 515.15.

38. *Khiṭaṭ*, vol. 1, 454.19, 23 (not reported in *Ṣubḥ*) and *Khiṭaṭ*, vol. 1, 455.32 and *Ṣubḥ*, vol. 3, 509.16, where he ascends to the seventh step.

39. During general audience: *Khiṭaṭ*, vol. 1, 386.19–20; *Ṣubḥ*, vol. 3, 495.20–21, upon entering, and *Khiṭaṭ*, vol. 1, 386.34, upon leaving. During Ramaḍān, in the mosque during prayer: *Khiṭaṭ*, vol. 2, 281.19–20; *Ṣubḥ*, vol. 3, 506.20. On New Year's: *Khiṭaṭ*, vol. 1, 448.1 and *Ṣubḥ*, vol. 3, 501.6.

40. Festival of Fast Breaking, when al-Ma'mūn ascends minbar to join caliph, *Khiṭaṭ*, vol. 1, 454.18 (twice).

41. Festival of Fast Breaking, when the wazir ascends minbar until he is level with the caliph's feet, then kisses them so that all in attendance will see: *Khiṭaṭ*, vol. 1, 455.32 and *Ṣubḥ*, vol. 3, 509.16.

42. During the celebration of the inundation of the Nile, *Khiṭaṭ*, vol. 1, 473.17–18 and 23. *Sīrat al-ḥājib Ja'far*, p. 125, where the missionary Abū 'Abd Allāh prostrates himself and then kisses al-Mahdī's stirrup.

43. Gestures with hand toward the ground (*yakhdum bi-yadih fī al-arḍ thalātha marrāt*): *Khiṭaṭ*, vol. 1, 447.37; *Ṣubḥ*, vol. 3, 501.12; *Nujūm*, vol. 4, 83.15–16.

44. During the Nile procession: *Khiṭaṭ*, vol. 1, 474.7 (*al-īmā' bi-taqbīl al-arḍ amāmhu fa-radd 'alayhi bi-kummih al-salāma* [he gestured as if to kiss the ground and the caliph returned the greeting to him with his sleeve]). During the New Year's procession, the wazir bows his head: *Khiṭaṭ*, vol. 1, 450.14; *Ṣubḥ*, vol. 3, 504.16; *Nujūm*, vol. 4, 90.12 (*yaska'a lahu sak'a ẓāhira*). The text of *Nujūm* reads, "wa-yaska'u al-wazir li-yuẓhir li'l-nās khidmatih," where n. 6 should be corrected as per Dozy, *Supplément aux Dictionnaires Arabes*, 2 vols. (Leiden, 1881), vol. 1, 668b, where *saka'a* is defined as "saluer quelqu'un en baisant la tête." On *'īd al-fiṭr*, where the phrase indicating the wazir's homage has clearly dropped out of the text and only the caliph's return of the greeting is preserved: *Khiṭaṭ*, vol. 1, 454.7 (restituted as per *Khiṭaṭ*, vol. 1, 474.7).

45. *Khiṭaṭ*, vol. 1, 386.32 and *Ṣubḥ*, vol. 3, 496.13.

46. Byzantine ambassador kisses ground continuously in an audience with al-Muʿizz, *Ittiʿāẓ*, vol. 1, 208–9. See below for more details on receptions of ambassadors. And see *Ittiʿāẓ*, vol. 2, 39–40.

47. According to al-Maqrīzī, these offices were introduced only under the caliph al-Ḥāfiẓ: *Khiṭaṭ*, vol. 1, 403.17ff.

48. *Khiṭaṭ*, vol. 1, 403, 461.

49. Al-Musabbiḥī, *Akhbār Miṣr*, p. 29. See also *Rusūm*, pp. 11–14, one of the most elaborate accounts we have of any Abbasid ceremony.

50. *Ittiʿāẓ*, vol. 2, 11.

51. For example, during a Nile procession, when the bearers of the caliph's sword and lance as well as the "young men of homage" (*ṣibyān al-salām*), who are part of the caliph's personal bodyguard, are summoned: *Khiṭaṭ*, vol. 1, 474.89.

52. See, for example, the account of the tenure of Abū al-Ḥasan al-Khiraqī, who was made chief qadi of Baghdad by the Abbasid caliph al-Muttaqī. The family, including his father and paternal uncle, were cloth merchants and served as notary witnesses (*shuhūd*) for the qadis of Baghdad because of their service to a much beloved concubine of al-Muqtadir. When al-Muttaqī became caliph, he wished to reward this faithful service and "to elevate his name and raise him to a station that no one in his family had previously attained so he invested him with the post of qadi," in spite of his complete lack of training or experience. Much to the surprise of observers, the unqualified al-Khiraqī executed his judicial duties himself rather than appointing a deputy, as custom dictated; much to their delight, he fulfilled those duties competently. Nonetheless, when al-Muttaqī went to Mawsil for a period of time, the qadi went into hiding and appointed Ibn Abī al-Shawārib to look after affairs. He did not resume his duties until al-Muttaqī returned to the capital city. (Al-Khaṭīb al-Baghdādī, *Tarīkh Baghdād*, 14 vols. [Cairo, 1931], vol. 5, no. 2976).

53. Stern, "The Epistle of the Fatimid Caliph al-Āmir (al-Hidaya al-Āmiriyya), its Date and its Purpose," *JRAS* (1950): 20–31, points out that al-Mustaʿlī was only a lad at the time. But what interests us here is the way the piece of information, with a clear and logical explanation, could be invested with a new, political meaning. Closeness to the capital was also, of course, a succession issue for the Fatimids, just as it was for the later Ottomans.

54. *Ittiʿāẓ*, vol. 3, 37, 40.

55. *Ittiʿāẓ*, vol. 2, 81. The story smacks of fancy, but certainly

reveals something of what must have been the prevalent attitude toward Christians in government. They attained to the highest ranks of government, but did not have the same social status as Muslims.

56. *Al-Hidayatu'l Āmiriyya*, ed. A. A. A. Fyzee, Islamic Research Association Series, no. 7 (Oxford, 1938), p. 13. See also S. M. Stern's incisive analysis of the book "Epistle," pp. 20–31.

57. al-Yamanī, *Sīrat al-ḥājib Jaʿfar*, pp. 125ff.

58. See the discussion of riding mounts in Goitein, *Mediterranean Society*, vol. 4, pp. 261–66.

59. The story of Mordecai in the Book of Esther comes to mind as a particularly good example of this ancient tradition. To King Ahasuerus' question about the proper way to honor a man, Haman replies, "For the man whom the king desires to honor, let royal garb which the king has worn be brought and a horse on which the king has ridden and on whose head a royal diadem has been set; and let the attire and the horse be put in the charge of one of the king's noble courtiers. And let the man whom the king desires to honor be attired and paraded through the city square, while they proclaim before him: This is what is done for the man whom the king desires to honor!" (chap. 6, pp. 7–10, translation of the Jewish Publication Society of America, 1969).

60. *Khiṭaṭ*, vol. 1, 451.38. For ʿAḍud al-dawla, see *Rusūm*, pp. 80–81.

61. *Ittiʿāẓ*, vol. 1, 209.

62. Ibid., vol. 2, 6.

63. Ibid., 11.

64. Ibid., 113.

65. Ibid., 14.

66. Ibid., 57.

67. Ibid., vol. 3, 11–12. The word translated here as "dirty" is the highly charged Arabic *najas*, "ritual impurity."

68. See Canard's discussion in "Ceremonial," pp. 387–93 and D. Sourdel, "Questions de cérémonial ʿabbaside," *Revue des études islamiques* 1960: 121–48; Oleg Grabar, "Notes sur les cérémonies umayyades," in *Studies in Memory of Gaston Wiet*, ed. M. Rosen-Ayalon, pp. 51–60 (Jerusalem, 1977).

69. Until a comprehensive study of insignia of sovereignty has been undertaken, we cannot determine with certainty the time at which some

objects came to be adopted as symbols of caliphal authority or their true provenance. The issue is as problematic for the Abbasids as it is for the Fatimids, since systematic discussions of a category of objects known as insignia of sovereignty seem to be characteristic of later sources. There is no evidence that such a collective category existed in the earlier years, even though several objects had clearly come to symbolize caliphal authority. Al-Qalqashandī (*Ṣubḥ*, vol. 3, 269–72) discusses the insignia of sovereignty of the Umayyads and Abbasids, calling them collectively "*shiʿār al-khilāfa.*" When discussing them in the context of the Fatimid processions, he uses the term *al-ālāt al-mulūkiyya al-mukhtaṣṣa bi'l-mawākib al-ʿiẓam* (royal implements specific to grand processions) (*Ṣubḥ*, vol. 3, 468ff.). A general discussion of insignia of sovereignty may be found in Ibn Khaldun (d. 808/1405–6), *The Muqaddimah*, tr. Franz Rosenthal, 3 vols. (Princeton, 1958), vol. 2, pp. 48–73. See also the discussion by Canard in "Ceremonial," pp. 387–93; D. Sourdel, "Questions," pp. 121–48; O. Grabar, "Notes," pp. 51–60.

70. *EI2*, vol. 4, pp. 1102–5.

71. *EI2*, vol. 1, pp. 1314–15. This cloak is said to have been a gift from the Prophet to the poet Kaʿb b. Zuhayr. It was then purchased from Kaʿb's son by Muʿāwiya (according to al-Māwardi, as quoted by Qalqashandī, for ten thousand dinars) and preserved in the Abbasid treasury until Mongol times. Ibn Isḥāq, *Sīrat rasūl Allāh*, 2 vols. in 3 (Göttingen, 1858–60) tells the story of Kaʿb's poem but makes no mention of the gift of the *burda* (trans. Alfred Guillaume, *The Life of Muhammad* (Oxford, 1970], pp. 597–601. For additional details, see also Dozy, *Dictionnaire détaillé des noms des vêtements chez les Arabes* [Amsterdam, 1845], pp. 59–64 [henceforth *Vêtements*]).

72. The *qaḍīb* had become a sign of the caliph's authority in Umayyad times; by the tenth century, descriptions of caliphal audiences regularly mention the staff, which was considered to belong to the Prophet. See *EI2*, vol. 4, pp. 377–78; Sourdel, "Questions," p. 135 and n. 100; E. Tyan, *Institutions de droit publique musulmane*, vol. 2 (Paris, 1954–56), pp. 490–92.

73. Ar. *julūs al-khulafā' wa-mā yalbasūnah fi'l-mawākib wa-yalbasuh al-dākhilūn ʿalayhim min al-khawāṣṣ wa-jamīʿ al-ṭawā'if* (*Rusūm*, pp. 90–92; Salem trans., pp. 73–75).

74. Ar. *al-ṭurūs allatī yuktabu fīhā ilā al-khulafā' wa'l-kharā'iṭ allatī tuḥmal al-kutub ṣādiratan wa-wāridatan fīhā wa'l-khutūm allatī tuwaqqaʿu ʿalayhā* (*Rusūm*, pp. 126–27; Salem trans., pp. 103–4).

75. Ar. *fī al-ālāt al-mulūkiyya al-mukhtaṣṣa bi'l-mawākib al-ʿiẓām* (*Ṣubḥ*, vol. 3, 540–44).

76. The distinctive headgear of the Abbasids, for example, was the *qalansuwa* (see Adam Mez, *The Renaissance of Islam*, trans. K. Bakhsh and D. S. Margoliouth [Patna, 1937], p. 132). This high-pointed conical cap was worn by the noble families of the Sasanian empire and adopted by the Umayyads. When it was adopted by men beyond the court, the caliph distinguished his *qalansuwa* by the distinctive way in which his turban was wound around it. For the history of the *qalansuwa*, see Boaz Shoshan, "On Costume and Social History in Medieval Islam," *Asian and African Studies* 22 (1988): 35–51, and the comprehensive references provided there. In *Rusūm*, the description of ʿAḍud al-dawla's investiture, the term *tāj* is used in a similar vein, when the text says, "He was invested with abundant robes of honor and crowned" (*tufāḍu ʿalayhi al-khilaʿ wa-yutawwaj*), where the meaning of "crowned" is explained further by the phrase "*ʿuṣiba ʿalayhi al-tāj*" (the crown was wound around [his head]) (*Rusūm*, p. 84).

77. *Ṣubḥ*, vol. 3, 468ff. and Canard, "Ceremonial," pp. 390–93. For a general description of the turban (*ʿimāma*), see Dozy, *Vêtements*, pp. 305–11; *EI*, s.v. "turban."

78. *Nujūm*, vol. 4, 94. The term may be translated literally as "the unique."

79. New Year, *Khiṭaṭ*, vol. 1, 448.5.

80. For numerous references, see al-Musabbiḥī, index no. 5, p. 147.

81. See, for example, *Ittiʿāẓ*, vol. 2, 157, where the *miẓalla* was carried over a pretender.

82. *Ittiʿāẓ*, vol. 1, 208.

83. Ibid., 237.

84. Ibid., 279; *Khiṭaṭ*, vol. 2, 277.24–25.

85. *Ittiʿāẓ*, vol. 2, 150–51. This is a significant detail for the palace procession on Ghadīr Khumm, treated below in chap. 6.

86. *Khiṭaṭ*, vol. 1, 407. See also Mez, *Renaissance*, p. 133.

87. Al-Musabbiḥī, *Akhbār Miṣr*, p. 62.

88. Ibid., p. 64.

89. Ibid., p. 66.

90. For details of the New Year's procession, see below, chap. 4 and the description in *Khiṭaṭ*, vol. 1, 447ff.

91. *Khiṭaṭ*, vol. 1, 449.1 and 9; 473.25 and 27. And a similar detail in *Rusūm*, p. 84 n. 1. See also *Khiṭaṭ*, vol. 1, 440.13.

92. *Itti'āẓ*, vol. 2, 71–72; and citations in Canard, "Ceremonial," p. 380 n. 2.

93. *Itti'āẓ*, vol. 2, 153.

94. On names in general, see *EI2*, s.v. "ism," "kunya," "nisba." See also Annemarie Schimmel, *Islamic Names* (Edinburgh, 1989).

On titulature, see *EI2* s.v. "laqab"; H. F. Amedroz, "The Assumption of the Title Shahanshah by Buwayhid Rulers," *Num. Chron.*, ser. 4, vol. 5 (1905): 393–99; idem, "On the Meaning of the laqab 'al-Saffah' as Applied to the First Abbasid Caliph," *JRAS* (1907): 660–63; P. Balog, "Pious invocations probably used as titles of office or as honorific titles in Umayyad and 'Abbasid times," in *Studies in memory of Gaston Wiet*, ed. M. Rosen-Ayalon (Jerusalem, 1977), pp. 61–68; A.-C. Barbier de Maynard, "Surnoms et sobriquets dans la litterature arabe," *Journal Asiatique*, ser. 10, vol. 9 (Jan.–June 1907): 173–244, 365–428; vol. 10 (July–Dec. 1907): 55–118, 193–273; C. E. Bosworth, "The Titulature of the Early Ghaznavids," *Oriens*, vol. 15 (1962): 210–33; M. Kabir, "The Assumption of the Title Shahanshah by the Buwayhid Rulers," *JASP*, vol. 4 (1959); J. H. Kramers, "Les Noms musulmans composés avec Din," *AO*, 5 (1927): 53–67; Bernard Lewis, "The Regnal Titles of the First Abbasid Caliphs," *Dr. Zakir Husain Presentation Volume* (New Delhi, 1968), pp. 13–22; Wilferd Madelung, "The Assumption of the Title Shahanshah by the Buyids and 'The Reign of Daylam' (Dawlat al-daylam)," *JNES*, vol. 28 (1969): 84–108, 168–83; F. Omar, "A Note on the Laqabs (i.e., Epithet) of the Early 'Abbasid Caliphs," in Farouk Omar, *'Abbasiyyat: Studies in the History of the Early 'Abbasids* (Baghdad, 1976), pp. 141–47; S. M. Stern, *Fāṭimid Decrees: Original Documents from the Fāṭimid Chancery* (London, 1964), section "Diplomatic Commentary," sect. 9 ("The Signature").

95. See *Tāj*, pp. 87–88 and *Rusūm*, p. 58.

96. See Schimmel, *Islamic Names*, pp. 4–8 for a complete discussion of the characteristics of the *kunya* and its various uses.

97. *Itti'āẓ*, vol. 1, 147. On the concept of *sharaf*, see the account of an audience in North Africa in which four imams were present, ibid., 135.

98. *Sīrat al-ustādh jūdhar (Jawdhar)*, M. Kāmil Ḥusayn and 'Abd al-Hādī Sha'īra (Cairo, 1954), p. 137.

99. *Khiṭaṭ*, vol. 1, 453.3–5. It is likely that the political expedience of this appearance was uppermost in the mind of the new wazir, who was no doubt eager to establish his authority with the troops. But what interests us here is the language used to express his desire in terms that

would have been acceptable to the caliph, terms that reflect the Fatimid preoccupation with *baraka*.

100. Ibid., 453.6–11.

101. Ibid., 475.10.

102. Ibid., 387–88.

103. *Sīrat al-ustādh jūdhar (Jawdhar)*, p. 138.

104. The sources ordinarily give only the vaguest and most general kinds of information about these distributions, their recipients, and their value. But the inventory of the clothing for the years 516/1122 and 517/1123 provides a full accounting of the expenditures for the occasion. The sums are staggering. A total of 14,305 pieces (*qiṭaʿ*) were distributed in 516/1122, more, Ibn al-Ma'mūn (d. 588/1192) tells us, than in all the days of al-Afḍal until the year 513/1119, i.e., 8,775 pieces. Here there is a slight discrepancy in the arithmetic. Ibn al-Ma'mūn calculates the excess at 5,634 pieces, but the total distributions during the year 516/1122 would then be 14,409. This is probably to be explained by scribal error or by misreadings during publication. In any event, the discrepancy of 104 pieces should not be regarded as significant, given the large numbers involved. The text is in *Khiṭaṭ*, vol. 1, 410. Furthermore, the costumes for this festival were double the number that they had been during the days of al-Afḍal. Their value was given at approximately twenty thousand dinars. This will seem an even more impressive sum if we take into account the value of the dinar during the Fatimid period. Goitein estimated its purchasing power by establishing a monthly income sufficient for a lower middle class family of two dinars (*Mediterranean Society*, vol. 1, 359 [App. B, no. 2]).

105. Abū al-Faḍl Jaʿfar b. ʿAli al-Dimashqī, *Al-Ishāra ilā Maḥāsin al-tijāra* (Cairo, 1900–01), p. 69 and n. 71.

106. Al-Musabbiḥī, *Akhbār Miṣr*, p. 57 (Shaʿbān 415/1024).

107. Ibid., p. 58.

108. See Goitein, *Mediterranean Society*, vol. 4, pp. 185–86. On the general economic and social safeguards of Jewish women in marriage, see ibid., 3, pp. 118–59.

109. Ibid., 4, p. 185.

110. Ibid., p. 184.

111. R. S. Lopez has established a direct connection between the acceptance of the notion of "hierarchy through clothing" and the development of imperial factories. This notion, as a sign of the absolutism of

the Byzantine emperors, was widely accepted by the end of the ninth century ("The Silk Industry in the Byzantine Empire," *Speculum* 20 [1945]: 1–42; reprinted in R. S. Lopez, *Byzantium and the World around it: Economic and Institutional Relations* [London, 1978]).

112. Lopez, "Silk Industry," pp. 2–10.

113. *Nujūm*, vol. 4, 99, reports that a Fatimid wazir received as a *khil'a* a red garment of the caliph. Hilāl al-Ṣābi' warns against wearing red in the caliph's residence "[because it] is the color of the caliph's dress as well as those who rebel against him" (*Rusūm*, p. 75). See also *EI2*, s.v. "marāsim."

114. See the proclamations in Norman Stillman, *The Jews of Arab Lands* (Philadelphia, 1979), for examples from both the Abbasid and Fatimid dynasties.

115. See Goitein, *Mediterranean Society*, vol. 4, pp. 195–96.

116. Ibid., p. 195 n. 329. But a general preoccupation with vivid colors is also characteristic of the period, see Goitein's discussion of the "color intoxication" of the classical Geniza period (ibid., pp. 172–77 and ibid., 1, pp. 106–8. I have not found any specific prohibition of wearing white, the dynastic color of the Fatimids, in Fatimid sources.

117. See ibid., 5, pp. 254–72.

118. See Mottahedeh, *Loyalty and Leadership*, chap. 4, "Justice, Kingship, and the Shape of Society," for a thought-provoking discussion of these issues in the context of Buyid society. Mottahedeh emphasizes the fact that the Buyid king stood outside of society, the only position from which he could balance the overlapping loyalties that were considered to be necessary to social and political order.

119. Al-Qalqashandī divides Fatimid ceremonial into two categories: processions (*rukūb*) and audiences (*julūs*). All of these ceremonies are subsumed under the rubric of *mawākib*. The term *mawkib* (pl. *mawākib*), which actually means a "procession" or "parade," comes from the verb *wakaba*, "to walk slowly." Thus *mawkib* is used to designate the ceremonial occasion of a procession, as well as the cortege itself. In the Fatimid usage, however, it seems to have the sense as well of any ceremonial and solemn occasion. See the usage of al-Qalqashandī in *Ṣubḥ*, vol. 3, 494ff., where he establishes the categories of *al-mawākib al-'iẓam* and *al-mawākib al-mukhtaṣara* for major and minor processions. Within these categories, ceremonies are divided into *rukūb* and *julūs*. All the ceremonies have at least some processional elements, be they formal parades or the solemn and deliberate manner in which one entered and exited from the caliph's presence. Al-Qalqashandī called

these *"al-julūs fi'l-mawākib."* There is no evidence, however, that such distinctions of category were made by the Fatimids themselves.

120. Ibid., 480–88.

121. Ibid., 495 and *Khiṭaṭ*, vol. 1, 386. The material used changed from one season to another. In the winter, brocade (*dībāj*) curtains and silk carpets were used; in the summer, *dabīqī* linen curtains and Ṭabaristān Ṭabarī carpets with gold were used. The throne was covered with Qurqūbī.

122. *Ṣubḥ*, vol. 3, 496 and *Khiṭaṭ*, vol. 1, 386. It is described as *ifrīz ʿālin ʿan arḍ al-qāʿa.*

123. This part of a room is conventionally referred to as the "*ṣadr,*" that is, the end or uppermost part of the sitting room, often elevated.

124. *Ṣubḥ*, vol. 3, 496.

125. Nearly the same ceremony took place when the caliph sat in the grilled loge (*shubbāk*) to review the parade of horses for the New Year's procession, as well as on the Festival of Fast Breaking (*Khiṭaṭ*, vol. 1, 447.27ff., 452.24ff.). Ibn al-Ma'mūn mentions the review of horses for the festival, but Ibn al-Ṭuwayr does not. See also Canard, "Ceremonial," p. 410 n. 2.

126. The common European ceremonial context in which courtiers witness the king being dressed is unthinkable in an Islamic context. For a description of the king's *levée*, see Elias, *Court Society*, pp. 83ff.

127. See *Tāj*, pp. 75–76. For the Fatimids, the details of prayer during Ramaḍān, when the caliph is concealed while he sermonizes and his concealment during banquets, see chap. 3. For a comparative approach to this issue in a later period, see Fatma Müge Goçek, *East Encounters West: France and the Ottoman Empire in the Eighteenth Century* (New York and Oxford, 1987), pp. 30–38.

128. For discussions of the gestures the caliph uses, see *Tāj*, pp. 7–8 and *Himma*, pp. 115–16.

129. *Khiṭaṭ*, vol. 1, 432.34ff.; *Ṣubḥ*, vol. 3, 498.20ff. A *mawlid* may mark the anniversary of either the birth or the death of the Prophet, a member of his family, or a saint.

130. *Khiṭaṭ*, vol. 1, 432–33 and mentioned in passing, *Ṣubḥ*, vol. 3, 14.

131. *Khiṭaṭ*, vol. 1, 466.20ff.; *Ṣubḥ*, vol. 3, 497ff.

132. *Khiṭaṭ*, vol. 1, 432–33.

133. Reported by Ibn al-Ṭuwayr.

134. *Itti'āẓ*, vol. 2, 71–72.

135. *Khiṭaṭ*, vol. 1, 477.10–12.

136. *Itti'āẓ*, vol. 3, 99–100.

137. *Himma*, pp. 116–19; *Tāj*, pp. 77–82; *Rusūm*, pp. 86–89.

138. See in particular the emphasis on this in *Himma*, p. 116.

139. See Marmon, *Eunuchs and Sacred Boundaries*, passim.

140. On these points, Richard Trexler's "Ritual Behavior in Renaissance Florence: The Setting," *Medievalia et Humanistica*, n.s., 4 (1973): 125–44, is suggestive, particularly with respect to the "sacralization" and "desacralization" of space.

CHAPTER 3

1. Ibn 'Idhārī, *Al-Bayān al-mughrib fī akhbār al-maghrib,* ed. R. Dozy (Leiden, 1848–49), p. 188. One copyist glossed the poem, saying that the poets praised the imam to such an extent that they nearly committed unbelief (*kufr*), but mentioning this was not intended to place al-Mahdiyya on an equal footing with Mecca (p. 183 note *b*).

2. Ibn Hāni', *Dīwān* (Cairo, 1933), no. 9: 12,13,15.

3. Ibid., no. 4: 56, 57.

4. Ibid., no. 1.

5. Ibid., no. 1: 31; Marius Canard, "L'Imperialism des Fāṭimides et leur propagande," *Annales de l'Institut d'Études Orientales de la Faculté des Lettres d'Alger* 6 (1942–47): 156–93 (reprinted in Marius Canard, *Miscellanea Orientalia* [London, 1973], p. 161 n. 21.

6. Ibn Hāni', *Dīwān*, no. 1: 44. See also Canard, "L'Imperialism," p. 161 n. 19.

7. See below, pp. 122–24.

8. None of the palace inscriptions are preserved in literary sources and none reported in either *CIA* or *RCEA*.

9. Ibrahim b. M. Ibn Duqmāq, *Kitāb al-Intiṣār li-wāsiṭat 'iqd al-amṣār*, vol. 4, p. 127.

10. K. A. C. Creswell, "The Founding of Cairo," in *Colloque Inter-*

national sur l'Histoire du Caire (Cairo, 1972), p. 127; H. C. Kay, "Al-Kahira and Its Gates," *JRAS* (1882): 233.

11. Ar. *al-turba al-muʿizziyya* or *turbat al-zaʿfarān*; see *Khiṭaṭ*, vol. 1, 407.

12. The imamate passed through an unbroken line from father to son. W. Ivanow, in *Ismaili Tradition Concerning the Rise of the Fatimids* (Bombay, 1942), pp. 102–3, reports this prophetic tradition from al-Qāḍī al-Nuʿmān's *Sharḥu'l-akhbār* (listed as number twenty-eight of fifty traditions): "I [i.e., al-Qāḍī al-Nuʿmān] heard the imam al-Muʿizz narrate a story about al-Mahdī. He said: once a certain important man asked him: art thou [really] the expected Mahdī, under whose authority God shall gather His slaves, making him the king of the whole earth, and shall the religion of the world become one under thee? He [al-Mahdī] replied to him: the mission of the Mahdī is enormous. I have a considerable share in it, and those who are coming after me shall also share it. [And al-Muʿizz added]: if it should be the lot of one person only, how could anything from it come to me? Then al-Muʿizz continued: al-Mahdī was the key which opened the lock of the Divine bounty, mercy, blessing, and happiness. By him God has opened all these to His slaves. And this shall continue after him in his successors, until the promise of God which He made to them in His bounty, might and power, will be fulfilled."

This is a striking contrast to the malicious anecdote reported by Sunni writers to discredit the Fatimids (reported, among others, in *Nujūm*, vol. 4, 77). In it, al-Muʿizz, questioned about his lineage (*nasab*) and his proof, drew his sword and proclaimed, "This is my pedigree." And, scattering a handful of gold dinars, proclaimed further, "This is my proof." The anecdote is mentioned by Bernard Lewis, in "An Interpretation of Fatimid History," *Colloque International sur l'Histoire du Caire* (Cairo, 1972): 287.

13. *EI2*, vol. 1, p. 825.

14. For a brief discussion of the special marks of the imam in Twelver Shiʿism, see the Introduction of Abdulaziz Abdulhussein Sachedina's *Islamic Messianism* (Albany, 1981). The Twelver Imam inherited both the weapons of Prophethood and its knowledge. The Imam was entrusted with books (*kutub*), knowledge (*ʿilm*), and weapons (*silāḥ*). This is true also in the Ismāʿīlī system.

This may throw light on the often-reported audience held by al-Muʿizz in North Africa shortly before the conquest of Egypt, when he received the notables of the Kutāma in his audience halls, with the doors to his libraries open, and exhorted them to devote themselves to their mission. The incident is reported in *Khiṭaṭ*, vol. 1, 352.5–19.

15. *Itti'āẓ*, vol. 1, 285 (s.a. 385) and *Khiṭaṭ*, vol. 1, 391. Stern identifies these lectures as the book *Da'ā'im al-islām*; see his "Cairo as the Center of the Ismā'īlī Movement," *Colloque International sur l'Histoire du Caire* (Cairo, 1972): 437–50 (reprinted in S. M. Stern *Studies in Early Isma'ilism* [Jerusalem, 1983], pp. 234–56).

16. The lectures at the Azhar were delivered to women (*Khiṭaṭ*, vol. 1, 391; Stern, "Cairo," pp. 440–41).

17. See the letter of appointment of a chief missionary preserved in al-Qalqashandī, *Ṣubḥ*, vol. 10, 434ff. Stern discusses the letter in "Cairo," pp. 440–41.

18. On the mosque as a political and religious center, see *EI2*, s.v. "masdjid," "architecture."

19. *EI2*, s.v. "masdjid." For a fuller discussion of the history of the *dār al-imāra*, see Jere L. Bacharach, "Administrative Complexes, Palaces, and Citadels: Changes in the Loci of Medieval Muslim Rule" in Irene Bierman, Rifa'at Abou-El-Haj, Donald Preziosi, *The Ottoman City and its Parts: Urban Form and Social Order*, pp. 111–28 (New York, 1991).

20. *Khiṭaṭ*, vol. 2, 365.

21. *EI*, vol. 3, p. 349a.

22. *Khiṭaṭ*, vol. 2, 117.

23. For example, the reading of the proclamation (*sijill*) of the qadi al-Fāriqī took place at the Mosque of 'Amr. Later, this mosque became a site of Fatimid Friday prayer.

24. Al-Kindī, *Kitāb al-wulāt wa-kitāb al-quḍāt*, ed. Rhuvon Guest (Beirut, 1908), p. 269.

25. Ibid., pp. 134, 274–75.

26. Goitein, *Mediterranean Society*, vol. 4, pp. 12–13, 26.

27. *Itti'āẓ*, vol. 1, 114–15 (Ibn Zūlāq).

28. Cf. the prayer by 'Abd al-Samī', *Nujūm*, vol. 4, 32.

29. *Itti'āẓ*, vol. 1, 114–15. See the discussion of these events by Yaacov Lev, "The Fāṭimid Imposition of Isma'ilism on Egypt (358–386/969–996)," *ZDMG* 138, no. 2 (1988): 315–17.

30. Yaacov Lev discusses this document in *State and Society in Fatimid Egypt* (Leiden, 1991), pp. 15–16.

31. Lev's analysis of this issue is somewhat different from mine. See his "Fāṭimid Imposition," pp. 313–25 and *State and Society*, pp. 133ff.

32. *Itti'āẓ*, vol. 1, 119. Cf. al-Shāfi'ī (*Kitāb al-Umm*, 7 vols. [Cairo, 1903–7], vol. 1, 205), prefers reading suras 62 and 63 during the Friday prayer, but reports a tradition in which suras 87 and 88 were read. Perhaps this was actually the practice in Egypt, where the Shāfi'ī (and Mālikī) schools predominated during the tenth century.

33. *Itti'āẓ*, vol. 1, 116–17. Ismā'īlīs reckon their calendar by astronomical calculation, Sunnis by sighting of the new moon.

34. The *muṣallā* (lit. "place for prayer") may refer to any place of prayer but usually designates an outdoor area set off for prayer. In the first century of the hijra, the *muṣallā* was a typical feature of Islamic cities. The Prophet held prayer and slaughtered animals there on the Sacrificial Feast (*'īd al-naḥr*); it was also the site for the prayer for rain (*istisqā'*) and for the dead. See *EI2*, s.v. "muṣallā" and "masdjid." By the tenth century, *muṣallās* seem to have been rare except in North Africa and the Hijaz. See also A. J. Wensinck, "Some Semitic Rites of Mourning and Religion," *Verhandelingen der Koninklijke Akademie van Wetenschappen te Amsterdam*, Afdeeling Letterkunde, 18, no. 1 (1917): 1–101, on the relationship between the thrashing floor and the *muṣallā*.

35. *Da'ā'im al-islām*, 1, 187 (paras. 606, 607, 608).

36. However, al-Kindī has numerous references to the *muṣallā* in *Wulāt*.

37. *Itti'āẓ*, vol. 1, 113; *Khiṭaṭ*, vol. 1, 451.

38. *Itti'āẓ*, vol. 1, 70 and 117; *Zahru'l-ma'ānī* in Ivanow, *Rise of the Fatimids*, p. 262. The Khārijī rebellion, which broke out in 332/943–44, is discussed fully in Farhat Dachraoui, *Le Califat fatimide au maghreb, 296–362 H./909–973 J.C.: Histoire politique et institutions* (Tunis, 1981), esp. pp. 133ff., 161–82, 347–51; R. Le Tourneau, "La Révolte d'Abu Yazid au Xe siècle," *Cahiers de Tunisie* 2 (1953):103–25.

39. Bāb al-Naṣr (Gate of [God's] Help or Gate of Victory) and the other northern gate of Cairo, Bāb al-Futūḥ (Gate of Conquest) stand as a sort of monumental expression of the Fatimid slogan, "Help from God and near victory" (*naṣrun min allāh wa-fatḥun qarībun* [Q. 61:13]).

40. *Itti'āẓ*, vol. 1, 120–21; *Nujūm*, vol. 5, 356. The Sunni call to prayer consists of the following formula: "God is most great; I testify that there is no god but God; I testify that Muhammad is the messenger of God; Hurry to prayer; Hurry to salvation; Prayer is better than sleep [recited only in the dawn prayer]; God is most great; There is no god but God." The Shi'is omit the phrase "Prayer is better than sleep" and instead recite "Hurry to the best of works" in each call to prayer. See I.

K. A. Howard, "The Development of the *Adhān* and *Iqāma* of the *Ṣalāt* in Early Islam," *Journal of Semitic Studies* 26, no. 2 (1981): 219–28.

41. *Daʿāʾim al-islām*, vol. 1, par. 601, prescribes the recitation of these suras.

42. Ritual prayer (*ṣalāt*) consists of a prescribed sequence of postures and associated recitations and utterances, performed either alone or congregationally, while facing the direction of Mecca (*qibla*). The basic cycle, the *rakʿa*, is made up of genuflections (*rukūʿ*) and prostrations (*sujūd*), Qur'anic recitation, and other prescribed statements, including the *takbīr* (God is most great). The *ṣalāt* is composed of a series of *rakʿa*s, the exact number of which may vary depending upon the time of day or the occasion for the prayer. The four Sunni legal schools of law (*madhāhib*) differ slightly in their ritual practices, as do various Shiʿi rites. For a clear, concise description of basic Sunni practice, see Frederick Mathewson Denny, *An Introduction to Islam* (New York, 1985), pp. 105–11.

43. That is, four *rakʿa*s with no *khuṭba*, as prescribed in *Daʿāʾim al-islām*, vol. 1, par. 603. See also al-Muḥaqqiq al-Ḥillī, *Sharāʾiʿ al-islām* (trans. A. Querry, *Droit musulman: Recuil de lois concernant les Musulmans schyites* [Paris, 1871–72]), vol. 1, 228, 274, 392.

44. On the value of Friday prayer as compared with regular prayer, see *Daʿāʾim al-islām*, vol. 1, 182.

45. Saturday, 24 Jumādā I 359/4 April 970. See *Khiṭaṭ*, vol. 2, 273ff.; Jalāl al-dīn al-Suyūṭī, *Ḥusn al-muḥāḍara fī ta'rīkh miṣr wa'l-qāhira*, 2 vols., ed. M. Abu'l-Faḍl Ibrāhīm (Cairo, 1967), vol. 2, 183; Creswell, "Founding of Cairo," pp. 129–30; *EI2*, s.v. "Azhar" and "masdjid."

46. *Khiṭaṭ*, vol. 2, 273.

47. *Ittiʿāẓ*, vol. 3, 136–37.

48. Ibid., 137–38.

49. Ibid., 140–41.

50. Ibid., 141–42.

51. *ʿĪd al-fiṭr* and *ʿīd al-aḍḥā* are the only two canonical festivals in the Muslim calendar. Although two entirely separate festivals, they share a number of common features, of which the most significant is the form of public prayer on these occasions, *ṣalāt al-ʿīdayn* (prayer of the two festivals). The law books devote a separate chapter to the regulations for this special communal prayer. Like the Friday prayer, the festi-

val prayer must be led by an imam and is obligatory only for those Muslims living in a city large enough for a congregational mosque (*jāmiʿ*). But there are important differences. The prayer takes place between sunrise and noon, unlike the Friday prayer, which takes place just after noon. There is neither the customary first nor the second call to prayer (*adhān, iqāma*); instead, the simple formula *al-ṣalāt jāmiʿatun* (lit. "The prayer is congregating," i.e., "Come to prayer!") is pronounced just before the beginning of the prayer. The *khuṭba* is delivered after, rather than before, the prayer. Finally, the prayer often takes place in a *muṣallā* rather than a mosque. For general description of the *ʿīd*, see *EI2*, s.v. "ʿīd." For the Ismāʿīlī regulations, see *Daʿāʾim al-islām*, vol. 1, 186–90.

52. *Ittiʿāẓ*, vol. 1, 137–38; *Khiṭaṭ*, vol. 1, 451.

53. This is called in Arabic "*taslīm.*"

54. The same practice was used in the Friday prayer during Ramaḍān.

55. *Dībāj* is often found as a material in curtains, pillows and other furnishings for ceremonies. Brocades are mentioned mostly as materials for furnishings in the Geniza, see Goitein, *Mediterranean Society*, vol. 4, pp. 110, 115, 116, 119, 120, 124, 126, 168.

56. Elephants and giraffes were commonly included in these and other processions, as, for example, in Nile processions.

57. ʿAlī b. Mūsā Ibn Saʿīd, *Kitāb al-mughrib fī ḥula al-maghrib*, vol. 4, ed. Knut L. Tallquist (Leiden, 1899), p. 16.

58. See, *EI*, s.v. "Ramaḍān."

59. His obituary states that he was the first of the caliphs to ride in procession to lead prayer on the Fridays during Ramaḍān (*Ittiʿāẓ*, vol. 1, 295).

60. Details of the costume in *Khiṭaṭ*, vol. 2, 280. The event is reported in less detail in *Ittiʿāẓ*, vol. 1, 267.

61. Cf. the prayer of al-Ḥākim in 403/1013, discussed below.

62. *Ittiʿāẓ*, vol. 1, 272; *Khiṭaṭ*, vol. 2, 277. He wore a *ṭaylasān*, held the staff, and wore sandals.

63. *Ittiʿāẓ*, vol. 1, 272; *Khiṭaṭ*, vol. 2, 277.

64. *Ittiʿāẓ*, vol. 1, 276.

65. Ibid., 279; *Khiṭaṭ*, vol. 2, 277.

66. *Ittiʿāẓ*, vol. 1, 283.

67. The troops mentioned are the Turks, Daylam, ʿAzīziyya, Ikhshidiyya, and Kāfūriyya. Curiously, no Kutāma are mentioned here, although they are mentioned in descriptions of processions during the reign of al-Ḥākim.

68. A common combination in jewelry; see Goitein, *Mediterranean Society*, vol. 4, p. 207.

69. One of the insignia of sovereignty, see chap. 2, above.

70. *Khiṭaṭ*, vol. 2, 277.

71. He had chits (*riqaʿ*) with their names written on them.

72. *Khiṭaṭ*, vol. 1, 451 and *Ittiʿāẓ*, vol. 1, 267.

73. *Ta'wīl al-daʿā'im*, vol. 1, 260 (*takbīrat al-iḥrām*).

74. In Ismaʿili thought, all phenomena are considered to have an apparent, exoteric meaning (*ẓāhir*), which can be easily comprehended by the believer, and an esoteric or hidden meaning (*bāṭin*), which is apprehended by means of allegorical interpretation (*ta'wīl*). *Daʿā'im al-islām* is al-Qāḍī al-Nuʿmān's treatise on Ismaʿili jurisprudence and falls into the category of the *ẓāhir*. *Ta'wīl al-daʿā'im* is al-Qāḍī al-Nuʿmān's allegorical interpretation of the precepts of the *Daʿā'im al-islām*.

75. *Daʿā'im al-islām*, vol. 1, 188; *Ta'wīl al-daʿā'im*, vol. 1, 316ff.

76. The *mahdī*, or divinely guided one, is a messianic figure who is expected to return at the end of time. The concept is of Shiʿi origin, but it was accepted by Sunnis. There are variations in the specifics of the doctrine concerning the *mahdī* among different Muslims groups. He is generally believed by Shiʿis to be the hidden imam who will reappear to restore justice and order to the world. The doctrine of the *mahdī* underwent significant change in the early Fatimid period. See *EI2*, s.v. "Ismāʿīliyya," "Mahdī"; Farhad Daftary, *The Ismāʿīlīs: Their History and Doctrines* (Cambridge, 1990), passim. *Ta'wīl al-daʿā'im*, vol. 1, 316, likens the exposure of the *mahdī*'s mission and the delight of the Believers whose trials are removed by it to the joy of those breaking the fast in the *fiṭr*.

77. The term *qā'im* is generally synonymous with *mahdī* among Shiʿis.

78. *Ta'wīl al-daʿā'im*, vol. 1, 322.

79. Ibid. See also the Introduction in Sachedina's *Islamic Messianism*, on prophetic weapons.

80. This is also expressed in the formula: *mathal al-khurūj ilā al-ʿīdayn mathal al-khurūj ilā jihād al-aʿdā'* (ibid.).

81. Ibid. (top).

82. See above, p. 45.

83. On his campaigns, see the brief outline in *EI2*, s.v. "al-ʿAzīz billāh" and Lev, *State and Society*, pp. 23–25. He never relinquished his ambition to secure Syria.

84. On their relationship, see Yaacov Lev, "The Fatimid Vizier Yaʿqub ibn Killis and the Beginning of the Fatimid Administration in Egypt," *Der Islam* 58 pt. 2 (1981): 237–49.

85. On the position of the Kutāma and al-ʿAzīz's military reforms, see Lev, *State and Society*, pp. 81ff.

86. *Ittiʿāẓ*, vol. 1, 267 and *Khiṭaṭ*, vol. 2, 280.

87. *Ittiʿāẓ*, vol. 1, 294.

88. On his accession, see *Ittiʿāẓ*, vol. 2, 3–4 and M. B. ʿAli Ibn Muyassar, *Akhbār Miṣr*, ed. Ayman Fu'ad Sayyid (Cairo, 1981), p. 177.

89. Bilbays was an important town on the natural invasion route of Egypt and was the first stop on the route of troops leaving the capital for Palestine. See *EI2*, vol. 1, p. 1218.

90. The position that he held was that of *wāsiṭa* (intermediary), an office that later came to be known as *wizāra* (wazirate). On the power struggle between Ibn ʿAmmār and Barjawān, see Lev, *State and Society*, pp. 25–26; Daftary, *Ismāʿīlīs*, pp. 186–88; *Ittiʿāẓ*, vol. 1, 292 and vol. 2, 4.

91. *Ittiʿāẓ*, vol. 2, 5–6.

92. It is curious that al-Ḥākim did not attend the festival prayer himself. The fact that he was a minor was not an obstacle. See Abu'l-Fawāris Aḥmad ibn Yaʿqūb, *Al-Risāla fi'l-imāma*, ed. and tr. Sami N. Makarem, *The Political Doctrine of the Ismaʿilis* (New York, 1977), chap. 12. Six weeks later, he led the prayer for *ʿīd al-aḍḥā*; see *Ittiʿāẓ*, vol. 2, 7.

93. For the description of the prayer at the *muṣallā*, see *Ittiʿāẓ*, vol. 1, 292.

94. *Ittiʿāẓ*, vol. 1, 292 (obituary of al-ʿAzīz) and vol. 2, 2.

95. *Ittiʿāẓ*, vol. 2, 20.

96. As in the years 389/999, 390/1000, 394/1004, 396/1006 (*Ittiʿāẓ*, vol. 2, 24, 5, 49, 68).

97. Prayer for both *ʿīd al-fiṭr* and *ʿīd al-naḥr* was still being held at the *muṣallā* in 395/1005. *Ittiʿāẓ*, vol. 2, 58 and 59.

98. *Itti'āẓ*, vol. 2, 20.

99. *Itti'āẓ*, vol. 1, 137–38.

100. *Khiṭaṭ*, vol. 2, 282–83 for the history of the mosque. It was built originally in baked brick (*ṭūb*), destroyed, then rebuilt in stone, at which time the Friday prayer was held there (*wa-uqīmat bihi al-jum'a*).

101. *Khiṭaṭ*, vol. 2, 282 and *Itti'āẓ*, vol. 2, 58. Al-Maqrīzī states that al-Ḥākim rode to the newly completed and outfitted Rāshida mosque on Thursday evening (*'ashīyat yawm al-jum'a*) and looked it over (*wa-ashrafa 'alayh*). He does not state explicitly that al-Ḥākim led prayer there. In *Itti'āẓ*, the editor includes in the same paragraph both the statement that the mosque was furnished during Ramaḍān 395/1005 and the description of al-Ḥākim's procession to prayer on the festival. This creates the false impression that the festival prayer was held at this mosque. The *Khiṭaṭ* text has no reference to festival prayer, and there is no other evidence that al-Ḥākim deviated from standard Fatimid practice in leading festival prayer at the *muṣallā*.

102. Ibn Duqmāq, *Kitāb al-intiṣār li-wāsiṭat 'aqd al-amṣār*, ed. K. Vollers (Būlāq, 1891–92, reprint, Beirut, n.d.), pp. 78–79. See also *Khiṭaṭ*, vol. 2, 283.18–19. This mosque should not be confused, however, with the Mosque of al-Ḥākim, which became the premier mosque of Cairo during al-Ḥākim's reign.

103. Ibn Duqmāq, *Kitāb al-intiṣār*, vol. 4, 78.

104. Irene Bierman, *Writing Signs: The Fatimid Public Text* (forthcoming).

105. On the meaning and function of inscriptional programs and writing, see the work of Irene Bierman, whose interpretation of these writing practices has been essential to my own understanding of the inscriptional program of the mosque. I am grateful to her for allowing me access to the manuscript of her forthcoming book, *Writing Signs*.

106. Here, I do not agree with Jonathan Bloom's analysis of the interior inscriptional program of this mosque. He does not believe the program had ideological content ("The Mosque of al-Hakim in Cairo," *Muqarnas* 1 [1982]: 18). However, I believe that the inscriptional program was a highly charged ideological expression of the Isma'ili ritual city.

107. Bloom, "Mosque of al-Hakim," Appendix, Inscriptions: Q. 11:73, 9:18, 9:128, 24:35–38, 5:55 and 2:257, 17:80.

108. *Da'ā'im al-islām*, vol. 1, 149. The relative value of prayer at different mosques is a convention of medieval Islamic tradition. For a

comprehensive discussion of early traditions, see M. J. Kister, "'You Shall Only Set Out for Three Mosques': A Study of an Early Tradition," *Le Muséon* 82 (1969): 173–96; reprinted with additional notes in M. J. Kister, *Studies in Jāhiliyya and Early Islam* (London, 1980).

109. *Ta'wīl al-da'ā'im*, vol. 1, 225–26; vol. 3, 60.

110. On the *dār al-ḥikma* (also known as *dār al-ʿilm*), see *Khiṭaṭ*, vol. 1, 391 (on *majālis al-ḥikma*), 445 and 458–59; *Ittiʿāẓ*, vol. 2, 56; D. Sourdel, "Dār al-Ḥikma", *EI2*, vol. 2, pp. 126–27; Sadik A. Assaad, *Reign of al-Ḥākim bi Amr Allah (386/396–411/1021): A political Study* (Beirut, 1974), pp. 88–93.

111. Bierman, *Writing Signs* (forthcoming).

112. *Ittiʿāẓ*, vol. 2, 68.

113. See Assaad, *Reign of al-Ḥākim*, chap. 5, for a detailed study of these rebellions.

114. On these edicts, see Heinz Halm, "Der Treuhänder Gottes: Die Edikte des Kalifen al-Ḥākim," *Der Islam* (1986): 11–72.

115. *Ittiʿāẓ*, vol. 2, 69.

116. Ibid., 78.

117. *Ittiʿāẓ*, vol. 2, 82. The Shiʿi call to prayer was again imposed in 401/1010 (ibid., 86).

118. Ibid., 87 and 95. See also Marius Canard's reconstruction of events in *EI2*, s.v. "Djarrāḥid," "al-Ḥākim bi-Amr Allāh"; Assaad, *Reign of al-Ḥākim*, pp. 146–55.

119. Curiously, there does not seem to be any mention of the Jarrāḥid revolt in *Ittiʿāẓ*

120. *Khiṭaṭ*, vol. 2, 277. Creswell identifies the *arkān* as the salients around the minarets, K. A. C. Creswell, *The Muslim Architecture of Egypt* (Oxford, 1952), vol. 1, pp. 65, 85–90; Bloom, "Mosque of al-Hakim," pp. 20–21, discusses these *arkān* from the point of view of the history of minarets.

121. See Bloom, "Mosque of al-Hakim," pp. 18, 36.

122. Bloom, "Mosque of al-Hakim," p. 20, disagrees with Flury's dating of the inscriptions to before 393/1003, primarily on the similarity of tone in the salients and the interior inscriptions.

123. Bloom, "Mosque of al-Hakim," inscription no. 13.

124. See the discussion in *EI2*, s.v. "masdjid."

125. Bierman reads this inscriptional program as a response to the Jarrāḥid *sharīf's* citation of Qur'an 28:1–6, implicitly likening al-Ḥākim to Pharaoh (see Bierman, *Writing Signs*, chap. 3).

126. Creswell, *Muslim Architecture of Egypt*, vol. 1, p. 37 states that al-Ḥākim suppressed the *khuṭba* in the Azhar after building his new mosque. According to al-Maqrīzī, *Khiṭaṭ*, vol. 2, 275–76, the communal Friday prayer and *khuṭba* were suppressed in the Azhar during the time of Saladin, because the Shāfi'ī school did not permit congregational prayer in more than one mosque in a city. There is overwhelming evidence that congregational prayer and the *khuṭba* continued to be held in more than one mosque throughout the Fatimid period.

127. *Khiṭaṭ*, vol. 2, 282 and *Itti'āẓ*, vol. 2, 96–97.

128. Cf. the procession of al-'Azīz in 380/990, reported in *Khiṭaṭ*, vol. 2, 280.

129. The Jarrāḥid revolt in Palestine began two years earlier, but in 403/1012, the *sharīf* of Mecca was raised as an anti-caliph. See *EI2*, s.v. "Djarrāḥid."

130. Al-Ḥākim's insistence on judging petitions himself was part of his attempt to maintain control over his administration after the death of Barjawān. On his administration, see *Itti'āẓ*, vol. 2, 28, 30; *Khiṭaṭ*, vol. 2, 14–15; Assaad, *Reign of al-Ḥākim*, pp. 69–71.

131. *Itti'āẓ*, vol. 2, 38.

132. On Egyptian *dabīqī* linen, see Goitein, *Mediterranean Society*, vol. 4, 165–66.

133. *Khiṭaṭ*, vol. 2, 277.

134. *Itti'āẓ*, vol. 2, 97. Compare the austerity also of the Ramaḍān prayers in that year.

135. Ibid., 98–99.

136. Ibid., 103.

137. Ibid., 101.

138. See Abu'l Fawāris Aḥmad b. Ya'qūb, *Al-Risāla fi'l-Imāma*, esp. chap. 11. After the Ṭayyibī schism, the designation of 'Abd al-Raḥīm acquired a new significance, see below, chap. 6.

139. *Itti'āẓ*, vol. 2, 109.

140. Ibid., 96 and *Khiṭaṭ*, vol. 2, 288. This section is translated by Bernard Lewis, *Islam from the Prophet Muhammad to the Conquest of*

Constantinople (New York and Oxford, 1974), vol. 1, pp. 46–59. I have relied on some of his usages in my translation.

141. *Itti'āẓ*, vol. 2, 99.

142. Ibid., 96.

143. In recent years, there have been several important reconsiderations of al-Ḥākim's reign. See Halm, "Treuhänder Gottes," pp. 11–72 and Josef van Ess, *Chiliastische Erwartungen und die Versuchung der Göttlichkeit: Der Kalif al-Ḥākim (386–411 H.)* (Heidelberg, 1977).

144. On Sitt al-mulk, see Yaacov Lev, "The Fāṭimid Princess Sitt al-Mulk," *Journal of Semitic Studies* 32 (1987): 319–28.

145. *Itti'āẓ*, vol. 2, 124. The text notes that three hours passed between the prayer for al-Ḥākim and the oath to al-Ẓāhir.

146. Ibid., 158–59 and al-Musabbiḥī, *Akhbār Miṣr*, p. 61. Masjid Tibr was located outside of Cairo along the canal (*khandaq*), close to Maṭariyya. It was originally built in 145/762–63 and was renovated by a high-ranking Ikhshidid amir named Tibr, after whom it was then called. Al-Musabbiḥī's eyewitness account is the only report of a procession on the first of Ramaḍān that we possess before the time of Ibn al-Ṭuwayr (d. 617/1220), who notes only that the caliph went out in procession on the first day of Ramaḍān and that the procession was identical in every respect to the New Year's procession. There are no descriptions of a New Year's procession from this early period, and it is likely that Ibn al-Ṭuwayr's comment that the procession for the first of Ramaḍān was exactly like that of the elaborate New Year's procession reflects a much later development. See *Khiṭaṭ*, vol. 1, 491 and *Ṣubḥ*, vol. 3, 509.

147. On the term *mudhahhab* (with gold threads), see Goitein, *Mediterranean Society*, vol. 4, p. 166. The Ṣaqlabī eunuch was Bahā' al-dawla Muẓaffar, mentioned often in this capacity by al-Musabbiḥī. The Ṣaqlabīs were associated, like the Kutāma, with the North African period of Fatimid rule. I interpret all references to Ṣaqlabīs in the Fatimid army as meaning "eunuch," based on David Ayalon's analysis of the important passage from Abu'l-Qāsim Ibn Ḥawqal, *K. ṣūrat al-arḍ*, 2d ed., ed. J. H. Kramers (Leiden, 1938–39), p. 110. Ayalon has demonstrated that the Ṣaqlabīs who entered the lands of Islam through Spain were castrated, unlike those who entered through the eastern frontiers. Ayalon's interpretation is especially important, since Ibn Ḥawqal's work was completed around 378/988 and he may himself have been a Fatimid agent. See David Ayalon, "On the Eunuchs in Islam," *Jerusalem Studies in Arabic and Islam*, 1 (1979): 67–124, esp. pp. 92–109.

148. That is, the Azhar Mosque and the Mosque of al-Ḥākim, now

called by al-Musabbiḥī by the epithets "al-Azhar" and "al-Anwar," respectively (*Ittiʿāẓ*, vol. 2, 159, 160); details on clothing only in al-Musabbiḥī, *Akhbār Miṣr*, pp. 62, 64.Costume going to the Azhar Mosque: *ṭaylasān sharb mufawwaṭ / ʿimāma qaṣab bayāḍ mudhahhaba / thiyāb dabīqī bayāḍ / miẓalla dabīqī mudhahhaba*; returning: *miẓalla dabīqī bayāḍ mukhawwama mudhahhaba*. Costume going to the Mosque of al-Ḥākim: *ridā' bayāḍ muḥashshā qaṣaban / thiyāb bayāḍ dabīqī / thawb muṣmat abyaḍ / ʿimāma bayāḍ mudhahhab / al-qaḍīb al-jawhar / al-miẓalla al-mudayyara bi'l-ḥumra*; returning: *al-miẓalla al-mudayyara bi'l-dhahab*.

149. Ibrāhīm is referred to as *"al-jalīs al-mu'addib."* George Makdisi, *The Rise of Humanism in Classical Islam and the Christian West* (Edinburgh, 1990), pp. 272ff., counts tutors and boon-companions among the professional humanists and lists a number of men who served at the Abbasid court first as tutors and then as boon-companions. I assume this to have been the case with al-Ẓāhir, for whom Ibrāhīm must have been a tutor who was promoted to boon-companion upon his accession.

150. On concealing the caliph during the *khuṭba*, see above, n. 99.

151. Al-Musabbiḥī, *Akhbār Miṣr*, p. 66, refers to them as *quwwād al-atrāk wa'l-khadam al-muṣṭanʿa fi'l-silāḥ*, i.e., the commanders of the Turks and the eunuchs upon whom patronage had been bestowed. For further discussion of patronage, see Lev, *State and Society*, p. 88.

152. *Ittiʿāẓ*, vol. 2, 161.

153. Ibn Abi'l-ʿAwwām was a Ḥanbalī jurist. He was appointed chief qadi by al-Ḥākim in 405/1014, with the stipulation that four Ismaʿili jurists attend his court in the event that a case involving Ismaʿili law was heard. Ibn Ḥajar al-ʿAsqalānī (d. 852/1448), *Rafʿ al-ʿiṣr ʿan quḍāt miṣr*, in *The Governors and Judges of Egypt,* ed. Rhuvon Guest, pp. 610–12; *Ittiʿāẓ*, vol. 2, 108–9; al-Musabbiḥī, *Akhbār Miṣr,* p. 10.

154. He is Jaʿfar b. Yūsuf Ibn Abi'l-Ḥusayn, the Kalbid governor of Sicily. He is mentioned only once by al-Maqrīzī (*Ittiʿāẓ*, vol. 2, 99). He ruled Sicily from 388/998 to 410/1019, when he was replaced by his son al-Akḥal. In 415/1025, Jaʿfar and his father Yūsuf retired to Egypt. The Kalbid dynasty is discussed in more detail by Leonard C. Chiarelli, "Sicily during the Fatimid Age" (Ph.D. diss. Utah, 1986), pp. 43–69.

155. Ar. *al-khadam al-muqawwadūn*. Al-Musabbiḥī, *Akhbār Miṣr*, p. 66, names Miʿḍād, Nāfidh, and ʿAnbar. Miʿḍād, a black eunuch, was a particularly honored member of the caliph's court. On him, see Lev, *State and Society*, pp. 74–77.

156. Al-Musabbiḥī, *Akhbār Miṣr*, pp. 80–82.

157. Two weeks later, the black slave troops plundered the grain port of Fustat. On the black slave troops (*'abīd*) and these riots, see Yaacov Lev, "Army, Regime, and Society in Fatimid Egypt, 358–487/968–1094," *IJMES* 19 (1987): 340–42; idem, "The Fāṭimid Army, A.H. 358–427/968–1036 C.E.: Military and Social Aspects," *Asian and African Studies* 14 (1980): 188–90.

158. Masjid Tibr is mentioned by al-Musabbiḥī several times as the destination of the caliph's excursions, usually accompanied by his troops. See al-Musabbiḥī, *Akhbār Miṣr*, pp. 15, 32, 38 (where it is noted that the caliph rode without a parasol with his army and entourage), 45, 46.

159. See al-Musabbiḥī, *Akhbār Miṣr*, pp. 29–30 and Lev, *State and Society*, pp. 75–76.

160. This is a tentative judgment, at best. The sources for the reign of al-Ẓāhir are highly fragmentary. Only one slim volume of the court historian al-Musabbiḥī's (d. 420/1029) chronicle survives, and it covers a period of only about eighteen months. The only year that is documented in detail in al-Maqrīzī's (d. 845/1442) *Itti'āẓ al-ḥunafā'* is 415/1024, corresponding to the surviving volume of al-Musabbiḥī. This situation suggests that only a small part of al-Musabbiḥī's vast history survived into the Mamluk period. The history of al-Musabbiḥī contains detailed information about the textiles and costumes used in Fatimid ceremonies during the reign of al-Ẓāhir. Although such detail scarcely exists for the earlier caliphs, this does not necessarily indicate a lack of ostentatious costuming. Indeed, the reports that al-Ḥākim took to wearing plain clothes, sometimes of wool, at the end of his life may indicate both that elaborate caliphal costuming was the norm and that any deviation was noteworthy. Accounts of earlier ceremonies do not speak with specificity about the costumes, and there is only spotty evidence about insignia of sovereignty. Al-Musabbiḥī's meticulous reports may reflect a personal bias in reporting rather than a significant shift in Fatimid material culture. In any case, a reliable and meaningful chronology of costuming and insignia of sovereignty seems at present to be beyond our reach.

161. *Khiṭaṭ*, vol. 1, 451–52.

162. See ibid.; *Itti'āẓ*, vol. 3, 82–83 (for *'īd*); *Khiṭaṭ*, vol. 1, 432 (for *mawlids*).

163. *Khiṭaṭ*, vol. 1, 452.4 (Ar. *barakat naẓar mawlānā*).

164. *Itti'āẓ*, vol. 3, 61–64.

165. Ibid., 63–64. Compare for year 516/1122, *Khiṭaṭ*, vol. 1, 453.

166. The sermon was delivered from the third step. Cf. the account of Ibn al-Ṭuwayr in *Khiṭaṭ*, vol. 1, 455.32–33, where the chief qadi ascends the minbar to the seventh step. I have not been able to determine the significance of the detail.

167. *Ittiʿāẓ*, vol. 3, 114–15. For another example of the subversion of protocol by political intrigue, see above, chap. 2.

168. Ibn al-Ma'mūn al-Baṭā'iḥī, son of the wazir al-Ma'mūn al-Baṭā'iḥī, has left spectacular descriptions of the clothing, food, and other material goods that appeared in Fatimid ceremonies during the years 515–19/1121–25. See *Khiṭaṭ*, vol. 2, 282.

169. *Ittiʿāẓ*, vol. 3, 83.

170. Ibid., 102.

171. On perfuming, see al-Qāḍī al-Nuʿmān, *Daʿā'im al-islām*, vol. 2, 163ff. It was a praiseworthy custom, an imitation of the custom of the Prophet.

172. The *maqṣūra* was an enclosed chamber in which the caliph prayed at the mosque. On the history of the *maqṣūra* in Egypt, see *Khiṭaṭ*, vol. 2, 250–51; Ibn Khaldūn, *Muqaddimah*, vol. 2, pp. 69–73.

173. *Khiṭaṭ*, vol. 2, 282. In previous years, the costumes were different from one Friday to the next. See accounts of al-Musabbiḥī for the reign of al-Ẓāhir.

174. On these greetings, see chap. 2, above.

175. Both a sign of honor and a gesture of submission. But cf. *Khiṭaṭ*, vol. 1, 451.35; al-Afḍal paid homage in private so that no one could see him. The story should be interpreted in a negative light. What respectable wazir would not wish to make public his submission to the caliph he served? But al-Afḍal was no ordinary wazir.

176. Ibn al-Ṭuwayr describes the dome (*qubba*) as being like a *hawdaj*.

177. Suras 62 and 63; see above.

178. The caliph entered the mosque from the *maʿūna*, which had a door that led to the *qāʿat al-khiṭāba*.

179. Processions to festival prayer are mentioned several times in the letters of al-Mustanṣir to the Sulayḥids. Most of the literary specimens that remain are from the pen of the celebrated scribe Abu'l-Qāsim ʿAli b. Munjib Ibn al-Ṣayrafī. A few are preserved in *Al-Sijillāt al-Mus-*

tanṣiriyya, ed. ʿAbd al-Munʿim Mājid (Cairo, 1954): no. 1 (451/1059), no. 13 (445/1053), both for *ʿīd al-fiṭr*; no. 64 (476/1083) for *ʿīd al-naḥr*.

180. The history of this construction is recounted by Ayman Fu'ād Sayyid, "Al-Qāhira et al-Fusṭāṭ: Essai de reconstitution topographique," vol. 3 (Ph.D. diss., Paris, 1986).

181. Materials were taken from ruins in al-Qaṭā'iʿ to build houses in Cairo, see Sayyid, "Al-Qāhira et al-Fusṭāṭ," vol. 3, p. 509. On Armenians in the army, see William Hamblin, "The Fāṭimid Army during the Early Crusades" (Ph.D. diss., University of Michigan, 1984), pp. 19–27.

182. The *dār al-wakāla* is actually a warehouse for the representative of merchants, see Goitein, *Mediterranean Society*, vol. 1, pp. 186–96.

183. Sayyid, "Al-Qāhira et al-Fusṭāṭ," vol. 3, p. 511.

184. See Caroline Williams, "The Cult of ʿAlid Saints in the Fatimid Monuments of Cairo," *Muqarnas* 1 (1983): 37–52; 3 (1985): 39–60. But see also Christopher Taylor's critique in his *The Cult of the Saints in Late Medieval Egypt* (Ph.D. diss., Princeton, 1989), pp. 31–48.

185. According to the description of Ibn al-Ṭuwayr, see *Ṣubḥ*, vol. 3, 512–15; *Nujūm*, vol. 4, 94–97; *Khiṭaṭ*, vol. 1, 387–88, 451–57.

186. *Khiṭaṭ*, vol. 1, 452 (Ibn al-Ma'mūn) and p. 387 (Ibn al-Ṭuwayr).

187. Both Ibn al-Ma'mūn and Ibn al-Ṭuwayr report this sequence.

188. I assume that this refers to the provincial capitals, as listed in *Ṣubḥ*, vol. 3, 493–94 (Qūṣ, Sharqīya, Gharbīya, Alexandria).

189. This is not in the account of Ibn al-Ṭuwayr; perhaps it is unique to al-Ma'mūn's wazirate.

190. On mounts, see Goitein, *Mediterranean Society*, vol. 4, 261–66 for the common people.

191. Ibn al-Ma'mūn mentions two in particular: "Decked out fair to men is the love of lusts—women, children, heaped-up heaps of gold and silver, horses of mark, cattle and tillage. That is the enjoyment of the present life; but God—with Him is the fairest resort" (Q. 3:14) and "Say: 'O God, Master of the Kingdom, you givest the Kingdom to whom you will, and seize the Kingdom from whom you will, you exalt whom you will, and you abase whom you will; in your hand is the good; you are powerful over everything'" (Q. 3:26). After the parade of horses and various other animals, outfitted in brocades and fine linens and ornamented with gold and silver, the verses are almost an antidote to all of

this deliberate ostentation. The combination of the two verses is particularly interesting. On the one hand, men will be tempted by "lusts"—and the dynasty appeals to that material greed by displaying its wealth in the extreme, as a sign of its power. On the other hand, it is all for naught, because ultimately the fate of the dynasty rests with God. The verses marked a boundary between the ostentatious display of material wealth and the fulfillment of the ritual obligation.

192. On the use of sleeves as pockets, see Goitein, *Mediterranean Society,* vol. 4, p. 161.

193. *Khiṭaṭ*, vol. 2, 453. Many present did not accept that day as the festival. The Isma'ilis determined the date of the fast by astronomical calculations; the Sunnīs reckoned the festival by observation of the new moon.

194. *Khiṭaṭ*, vol. 2, 453. The wazir then went to his own residence and hosted a similar banquet.

195. In both Ibn al-Ma'mūn and Ibn al-Ṭuwayr. On the *maṣṭaba*s of al-ʿAzīz, see above, p. 49.

196. The parasol matched the costume, which is described as *al-thiyāb al-bayāḍ al-muwashshaḥa al-muḥawwama* (white garments embellished with ornamental stripes). For ornamental stripes, see Goitein, *Mediterranean Society*, vol. 4, 113 and n. 28 (where it refers to a cushion).

197. Ibn al-Ṭuwayr: *al-yatīma*; Ibn al-Ma'mūn: *al-jawhar fī mandīlih.*

198. Ibn al-Ma'mūn mentions the staff specifically; Ibn al-Ṭuwayr alludes to it by remarking on the presence of the insignia of sovereignty. (On them, see *Ṣubḥ*, vol. 3, 270, 468).

199. Ar. *al-rahajiyya.* The usage seems to be almost exclusive to Ibn al-Ma'mūn (*Khiṭaṭ*, vol. 1, 452.28, 33; 453.24, 38 and elsewhere.

200. On salutes, see above, chap. 2, on *al-adab fi'l-salām.*

201. Ibn al-Ṭuwayr says that he enters from east of the *muṣallā* unseen, as he does in the Azhar when he prays on Fridays.

202. In Ibn al-Ṭuwayr's account, the curtains contained sura 87 (instead of sura 91) and sura 88 (occasionally 93). Ibn al-Ma'mūn does not mention what was on the curtains. I assume that they contained suras 88 and 91.

203. The text states, "Only those whom the missionary recognized were permitted to enter into his presence," certainly a precaution against Nizārī assassins.

204. Ibn al-Ṭuwayr: wazir and qadi only. Ibn al-Ma'mūn: wazir, qadi, and missionary.

205. Ibn al-Ma'mūn emphasizes how closely guarded he was, clearly a response to the Nizārī threat.

206. Cf. above, on Ramaḍān ceremonies.

207. Ibn al-Ma'mūn: third step. Ibn al-Ṭuwayr: seventh. Cf. the reading of the text of the testamentary designation of ʿAlī (*waṣiyyat ʿalī*) on the festival of Ghadīr Khumm, where the chair (or lectern) of the missionary movement (*kursī al-daʿwa*) is set up with nine stairs (*Khiṭaṭ*, vol. 1, 388–89).

208. Ibn al-Ṭuwayr: *mudarraj*. Ibn al-Ma'mūn: *daʿw*.

209. *Khiṭaṭ*, vol. 1, 454.21

210. Ibid., 455.34ff.

211. Ibid., 407.

212. On *al-muḥawwal*, see ibid., 390–91 (the audience hall of the chief missionary. Ibn al-Ma'mūn does not mention *al-muḥawwal* by name.

213. These castles were common at Fatimid banquets. They were made in the palace kitchens (*dār al-fiṭra*), see ibid., 425. Ibn al-Ṭuwayr describes them (ibid., 388). Are the "plundered" palaces (*quṣūr*) of Ibn al-Ma'mūn's description sugar castles? See also the description of the sugar castles and figurines made for the cutting of the canal (ibid., 479).

214. Ibn al-Ṭuwayr (cited at ibid., 388): the caliph took off his festival costume (*al-thiyāb al-ʿīdīya*) with a *sima* in the turban and dressed in something from the Royal Wardrobe (*khazā'in al-kisawāt al-khāṣṣa*). Ibn al-Ma'mūn (cited at ibid., 455): he took off his costume and gave it to the wazir. On *khilʿa*, see chap. 2, above; *EI2*, s.v. "khilʿa"; *Mediterranean Society*, vol. 4, 11, 184.

215. The term does not appear in Dozy, *Vêtements*, but it is found in Goitein, *Mediterranean Society*, vol. 4, pp. 158, 398. In 516/1122, Ibn al-Ma'mūn described the costume (*kiswa*) of the *ʿīd* for the caliph's procession as follows: *badla khāṣṣ jalīla mudhahhaba thawbuhā muwashshaḥ mujāwam mudhāyal*. It comprised eleven pieces, including the two *lifāfa*s used to wrap it. It was valued at 166 1/2 dinars and required 357 1/2 *mithqāl*s of gold (spun at a cost of 1/8 dinar per *mithqāl*), as well as 2,994 *qaṣaba*s of *dhahab ʿirāqī*. Goitein, *Mediterranean Society*, vol. 4, 166 n. 116 defines a *thawb mudhahhab* as a garment with gold threads. Most *mudhahhab* garments had linen as their base material.

216. Cf. Ibn al-Ma'mūn's description of the costume for Ramaḍān, *Khiṭaṭ*, vol. 2, 282.4–9. The *khilʿa* (robe of honor) of the wazir: *badla mudhahhaba mukmala mawkibiyya* for the first day of Ramaḍān. Is this a *khilʿa* in the same sense? It is the only article listed as such.

217. Ibn al-Ṭuwayr, cited by *Khiṭaṭ*, vol. 1, 388.11–12, under *simāṭ al-fiṭr*.

218. Called thus twice by Ibn al-Ma'mūn for the year 516/1122, cited by ibid., 410.8–9 (*kiswa*) and 452.10 (*hay'at ṣalāt al-ʿīd*). Was this a popular designation? The term *ḥulla* appears rarely in Fatimid texts and then only to designate female clothing (see ibid., 410–11). But Goitein, *Mediterranean Society*, vol. 4, often cites the word *ḥulla* in the meaning of gala costume. It is possible that it was called so popularly because of the large number of costumes distributed to the women of the court.

219. See *EI2* s.v. "ʿīd" and "ḥadjdj."

220. *Khiṭaṭ*, vol. 1, 437.11–14. Compare this to the description of slaughtering, based on legal sources, in *EI2*, s.v. "dhabiḥa."

221. *Khiṭaṭ*, vol. 1, 437.10, 14–15.

222. Ibid., 436.12ff., esp. 15–17. See also on banquets, *Ittiʿāẓ*, vol. 3, 95–96 (516/1122–23); *Khiṭaṭ*, vol. 1, 387–88; *Nujūm*, vol. 4, 97–98; *Ṣubḥ*, vol. 3, 523–24.

The Sābāṭ Gate (*bāb al-sābāṭ*) was a gate of the Western Palace, located at the secret gate (*bāb sirr*) of the Manṣūrī hospital. It is also mentioned for the year 515/1122 (*Khiṭaṭ*, vol. 1, 436.15) and for the celebration of the Festival of Ghadīr Khumm (*Khiṭaṭ*, vol. 1, 458). In 515/1122, Ibn al-Ma'mūn lists 2,561 heads, of which 117 she-camels, 24 cattle, and 20 water buffalo were slaughtered by the caliph at the *muṣallā*, the *manḥar*, and the Sābāṭ Gate. The remaining 2,400 rams were slaughtered by the butchers. This is almost verbatim the account provided by Ibn Abī Ṭayyi (*Khiṭaṭ*, vol. 1, 437.22–25).

223. Compare this to the list of costumes under the rubric Costume Warehouses (*khazā'in al-kisawāt*) for Ibn al-Ma'mūn for the 516/1123 Festival of Fast Breaking. The *kātib al-dast* received a *badla mudhahhaba* of 5 pieces and a sleeve and an *'arḍī* (*Khiṭaṭ*, vol. 1, 411.32–33); the chamberlain (*mutawallī ḥajabat al-bāb*) received a *badla mudhahhaba* (*Khiṭaṭ*, vol. 1, 411.33–34). For the year 515/1122, the *kiswa* consisted of 107 pieces for amirs of the collar and the *muḥannak* eunuchs, the *kātib al-dast* and the *mutawallī ḥajabat al-bāb*, and other servants (*Khiṭaṭ*, vol. 1, 436.14–15).

224. Place for milling wheat, for warehouses of wood and iron. It was located behind the palace, contiguous to the large residence of the

wazir (*dār al-wizāra al-kubrā*). See *Khiṭaṭ*, vol. 1, 444.11–21 (*dār al-manākh al-saʿīd*); *Ittiʿāẓ*, vol. 3, 341; Ibn Mammātī, *Qawānīn al-dawānīn*, ed. A. S. Atiya (Cairo, 1943), p. 353 (in the sense of *al-ahrā'*); *Ṣubḥ*, vol. 3, 475 (storehouses). See also *Khiṭaṭ*, vol. 1, 439.5: *dār al-wizāra*, where it is placed to the south of the Madrasa of Qarāsunqur. This account seems to be the source for Ibn ʿAbd al-Ẓāhir, cited in *Khiṭaṭ*, vol. 1, 437.25–28. The details are almost identical, although some terminology is different.

225. *Khiṭaṭ*, vol. 1, 437.17–19.

226. Meaning, the Ṣulayḥid ruler, see ibid., 437.13.

227. See below, chap. 6, on the festival of Ghadīr Khumm and the sources cited there.

CHAPTER 4

1. For a complete discussion, see A. J. Wensinck, "Arabic New Year and the Feast of Tabernacles," *Verhandelingen der Koninklijke Akademie van Wetenschappen te Amsterdam*, Afdeeling Letterkunde, n.r., 25, no. 2 (1925): 1–41.

2. *Ittiʿāẓ*, vol. 1, 214, 224; *Khiṭaṭ*, vol. 2, 31.

3. *Nujūm*, vol. 4, 79. Marius Canard recognized that it must be a late introduction, but he did not explore the matter further. Canard translated al-Maqrīzī's text with comprehensive annotations in his article "La Procession du nouvel an chez les Fatimides" (*Extrait des Annales de l'Institut d'Études Orientales* 1952: 364–98), an expansion of the earlier work of Inostrantsev (in Russian).

4. *Ittiʿāẓ*, vol. 2, 25. It is possible that such audiences for New Year's greetings were held every year, but I am reluctant to make such an assumption in the absence of other evidence.

5. Ibn al-Ma'mūn's text reads: "The ceremony of greetings [*al-hinā'*] was on the morning of the festival in both the wazir's residence and the caliphal palace. Whoever's custom it was to attend came, and after them the poets attended in ranks" (*Khiṭaṭ*, vol. 1, 445–46).

6. The descriptions of the procession for the New Year are found in the *Khiṭaṭ* under the section on the mint (*dār al-ḍarb*). I will return to this point when discussing the significance of the procession later in this chapter.

7. Compare to the procession route described in greater detail below by Ibn al-Ṭuwayr, where the caliph left the palace through the

Festival Gate, exited from Bāb al-Naṣr, and reentered the city through Bāb al-Futūḥ.

8. That is, to the high-ranking functionaries, the *arbāb al-rusūm*, who lived in Cairo.

9. For summaries of Fatimid administration, see appropriate sections in *EI2*, s.v. "daftar," "dīwān," "Fatimids." More detailed analyses are found in ʿAbd al-Munʿim Mājid, *Nuẓum al-fāṭimiyyīn wa-rusūmuhum fī miṣr* (Cairo, 1973); Hassanein Rabie, *The Financial System of Egypt* (Oxford, 1972); Lev, "Fatimid Vizier Yaʿqub ibn Killis," pp. 237–49; Claude Cahen, *Makhzūmiyyāt: Études sur l'histoire économique et financière de l'Égypte médiévale* (Leiden, 1977); Claude Cahen and Y. Rāghib, *Kitāb al-minhāj fī ʿilm kharāj miṣr li-Abi'l-Ḥasan ʿAlī b. ʿUthmān al-Makhzūmī* (Cairo, 1986).

10. On his career, see Walter J. Fischel, *Jews in the Economic and Political Life of Medieval Islam* (London, 1937); Lev, "Fatimid Vizier Yaʿqub ibn Killis."

11. On the reforms in the monetary system, see Rabie, *Financial System of Egypt*, pp. 162–69.

12. For an erudite and readable discussion of gold trade and minting in West Africa, and its implications for Fatimid gold production, see J. Devisse, "Trade and Trade Routes in West Africa," in M. ElFasi, ed., *Africa from the Seventh to the Eleventh Century*, vol. 3 of *General History of Africa* (Berkeley, 1988), pp. 367–435 (includes maps).

13. Rabie, *Financial System of Egypt*, p. 169.

14. On the other hand, silver supplies had always been problematic for the Fatimids. The silver dirham in the late tenth and early eleventh century had depreciated considerably, apparently due to the difficulty of importing silver from the eastern parts of the Islamic world, on which Egypt had relied. There seems to have been a steady decline in the quality of silver coinage unti the end of the dynasty. Rabie, *Financial System of Egypt*, pp. 166–67 and references there.

15. Cf. Rabie, *Financial System of Egypt*, p. 165; A. S. Ehrenkreutz, "Arabic *Dīnārs* Struck by the Crusaders, A Case of Ignorance or of Economic Subversion," *JESHO* 7 (1964): 167–82.

16. *Khiṭaṭ*, vol. 1, 445; Ehrenkreutz, "Arabic *Dīnārs*," pp. 178–79; A. S. Ehrenkreutz, "Contributions to the Knowledge of the Fiscal Administration of Egypt in the Middle Ages," *BSOAS* 16 (1954): 502–14, esp. 506–9.

17. *Khiṭaṭ*, vol. 1, 445; *Ittiʿāẓ*, vol. 3, 92; Ibn Muyassar, *Akhbār*

Miṣr (Sayyid ed.), p. 92; Ibn Mammātī, *Qawānīn al-dawāwīn*, pp. 331–33; *Subḥ*, vol. 3, 365.

18. Ehrenkreutz, "Contributions," pp. 508–9, citing Ibn Baʿra; Sayyid, "Al-Qāhira et al-Fusṭāṭ," vol. 3, 529–31. For a brief time, the Fatimids also minted coins in the Upper Egyptian city of Qūṣ. See *Ṣubḥ*, vol. 3, 369; *Ittiʿāẓ*, vol. 3, 93.

19. Ehrenkreutz, "Contributions," pp. 510–11; *Khiṭaṭ*, vol. 1, 110.17–19, 445.21; *Ṣubḥ*, vol. 3, 461–62, 482.

20. Ehrenkreutz, "Contributions," p. 519; Sayyid, "Al-Qāhira et al-Fusṭāṭ," vol. 3, p. 531. For a complete discussion of the techniques used in minting, see the treatise of Ibn Baʿra, *Kashf al-asrār al-ʿilmiyya bi-dār al-ḍarb al-miṣriyya*, ed. ʿAbd al-Raḥmān Fahmī (Cairo, 1966). A discussion and partial translation of the manuscript was published by A. S. Ehrenkreutz, "Extracts from the Technical Manual on the Ayyūbid Mint in Cairo," *BSOAS* 15 (1953): 423–47. A nearly complete translation was done by Martin Levey, "Chemical Aspects of the Medieval Arabic Minting in a Treatise by Manṣūr Ibn Baʿra," *Japanese Studies in the History of Science*, supp. 1 (Tokyo, 1971).

21. There is a long and detailed description of the objects that were brought out of the various treasuries in the *Khiṭaṭ*, vol. 1, 445–46; it is abbreviated considerably in the *Nujūm*, and even more in *Ṣubḥ*. But this seems to be the source for much of al-Qalqashandī's information in his separate section on the insignia, *Ṣubḥ*, vol. 3, 468ff. Ibn al-Ṭuwayr designates the arms and parade equipment that were to be given to the various amirs, bodyguards, cavalry, and infantry in the procession. This long list constitutes an important document in the history of material culture for the Fatimid period.

22. Both *Ṣubḥ* and *Nujūm* say this was done in the usual swift manner, but *Khiṭaṭ* notes that the messenger rode a race horse and that his quick pace was contrary to his usual manner. On the basis of other instances in which the wazir was summoned, the reading of the former sources seems to be the better one.

23. These are the positions they took up outside the door of the Gold Hall during the audiences of the caliph. Both were *muḥannak* eunuchs.

24. Cf. the procession to cut the canal in chap. 5, below.

25. On these salutes, see chap. 2, above.

26. These must be the seventy race horses and thirty mules that Ibn al-Ṭuwayr mentions, *Khiṭaṭ*, vol. 1, 447.11ff., which were the *janāʾib*,

the horses led by hand in the caliph's cortege. Their harnesses were all of precious materials: either gold or a mixture of gold and silver inlaid with enamel. The cantles and pommels were also of gold or silver and ornamented with jewels. Around the necks of the horses were gold collars and amber chains and, sometimes, ankle bracelets of gold on their front and hind legs. Instead of leather in the saddles, red, yellow, and other colors of brocade and of siglaton were embroidered in different colors of silk thread. Each mount and its equipment was estimated at a value of one thousand dinars.

27. See the poem of 'Umāra al-Yamanī, who also compares the horses paraded in processions to brides, ibid., 495–96. Horses were also led by hand through the Iwan during the festivities for the Festival of Fast Breaking, ibid., 452.28ff.

28. There seems to be some confusion in the versions at this point. Ibid., 448.6–7, describes the *yatīma* as a large gem, of inestimable value, that is placed in the midst of other, less precious gems arranged in the shape of a horseshoe (*al-ḥāfir*), of red rubies. These are surrounded by tubes of brilliant green emeralds (the term used to describe the color is *zumurrud dhubābī*, "horsefly emerald," referring to the brilliant green body of the horsefly). Canard ("Procession du nouvel an," p. 380 n. 61), believed that al-Qalqashandī erred in *Ṣubḥ*, vol. 3, 469, when he described the *ḥāfir* ornament as a crescent-shaped red ruby, surrounded by emeralds, that was placed on the head of the caliph's horse. But al-Qalqashandī may not have been mistaken, after all. There are two references to a *ḥāfir* in the *Kitāb al-dhakā'ir wa'l-tuḥaf* of Ibn al-Zubayr; both describe a crescent-shaped ornament made of red rubies. But the term *yatīma*, like *farīda* (the singular) is used almost exclusively to describe pearls, according to Marilyn Jenkins; see *EI2*, Supplement, s.v. "djawhar." See also *EI2*, s.v. "hilāl," where it is stated that the crescent or horseshoe as an equine decoration for royal horses goes back to Sassanian times and was known also by the Byzantines. Thus, either interpretation may be correct.

29. It was made of twelve panels (*shawrak*), each measuring a span across at the bottom and 3 1/3 cubits in length. The tops of the panels were very narrow and were attached to a circular rim at the top of the staff. The staff itself was a lance (*qunṭariyya*) made of beechwood and dressed in gold tubes (*anābīb al-dhahab*).

30. Like the staff of the parasol, these lances were dressed in gold tubes.

31. See also *Ṣubḥ*, vol. 3, 468.

32. The lance was in a cover ornamented with rows of pearls

(*manẓūm bi'l-lu'lu'*). The shield, decorated with gold studs (*kawāmikh, kawābij*), was attributed to Hamza b. ʿAbd al-Muṭṭalib.

33. These officials must be identical with the civil and military functionaries, identified by al-Qalqashandī, who served in the capital (*Ṣubḥ*, vol. 3, 478ff.). He lists among the officials of the sword the wazir, commander of the army (*isfahsalār*), porter of the parasol, sword-bearer, lance-bearer, arms-bearering mounted escorts (also known as *al-rikābiyya* or *ṣibyān al-rikāb*, numbering more than two thousand), the prefect of Cairo (who had a special place in the procession), and the prefect of Fustat (who was lower in rank and is not mentioned as having an assigned place in the procession; but cf. the procession to open the canal at the inundation of the Nile, where he has an important role).

The caliph's eunuchs constituted the second category of men of the sword. The highest-ranking eunuchs were known as the *muḥannak* eunuchs, so-called because of the fashion in which they wound their turbans under their chins. They included the turban-winder (*shādd al-tāj*), the master of the audience hall (*ṣāḥib al-majlis*, referred to sometimes as the "master of the curtain"), the messenger, the majordomo, the director of the treasury, the keeper of the register (*ṣāḥib al-daftar*), the bearer of the inkstand, and the officials responsible for the caliph's relatives and for their board. The non-*muḥannak* eunuchs included the commanders of the less-important regiments of the infantry, such as the Āmiriyya and Ḥāfiẓiyya, the black infantry, and the commander of the *ṣibyān al-ḥujar*, the young men who were boarded in the palace.

The men of the pen were divided into religious officials and bureaucratic (*dīwānī*) officials. The religious officials included the chief qadi and the chief missionary (*daʿi*), the market inspector (*muḥtasib*), the supervisor of the treasury, and the lieutenant of the chief chamberlain, as well as the Qur'an reciters. The bureaucratic officials were the heads of the numerous diwans.

34. These were stored in the treasury of parade equipment, the *khizānat al-tajammul*, which was a division of the Arms Treasury. There were nearly one hundred silver staffs (*qaṣaba*s) for the wazir, the amirs, and the commanders of the infantry and the cavalry. They were lances decorated with tubes (*anābīb*) of silver inlaid with gold, to which multicolored *sharb* linen cloths were attached and hung down like drapes. Two pomegranates of "puffed up" (*manfūkh*) gilded silver and crescents in which little bells hung decorated the tops of the staffs. *Khiṭaṭ*, vol. 1, 446.31–34.

The litters (*ʿammariyyāt*) resembled camel-borne litters. They were covered with curtains of red and yellow brocade, *qurqūbī*, and siglaton. Like the staffs, there were about one hundred of them.

35. *Khiṭaṭ*, vol. 1, 446.37ff.

36. The turban (*ʿimāma*) was made of a length of cloth wound around the head with one end or "tail" left hanging down. This tail could sometimes be quite long. Wearing a turban without a tail was considered to be a *bidʿa* (innovation) (*EI*, s.v. "turban"; M. M. Ahsan, *Social Life under the Abbasids* [London and New York, 1979], p. 32; Dozy, *Vêtements*, pp. 307–8 and n. 3 who served in the capital). The *muḥannak* eunuchs were distinguished by wrapping the tail of the turban under their chins (*taḥnīk*), a custom that had been adopted by the caliph al-ʿAzīz (see *EI2*, vol. 5, s.v. "libās").

37. The sword bearer was the only porter required to lower the end of his turban. He was a very high-ranking amir. Although it is not explicitly designated, he must have been one of the amirs of the collar (*al-muṭawwaqūn*) (see *Ṣubḥ*, vol. 3, 478; *Khiṭaṭ*, vol. 1, 448.29).

38. It is remarkable that their porters were already clearly mounted on horseback in the palace, a privilege granted only to the wazir; but even he could not ride into the audience hall on horseback. We might draw the tentative conclusion that these insignia were so closely associated with the person of the caliph that their bearers were considered to be almost like appendages to the objects and, therefore, were allowed a prerogative reserved only to the caliph himself.

39. *Khiṭaṭ* has *ilā jānib al-rāya*—which Canard identified as a misreading of *dābba* ("Procession du nouvel an," p. 389; cf. *Nujūm*: *ilā jānib al-dābba*).

40. Only in *Ṣubḥ*.

41. Compare this to the procession to open the canal, below in chap. 5. During the actual procession, the *muḥannak* eunuchs relinquished their duties to the *rikābiyya*.

42. Ar. *arbāb al-qaṣab* or *al-quḍub al-fiḍḍa*. *Ṣubḥ*, vol. 3, 476 says they carried silver rods that were stored in the *khizānat al-tajammul* (Treasury of Parade Arms). These must have been the bearers, then, of the silver rods described in the inventory of the Treasury of Parade Arms (*Khiṭaṭ*, vol. 1, 446.31–34), and destined for the wazir, the amirs of the ranks, and the commanders of the troops and of the regiments of cavalry and infantry. They were spears dressed with silver tubes (*anābīb*) inlaid with gold. The final two cubits had no tubes, but a number of multicolored fine (*sharb*) linen cloths with embroidered ends that were left hanging were attached to them. The head of the spear was decorated with two "puffed up" (*manfūkh*) gilded silver pomegranates and crescents, in which were hung little bells, which rang when they moved. There were almost one hundred of these rods.

43. There are three versions of this text: *furūʿ al-umarāʾ wa-awlāduhum wa-akhlāṭ baʿḍ al-ʿaskar al-amāthil ilā arbāb al-qaṣab ilā arbāb al-aṭwāq* (*Khiṭaṭ*, vol. 1, 449.28–29); *ajnād al-umarāʾ wa-awlāduhum wa-akhlāṭ al-ʿaskar amām al-mawkib wa-adwān al-umarāʾ yalūnuhum wa-baʿḍahum arbāb al-quḍub al-fiḍḍa min al-umarāʾ thumma arbāb al-aṭwāq minhum* (*Ṣubḥ*, vol. 3, 503); *akhlāṭ baʿḍ al-ʿaskar thumma al-amāthil thumma arbāb al-manāṣib thumma arbāb al-aṭwāq* (*Nujūm*, vol. 4, 88).

44. These arms are listed in the inventory of arms (*Khiṭaṭ*, vol. 1, 446).

45. Ar. *al-janāḥayn al-māddayn*. See George Scanlon, *A Muslim Manual of War* (Cairo, 1961), where it is a technical term used to describe the flanks of an army. The same term is used in the description of the Nile procession. In the rhymed prose letter of the scribe al-ʿAmīdī, describing an unidentified late Fatimid procession, the same term is used (see Paula Sanders, "A New Source for the History of Fāṭimid Ceremonial: The *Rasāʾil al-ʿAmīdī*," *Annales Islamologiques* 25 [1990]: 127–31).

46. Ar. *al-midhabbatayn*. The flywhisks, which were considered as insignia of sovereignty, were always carried by Ṣaqlabīs (who were also designated to assist in carrying the parasol).

47. These do not seem to be included in the inventory of the Arms Treasury. These swords were called "blood swords" (*suyūf al-damm*) because they were used in executions.

48. They are also called *"arbāb al-furanjiyyāt"* in *Nujūm* and *Khiṭaṭ*, but not in *Ṣubḥ*. The *furanjiyyāt* are designated in *Khiṭaṭ*, vol. 1, 446.28 and (for Nile procession) 473.33.

49. I assume that the banners, standards, and litters that had been part of his own procession to the palace earlier in the day were carried in front of him during this procession; they are not mentioned specifically in the description of the procession itself, but they are included in the inventory that precedes it.

50. Canard, "Procession du nouvel an," p. 392 n. 107, says that Inostrantsev took this to mean that the wazir did not want to lose sight of the caliph because of the *baraka* that seeing him conferred. It would have been difficult, with the caliph surrounded not only by the mounted escort, but also followed by more than three hundred armed men, for the wazir to see the caliph. But the "men of the small arms" were almost certainly on foot, making it considerably easier to see the caliph. Furthermore, the wazir, as others in the procession, would certainly have been able to see the parasol carried over the caliph.

51. Ibn al-Ṭuwayr notes that their numbers were so great that their music sounded like thunder. It is easy to understand why drums had been beat in the stables for several days before the procession to accustom the mounts to the noise.

52. A Berber group who were armed generally with only swords and spears. They formed a large part of the Syrian garrisons in the eleventh century and are mentioned first by Nasir-i Khusrau (*Sefer Nameh*, Schefer trans., pp. 124, 138). They had fallen into disfavor during the rule of Badr and al-Afḍal, but seem to have made a comeback under the wazir al-Ma'mūn, who laid out their quarter just outside of Bāb Zuwayla. See B. J. Beshir, "Fatimid Military Organization," *Der Islam* 55 (1978): 39; *Ṣubḥ*, vol. 3, 359; *Khiṭaṭ*, vol. 2, 20.

53. A regiment of black slaves whose quarter bordered on the Ḥusayniyya (another regiment of black slaves) quarter just north of Cairo. See *Khiṭaṭ*, vol. 2, 20–22.

54. The troops recruited by Badr al-Jamalī.

55. Associated originally with the first Fatimid wazir, Yaʿqūb b. Killis (*Khiṭaṭ*, vol. 2, 5, 14).

56. Al-Muʿizz is said to have established an academy in the palace to train soldiers, *Khiṭaṭ*, vol. 1, 443. But under his grandson al-Ḥākim, it was used primarily for training officers. Al-Afḍal had increased the institution after his defeats at the hands of the Crusaders. In the late Fatimid period, there were about five thousand *ḥujariyya*, divided according to age. See Beshir, "Fatimid Military Organization," pp. 47–48.

57. This designation here should probably be interpreted to mean Armenians. See ʿUmāra al-Yamanī, *al-Nukat al-ʿAṣriyya*, ed. Hartwig Derenbourg (Paris, 1897), where Bahram is given the *nisba al-ghuzzī* several times.

58. I have been unable to identify this place precisely. It is not mentioned in the description of the area outside of Bāb al-Naṣr (*Khiṭaṭ*, vol. 2, 138). Numerous mausolea were built there following the death and burial of Badr al-Jamalī in 487/1094, just north of the *muṣallā* (cf. ibid., 463. It then became a popular burial ground for the residents of the Ḥusayniyya quarter just outside of Bāb al-Futūḥ (see ibid., 20–22, 136); the Rayḥāniyya regiment lived there also.

59. The description of the long and short routes is found only in *Ṣubḥ*, vol. 3, 504.

60. *Nujūm* adds "to display his homage to the people" (*li-yuẓhir li'l-nās khidmatihi*).

61. *Ṣubḥ*, vol. 3, 476–77.

62. Ibid., 468. Al-Qalqashandī states that later it was carried by one of the *ʿadl* witnesses, but there is no independent evidence to corroborate this assertion.

63. Ibid., 468: *wa-lahu amīrun min aʿẓam al-umarāʾ*; *Khiṭaṭ*, vol. 1, 403.23.

64. *Ṣubḥ*, vol. 3, 470, 479–80, designates them as those who carry the caliph's arms and also as those who hold the office of *ḥaml al-silāḥ*, where the terms *ṣibyān al-rikāb al-khāṣṣ* and *rikābiyya* are given as synonyms. They are listed in *Khiṭaṭ*, vol. 1, 402, as the last of the pay ranks in the *dīwān al-rawātib*, where their twelve commanders, referred to here as *"muqaddam,"* are called collectively *"aṣḥab rikāb al-khalīfa"* and their monthly salary is put at fifty dinars.

65. *Ṣubḥ*, vol. 3, 482–85, under the discussion of the religious officials of the civilian administration, where al-Qalqashandī quotes Ibn al-Ṭuwayr as saying that the chief judge was not addressed as *qāḍī al-quḍāt*, because that is one of the titles (*nuʿūt*) of the wazir.

66. Ibid., 487–88, under discussion of the registrar's office (*al-tawqīʿ bi'l-qalam al-jalīl*).

67. *Khiṭaṭ*, vol. 1, 401.

68. See Lev, "Army, Regime, and Society," pp. 340–42, for a discussion of the *ʿabīd* prior to al-Afḍal.

69. Hamblin, "Fāṭimid Army," pp. 27–32.

70. Jere L. Bacharach, "African Military Slaves in the Medieval Middle East: The Cases of Iraq (869–955) and Egypt (868–1171)," *IJMES* 13 (1981): 482.

71. Bacharach, "African Military Slaves," pp. 484–85; Lev, "Army, Regime, and Society," p. 349.

72. Bacharach, "African Military Slaves," p. 487.

73. Hamblin, "Fāṭimid Army," pp. 42–47; Beshir, p. 47; Lev, *State and Society*, pp. 100–102.

74. *Khiṭaṭ*, vol. 1, 443–44; Hamblin, "Fāṭimid Army," p. 42.

75. Beshir, "Fāṭimid Army Military Organization," pp. 47–48.

76. See *Ṣubḥ*, vol. 3, 477, where he includes them in the category *khawāṣṣ al-khalīfa*, along with the eunuchs and the *ṣibyān al-khāṣṣ*.

77. Bacharach, "African Military Slaves," pp. 486–87; Hamblin, "Fāṭimid Army," pp. 51–54.

CHAPTER 5

1. For an excellent survey of pre-Christian Nile cults, see Danielle Bonneau, *La Crue du Nil, divinité égyptienne* (Paris, 1967).

2. *Khiṭaṭ*, vol. 1, 64.10–12: *fa-mā yūjad miṣr qāṭiʿ ṭarīq siwāh wa-lā marghūb marhūb illā iyyāh.*

3. *Khiṭaṭ*, vol. 1, 61, on the authority of Ibn Zūlāq (d. 386/996).

4. *Khiṭaṭ*, vol. 1, 60.

5. It is well to remember that the original city of Cairo had been built a considerable distance from the river; the city in the mid-twelfth century was even further from the water: the banks had silted up and the Nile shoreline had moved west.

6. *Khiṭaṭ*, vol. 1, 60, citing Ibn Muyassar.

7. The winter crops were wheat, barley, beans, bittervetch, lentils, flax, chick peas, clover, onions, garlic, and lupin. The summer crops were unripe melons, watermelons, kidney beans, sesame, cotton, sugar cane, colocasia, eggplant, indigo, radishes, turnips, lettuce, and cabbage. For more complete discussion, see Hassanein Rabie, "Some Technical Aspects of Agriculture in Medieval Egypt," in *The Islamic Middle East: 700–1900*, ed. A. L. Udovitch (Princeton, 1981), pp. 59–90; Claude Cahen, "Al-Makhzūmī et Ibn Mammāṭī sur l'agriculture égyptienne médiévale," originally published in *Annales Islamologiques* 11: 141–51 and reprinted in Cahen's *Makhzūmiyyāt*, pp. 179–89. The Arabic text translated and discussed there by Cahen is published in Abu'l-ḥasan ʿAlī b. ʿUthman al-Makhzūmī, *Kitāb al-Minhāğ fī ʿilm Ḫarağ Miṣr*, edited and annotated by Claude Cahen and Yūsuf Rāğib (Cairo, 1986), pp. 2ff. Most of this section is based on these sources.

8. Andrew Watson has argued that the early Islamic period witnessed an agricultural revolution, characterized by the introduction and diffusion of numerous new crops into the Islamic world. This diffusion, stimulated and enhanced by travel, migration, and conquest, was supported at court by kings who established botanical gardens where they cultivated exotic plants, many of them brought as gifts from foreign courts. By the tenth century, Muslim geographers chronicled vast changes in the countryside of their own times. This "green revolution" was possible in large measure because of the introduction of new agricultural techniques, the most important of which was irrigation. See Andrew Watson, *Agricultural Innovation in the Early Islamic World* (Cambridge, 1983); Andrew Watson, "A Medieval Green Revolution: New Crops and Farming Techniques in the Early Islamic World," in *The*

Islamic Middle East, 700–1900, ed. A. L. Udovitch (Princeton, 1981): 29–50. Watson's arguments were called into question by Michael Brett in his review in *BSOAS*, vol. 48 (1985): 126–28.

9. See Rabie, "Technical Aspects," p. 68, based on al-Nābulusī and al-Maqrīzī; Cahen, "Al-Makhzūmī," pp. 148–51.

10. Watson estimates, based on Ibn Mammātī's figures, that the rate fell between one-fifth and one-tenth of output. This is different from other systems of taxation. See *EI2*, s.v. "kharādj"; Claude Cahen, "Contribution à l'étude des impôts dans l'Égypte médiévale," in his *Makhzūmiyyāt*, pp. 22–56.

11. *Khiṭaṭ*, vol. 1, 61; *Ṣubḥ*, vol. 3, 293–94, 297. See Rabie, *Financial system of Egypt*, chap. 3, esp. pp. 73–79.

12. Omar Toussoun, *Mémoire sur l'histoire du Nil*, vol. 8 in *Mémoires présentés à l'Institut d'Egypte* (Cairo, 1925), p. 239.

13. M. b. Aḥmad al-Muqaddasī, *Aḥsan al-taqāsīm*, 2nd ed., ed. M. J. de Goeje [Leiden, 1906], pp. 200ff.

14. See Bonneau, *La Crue du Nil*.

15. *Khiṭaṭ*, vol. 2, 144.

16. Ibid., vol. 1, 71–72 lists nine canals: Minuf, Menha (in the Fayyum), Ashmum Tannah, Sardus, Alexandria, Damietta, Cairo, Abū Munajjā, and Nasiri. *Ṣubḥ*, vol. 3, 297–302, lists only six: Menha, Cairo, Sardus, Alexandria, Sakha, and Abu'l-Munajja. Toussoun, *Mémoire sur l'histoire du Nil*, pp. 195–264, collects and translates numerous sources on the history of the canals.

17. The canal of Abu'l-Munajjā was dug to replace the old canal of Sardus, which had previously supplied water to the Sharqiyya province. The administrator (*mushārif*) of the province was Abu'l-Munajjā, a Jew who dug the new canal at the request of the people. The work was begun, according to al-Maqrīzī, in 506/1112–13, when al-Afḍal sailed in a boat (*markab*), accompanied by the general (*qā'id*) Abū ʿAbd Allāh Muḥammad b. Fātik al-Baṭā'iḥī (later to become the wazir with the honorific title al-Ma'mūn) and his brothers. The troops (*ʿasākir*) marched alongside them on the shore along with local dignitaries (*shuyūkh al-bilād*). Al-Afḍal threw a bundle of reeds (*ḥuzum [min] al-būṣ*) into the water and the Nile boat (*ʿushārī*) followed it until the waves tossed it to the place where they dug the canal. In spite of al-Afḍal's attempts to have the canal named after him, it was always called after Abu'l-Munajjā (even after he fell into disfavor). When al-Ma'mūn became wazir, he initiated an opening of that canal like the opening of the Canal of Cairo.

Al-Ma'mūn built a pleasure palace overlooking the canal (*manẓara*) in which the caliph stayed. The ceremony of cutting the canal of Abu'l-Munajjā continued beyond the fall of the dynasty. Al-Qāḍī al-Fāḍil says that in 577/1181, Saladin rode to open the canal of Abu'l-Munajjā (*fatḥ baḥr abi'l-munajjā*). In 590/1193–94, the canal was cut seven days after the Christian Festival of the Cross (*'īd al-ṣalīb*, on which see *Khiṭaṭ*, vol. 1, 266–67). Al-Qalqashandī reports in *Ṣubḥ*, vol. 3, 303) that the cutting took place on the Festival of the Cross (17 Tūt) but was later switched to Nawruz on 1 Tūt on account of the desires of the people (*ḥirṣān 'alā rayy al-balad*). See *Ṣubḥ*, vol. 3, 300; *Khiṭaṭ*, vol. 1, 71–72, 487–88; on Abu'l-Munajjā, see Goitein, *Mediterranean Society*, vol. 2, 356–57.

18. *Khiṭaṭ*, vol. 1, 71; *Ṣubḥ*, vol. 3, 298–300. A longer and more detailed history of the canal is found in *Khiṭaṭ*, vol. 1, 139–44, under the rubric *khalīj miṣr*.

19. Attributed to al-Kindī in *Ṣubḥ*; reported without attribution in *Khiṭaṭ*. Apparently, the work took about six months.

20. I suspect that this appellation and the direct link between Egypt and the Hijaz that the canal provided might have contributed to Jawhar's choice of a site for the Fatimid palace. Perhaps he thought it an appropriate spot for his master, especially given the eastern ambitions of the dynasty. Al-Maqrīzī records four names for the canal: *khalīj amīr al-mu'minīn* (Canal of the commander of the faithful), khalīj al-qāhira (Canal of Cairo), *al-khalīj al-ḥākimī* (Canal of al-Ḥākim) and *khalīj al-lu'lu'* (Canal of the Pearl [Pavilion]). See *Khiṭaṭ*, vol. 1, 71. The name *al-khalīj al-ḥākimī* appears also in *Raf' al-Iṣr* in al-Kindī, *Kitāb al-wulāt*, p. 599 (citing al-Musabbiḥī). Al-Maqrīzī also reports in *Khiṭaṭ*, vol. 2, 139–40, that the canal was originally known as the *khalīj miṣr* (Canal of Egypt) and was renamed *khalīj al-qāhira* (Canal of Cairo) after the establishment of Cairo. See also W. B. Kubiak, *Al-Fustat: Its Foundation and Early Urban Development* (Cairo, 1987), pp. 118–20, for a summary of the history of the canal.

21. Al-Maqrīzī says, however, that navigation from Fustat to Qulzum continued until the time of the caliph Abu Ja'far al-Manṣūr, when he closed it in order to cut off food supplies from Muḥammad b. 'Abd Allāh, who revolted in Medina in 158/775.

22. Al-Maqrīzī reports, citing al-Musabbiḥī (*Khiṭaṭ*, vol. 1, 143), that in 401/1010–11, the caliph al-Ḥākim prohibited sailing in barges (*qawārib*) along the canal to Cairo and barricaded the gates of Cairo that led to the canal as well as the windows of the houses that over-looked the canal. It must have been common practice to sail from Fustat to Cairo along the canal. Perhaps this sheds some light on another pro-

hibition of the same year, when al-Ḥākim prohibited people from sitting at the gates of Cairo or entering the city.

In *Khiṭaṭ*, vol. 1, 467–468 (under the rubric of *manẓarat al-lu'lu'* [The Pearl Pavilion]), al-Maqrīzī says that this pavilion was the residence of the wazir Barjawān from 388/998 until he was killed in 402/1011–12, at which time al-Ḥākim ordered the pavilion destroyed. This is transmitted on the authority of both al-Musabbiḥī and Ibn Muyassar. It is further reported by Ibn Ḥajar in *Raf' al-iṣr*, p. 599, on the authority of al-Musabbiḥī, that the caliph al-Ḥākim gave a house (*dār*) to the qadi al-Ḥusayn b. 'Alī b. al-Nu'mān on the canal (called there *"al-khalīj al-ḥākimī"*). The qadi used to sail there in a Nile boat (*'ushārī*) during the inundation. His notary witnesses would ride alongside him on horseback on the bank of the canal.

23. *Khiṭaṭ*, vol. 2, 109.20, 146.10–19.

24. Ibid., 109.19–20, 113.32–35. According to al-Maqrīzī, the opening of the canal took place at the Bridge of the Dam (*qanṭarat al-sadd*) in Ayyubid times. This area was still covered with water in Fatimid times, but when the Nile receded, the bridge (*qanṭara*) at the Seven Reservoirs was abandoned and al-Malik al-Ṣāliḥ Najm al-Dīn Ayyūb (r. 637–47/1240–49) built the *qanṭarat al-sadd* in order to get to the Bustān al-Khashshāb on the west side of the canal (*Khiṭaṭ*, vol. 2, 146.10–19). Kubiak, *Al-Fustat*, pp. 44–47, offers a critique of al-Maqrīzī's reconstruction of the history of the Nile in the early Arab period.

25. On these warehouses, see Goitein, *Mediterranean Society*, vol. 1, 187–89.

26. A similar point, to which I shall return below, is made by F. E. Engreen in his article "The Nilometer in the Serapeum at Alexandria" (*Medievalia et Humanistica* 1943: 3–13), when discussing the role of the Nilometer in flood control and its relation to the transition from the pagan cult in Egypt to Christianity.

27. *Khiṭaṭ*, vol. 1, 470, citing Ibn Zūlāq: *"rakaba . . . li-kasr khalīj al-qanṭara"* (the canal of the bridge). Although there are no other references to a *khalīj al-qanṭara* in al-Maqrīzī, I surmise that the reference is to the Banī Wā'il canal. The text states clearly that he rode along the banks of the Nile to Banī Wā'il, and then to Birkat al-Ḥabash, which is also along the Banī Wā'il canal. On Birkat al-Ḥabash, see *Khiṭaṭ*, vol. 2, 152–53.

28. This can only be the defensive trench dug at the time of the Arab conquest of Egypt. According to Kubiak, *Al-Fustat*, p. 86, the eastern part of the trench ran from the Muqattam spur, through the cemeteries, south to Birkat al-Ḥabash.

29. *Itti'āẓ*, vol. 1, 214.

30. Ibid., 275 (s.a. 382 A.H.).

31. Ibid., 283.

32. Ibid., vol. 2, 100. This is quite a low level; perhaps this is the reason the report was recorded by al-Maqrīzī.

33. *Khiṭaṭ*, vol. 1, 470.36–38.

34. He continues by remarking on the drunken behavior of the women, who mingled with the men. The text of *Itti'āẓ*, vol. 2, 132, identifies the occasion as Easter. The text here has *mawkib* for the *Khiṭaṭ*'s *markab*.

35. Nasir-i Khusrau, *Sefer Nameh*, Schefer translation, pp. 136ff.; Thackston translation, pp. 48–51.

36. This seems to refer to the magnificent tent called "al-Qātūl," described below.

37. Nasir-i Khusrau explains *būqalamūn* as an "iridescent cloth that appears of different hues at different times of the day. It is exported east and west from Tennis" (Nasir-i Khusrau, *Sefer Nameh*, Thackston translation, p. 39). Goitein, *Mediterranean Society*, vol. 4, pp. 120, 324, 381 n. 63, translates the term as "chameleon-colored."

38. The *durrā'a* is a wide robe, slit in the front, with long, wide sleeves that expose part of the arm. The garment is worn by both men and women. Brocade *durrā'as* were popular with the Abbasids. See Yedida K. Stillman, *Female Attire of Medieval Egypt* (Ph.D. diss., University of Pennsylvania, 1972), p. 35; *EI2*, 5 s.v. "libās"; Dozy, *Vêtements*, pp. 177–81; Ahsan, *Social Life*, pp. 39–40.

39. This is the only instance in a description of a procession that describes the actions of the onlookers. It is significant that it was left to a traveler to report this fact. The descriptions of the Egyptian historians are written so completely from the point of view of the court that such a fact would naturally have been omitted.

40. These are transmitted only in the *Khiṭaṭ*, vol. 1, 470–75. The descriptions of both Ibn Taghrī Birdī and al-Qalqashandī are based entirely on the history of Ibn al-Ṭuwayr.

41. *Khiṭaṭ*, vol. 1, 470ff. Al-Maqrīzī says that it was built by al-'Azīz.

42. Ibn al-Ṭuwayr: seventy cubits.

43. Ibn al-Ṭuwayr says that it was called thus because a servant had

fallen from the top of its pole and died. Ibn al-Ma'mūn says that it was always set up under the direction of engineers and that the workers hated setting it up because of the danger involved; they wanted to strike one of the smaller tents instead. For a complete history of the tent, see ibid., 418–20, in the description of the Treasury of Tents (*khizānat al-khiyam*). See also Ibn al-Ṭuwayr's description (ibid., 477.18).

44. The term *arbāb al-rutab bi-ḥadrat al-khalīfa* (officials at the capital) is used by Ibn al-Ṭuwayr to designate a pay rank in the *dīwān al-rawātib* (central pay office) (see ibid., 401–2; *Ṣubḥ*, vol. 3, 486ff.). It is the third rank, after the wazir and the retinue (*hawāshī*) of the caliph. The officials listed under this rank and their salaries per month are: head of the chancery (*kātib al-dast al-sharīf*), salary reported as both 120 and 150 dinars (*Khiṭaṭ*, vol. 1, 401.32, 402.21); the scribes serving the head of the chancery, 30 dinars; chief chamberlain (*ṣāḥib al-bāb*), 120 dinars; sword bearer (*ḥāmil al-sayf*), 70 dinars; lance bearer (*ḥāmil al-rumḥ*, 70 dinars; other commanders (*zimām*), 30 to 50 dinars.

45. For the relation between proximity to the caliph and rank, see above, chap. 2.

46. A costly silk textile produced in Qurqūb, in southwestern Iran on the border with Iraq. There are references in the Geniza to Qurqūbī curtains in the trousseaux of Karaite brides; a Qurqūbī *shāshiyya* (long piece of fine cloth to be used for a turban or shawl); and Qurqūbī canopies. See Goitein, *Mediterranean Society*, vol. 4, 121, 196–97, 417 n. 337 (where there are further references).

47. *Khiṭaṭ*, vol. 1, 473 (citing Ibn al-Ma'mūn). The appearance of these figurines in processions seems to be unique to the Fatimids among Islamic dynasties. The Abbasids, also received such things as gifts from foreign rulers, but did not display them. This issue is discussed briefly by Oleg Grabar, "Imperial and Urban Art in Islam: The Subject Matter of Fatimid Art," in *Colloque International sur l'Histoire du Caire* pp. 173–90 (Cairo, 1972); reprinted in *Studies in Medieval Islamic Art* (London, 1976).

48. On *ṭamīm*, see R. B. Serjeant, *Islamic Textiles: Material for a History up to the Mongol Conquest* (Beirut, 1972), pp. 18, 160. The caliph's costume for the cutting of the canal in 415/1024 was made of gold brocade (*ṭamīm mudhahhab*), al-Musabbiḥī, *Akhbār Miṣr,* p. 11.

49. See above, chap. 2, for the comportment of those in attendance at audiences.

50. Ar. *wa-lā yakūn salāmu qarībin minhu wa-khalīlin ghayr al-wazīr illā bi-taqbīl al-arḍ min baʿīd min ghayr dunūw.*

51. They are always the designated bearers of the *midhābb*.

52. This seems to be a reference to the caliph's custom of visiting the treasuries before major processions and choosing the textiles, arms, and other insignia that would appear in a procession. See, *Khiṭaṭ*, vol. 1, 407, under the description of Ibn al-Ṭuwayr of the treasuries.

53. Ibn al-Ṭuwayr specifies that the *muḥannak* eunuchs walked with the caliph until he exited from the palace and then the cortege was organized as it had been for the New Year.

54. I take this to mean that the two rows that had been organized were disbanded and that those present took the places they occupied customarily in audiences.

55. Nor was it carried on the *'īd al-naḥr*.

56. Ar. *mā yajibū min farḍ al-salām*.

57. Ar. *urkhiyat 'adhabatuhu tashrīfan lahu muddata ḥamlihi khāṣṣatan . . . wa-shudda wusṭuhu bi'l-minṭaqa al-dhahab ta'adduban wa-ta'ẓīman li-mā ma'ahu* (*Khiṭaṭ*, vol. 1, 473.25). The sword bearer also lowered the tail of his turban in the New Year's procession. But there the term *dhu'āba* is used instead of *'adhaba*: *urkhiyat dhu'ābatuhu mā dām ḥāmilan* (449.9). The wazir's sons and brothers marched in front of him, each without passing the turban under his chin: *wa-kull minhum murkhā al-dhu'āba bi-lā ḥanak* (449.1) The wazir himself, however, wore his turban (*mandīl*) under his chin in this procession. Canard mentions the lowered tail of the turban in his two articles on Fatimid ceremonial, "Procession du nouvel an," p. 387 n. 86, p. 388 n. 94, and "Ceremonial," p. 382 n. 5.

According to Dozy, *Vêtements*, p. 420, the belt (*minṭaqa*) was always made of silver or gold. See also Serjeant, *Islamic Textiles*, p. 203; Ibn Zubayr, *Kitāb al-dhakhā'ir wa'l-tuḥaf*, ed. M. Ḥamīd Allāh (Kuwait, 1959), pp. 214ff.: one thousand girdles studded with gold (cited by Ahsan, *Social Life*, p. 53).

58. Ar. *lam yakun li'l-khidma al-madhkūra 'adhaba murkhāh wa-lā minṭaqa* (detail in Ibn al-Ma'mun's account).

59. Lev, *State and Society*, p. 94.

60. See R. Dozy, *Supplément aux Dictionnaires Arabes*, vol. 2, 228B and *Vêtements*, pp. 324–26, s.v. "ghunbāz."

61. He is called by Ibn al-Ma'mūn "*mutawallī al-sitr*"; in Ibn al-Ṭuwayr's description of palace audiences, this official is called either *ṣāḥib al-majlis* or *ṣāḥib al-sitr*). He was a eunuch. See above, chap. 2, p. 33.

62. On these gestures, see chap. 2, above.

63. Ar. *fa-radda ʿalayhi bi-kummihi al-salām.*

64. The text does not say that it was done according to rank, but it does specifically state that these officials were the last to dismount. The context makes it clear that it was done according to rank, as does our previous knowledge of the particular honor accorded to these officials.

65. Ibn al-Ṭuwayr says that the wazir had already entered the tent and that the caliph found him waiting at the door of the tent. The wazir walked ahead of him to the throne (*sarīr al-mulk*), where the caliph then dismounted.

66. The city of Jahram in Fars province was famous for its long carpets and wool rugs. Guy Le Strange, *Lands of the Eastern Caliphate* (Cambridge, 1905), pp. 254, 294; Yaʿqūb b. ʿAbdallāh Yāqūt, *Muʿjam al-buldān*, 6 vols., ed. F. Wüstenfeld (Leipzig, 1866–73), vol. 2, 167. I am grateful to Prof. Jerome Clinton, who informed me that Jahram was an important carpet center.

67. Ibn al-Ṭuwayr describes also the way the wazir sat: with his feet "scraping the ground" (*rijlahu tuḥikk*). *Ṣubḥ*, vol. 3, 516 has the dual form *yuḥikkān al-arḍ*.

68. Ibn al-Ṭuwayr states that the *muḥannak* eunuchs surrounded him and the *muṭawwaq* amirs came after them.

69. According to Ibn al-Ṭuwayr, the *arbāb al-rutab* stood in two rows to the side of the throne during the recitation.

70. Ibn al-Ṭuwayr says they were presented by the *ṣāḥib al-bāb*. He names three of these poets: Ibn Jabar, Masʿūd al-dawla b. Jarīr, and Kāfī al-dawla Abu'l-ʿAbbās. It is possible, perhaps, to date Ibn al-Ṭuwayr's account by these names. Al-Qalqashandī did not include these details in *Ṣubḥ*, vol. 3, 516.

71. These details, which are specific to the court of the caliph al-Āmir, are, of course, not in the description of Ibn al-Ṭuwayr.

72. In *Khiṭaṭ*, vol. 1, 402, the workmen in the royal gardens are listed among the employees (*mustakhdamūn*) in Cairo and Fustat (a category that includes the prefects of Cairo and Fustat); they received salaries ranging from five to twenty dinars per month.

73. Compare this with Nasir-i Khusrau's description, where the caliph actually went to the head of the canal and threw a short pike at the dam as a signal to break it. Ibn al-Ṭuwayr notes that one of the *muḥannak* eunuchs, not the wazir, gave the signal.

74. Ibn al-Ṭuwayr does not mention any recitation of the Qur'an or the *takbīr*. He says that drums and trumpets were sounded on the two shores: *wa-yakhdum bi'l-ṭabl wa'l-būq min al-barrayn.*

75. The *'ushārī* was a boat used primarily for river transport. According to Goitein, *Mediterranean Society*, vol. 1, p. 295, men of high standing often owned such boats and used them for travel, but they were also a form of commercial transport. This boat had a small cabin on the deck. Under the Fatimids, the Office of the Fleet (*dīwān al-'amā'ir*) was responsible for building not only warships, but also these Nile boats, which were used to transport grain and were also given to provincial governors. See Lev, *State and Society*, p. 119.

76. In discussing the preparations for the procession, Ibn al-Ma'mūn described the costumes of the captains of the Nile boats: Dimyāṭī linen cloths with Sūsī turbans and red silk wrappers (*al-shiqaq al-dimyāṭī wa'l-manādīl al-sūsī wa'l-fuwaṭ al-ḥarīr al-aḥmar*). The crew (*al-nawātiyya*) wore Alexandrian linen cloths and caps (*al-shiqaq al-iskandarāniyya wa'l-kalūtāt*) (*Khiṭaṭ*, vol. 1, 413.12–13, 472.36–38; Ayman Fu'ād Sayyid, *Nuṣūṣ min akhbār miṣr li-Ibn al-Ma'mūn* [Cairo, 1983], pp. 55, 74). Dozy, *Vêtements,* p. 387, defines the *kalūta* as a cap around which the turban is wound. It is first mentioned in the Fatimid period; in Ayyubid and Mamluk times, it was worn only by high-ranking officials. See the numerous references to the *kalūta* in L. A. Mayer, *Mamluk Costume* (Geneva, 1952), index s.v. "kalaftāh"; *EI2*, s.v. "libās."

77. *Ṣubḥ*, vol. 3, 516; *Khiṭaṭ*, vol. 1, 478.35ff. The lengthy description of this Nile boat is found in the discussion of the procession to perfume the Nilometer, *Khiṭaṭ*, vol. 1, 476.23ff. and *Ṣubḥ*, vol. 3, 513. It had an octagonal cabin made of ivory and ebony (*bayt muthamman min 'āj wa-abnūs*), which consisted of eight panels that were three cubits wide and the height of a grown man. The panels were joined together to form the *bayt* and surmounted by a dome of elegantly crafted wood covered with plates of silver and gold (*al-fiḍḍa wa'l-dhahab*), rendered in *Ṣubḥ* as *al-fiḍḍa al-mudhahhaba.* Ivory was a common material in carving panels of all sizes, see *EI2*, s.v. "'ādj."

78. *Ṣubḥ*, vol. 3, 517, says that there were seven. It adds, to the boats listed by al-Maqrīzī, one called "the green" (*al-akhḍar*).

79. Ar. *al-fiḍḍī.* This may be identical with the *'ushārī* made for the mother of the caliph al-Mustanṣir in 436/1044–45 by Abū Sa'īd Sahl al-Tustarī, known as *al-fiḍḍī.* It required 130,000 dirhems of silver and 2,400 dinars for workmanship, exclusive of the textiles used as curtains and drapes. In the same year, 400,000 dinars were spent on the orna-

mentation and implements for thirty-six Nile boats (Ibn al-Zubayr, *K. al-dhakhā'ir wa'l-tuḥaf*, cited in *Khiṭaṭ*, vol. 1, 479.11ff.).

80. It had been produced by a master carpenter, known as al-Ṣiqillī, and was named after him.

81. Ibn al-Ṭuwayr, cited in *Khiṭaṭ*, vol. 1, 482–83, describing the arsenal (*ṣinā'a*) at Fustat, says that there were fifty Nile boats and twenty other boats, of which ten were for the personal entourage of the caliph. Nasir-i Khusrau counted twenty-one Nile boats, decorated in gold, silver, precious stones, and satin curtains (Schefer translation, p. 142; Thackston translation, p. 51).

82. Ibn al-Ṭuwayr does not mention distribution of any robes of honor.

83. Ar. *badla mandīluhā wa-thawbuhā mudhahhabān wa-thawbān 'attābī wa-siqlāṭūn*. On *'attābī*, see Serjeant, *Islamic Textiles*, Index, s.v. "'Attābī"; Stillman, "Female Attire," p. 21. Siglaton is a heavy damask silk that was popular in the Middle Ages, see S. D. Goitein, *Letters of Medieval Jewish Traders* (Princeton, 1973), p. 77 n. 25.

84. These robes of honor do not seem to have been bestowed by the caliph or the wazir, who had already retired to private chambers in the pavilion. They must have been distributed by some lower-ranking functionary attached to the caliph's court. Had he been an official of real importance, he would have been designated by title or office.

85. The many tents of the *arbāb al-rutab* that were set up just north of "the Killer" (*al-qātūl*), mentioned by Ibn al-Ṭuwayr, but not specifically by Ibn al-Ma'mūn.

86. See *Ṣubḥ*, vol. 3, 516; *Khiṭaṭ*, vol. 1, 479.

87. *Ṣubḥ*, vol. 3, 516, says the *ṣāḥib al-mā'ida* is the equivalent in his own day of the *ustādār*. *Khiṭaṭ*, vol. 1, 402, counts the chief steward among the household servants of the caliph, whose duties include servicing the palace and the pavilions. He received approximately thirty dinars per month.

88. Ar. *shadda fi'l-ṭayāfīr al-wāsi'a fi'l-qawāwīr* (or: *'alayhā al-quwwārāt*) *al-ḥarīr wa-fawquhā al-ṭarrāḥāt al-nafīsa* (see *Ṣubḥ*, vol. 3, 516 [variant in *Khiṭaṭ*, vol. 1, 479.3]). I take the term *shadda* in the sense of a collection of separate items, as in Dozy, *Supplément*, vol. 1, 736b, "*Botte*, assemblage de choses liées ensemble." On the *ṭayfūr* (pl. *ṭayāfīr*), see Goitein, *Mediterranean Society*, vol. 4, p. 146 and nn. 56–57, where he notes that the term is common in the Geniza, but otherwise absent in Arabic dictionaries (but see also Ahsan, *Social Life*, p.

124 n. 448 for references from other sources). On the *quwāra* (round piece), see Goitein, *Mediterranean Society*, vol. 4, p. 384 n. 140, p. 392 n. 40, p. 463 n. 226, where the references refer especially to a covering for a table. I have translated *ṭarrāḥāt* here tentatively as "mats." All of the contemporary usages of the term *ṭarrāḥa* known to me (especially those from the Geniza) are of the *ṭarrāḥa* as a mat upon which one sits or sleeps. Goitein, *Mediterranean Society*, vol. 4, pp. 110–11, 115, describes it as a daybed, in thickness somewhere between the *martaba* and the *maṭraḥ*, and usually made of expensive brocades. Serjeant believes it to be a square carpet (*Islamic Textiles*, pp. 119, 212). In her translation of the sections in *Ṣubḥ al-aʿshā* on Fatimid ceremonies, however, Maryta Espéronnier understands the *ṭarrāḥāt* as covers made of fine cloth (see "Les Fêtes civiles et les cérémonies d'origine antique sous les Fatimides d'Egypte," *Der Islam* 65 [1988]: 46–59). I would suggest, in view of the evidence presented by Goitein and Serjeant, that the *ṭarrāḥāt* here may also be mats, brought along with the trays of food and given to their recipients to sit upon while eating the banquet.

89. *Khiṭaṭ*, vol. 1, 479.6.

90. On this custom of taking food from banquets, and the phrase *al-sharaf wa'l-baraka*, see the discussion of banquets for Ramaḍān and the two festivals, chap. 3, above.

91. Ar. *min jumlat badalāt al-jumaʿ*.

92. Described by Ibn al-Ma'mūn in the long inventory of the Wardrobe Treasury: *badla mawkibiyya ḥarīrī mukmala mindīluhā wa-ṭaylasānuhā bayāḍ* (*Khiṭaṭ*, vol. 1, 413.1–2). The *ṭaylasān*, a shawl-like garment worn over the shoulders and sometimes over the head, was especially popular in Abbasid society, where it was the prescribed costume for jurists and judges. See *EI2*, s.v. "libās"; Ahsan, *Social Life*, pp. 42–43; Hilāl al-Ṣābi', *Rusūm*, Ar. p. 91, Salem translation, p. 74; Dozy, *Vêtements*, pp. 278–80.

93. The text reads, *wa-dakhala min bāb al-khalīfa al-qiblī*. That is, the door of the tent that led directly to the door of the pavilion, the same door from which he had exited earlier when going to *manẓarat al-sukkara* (*Khiṭaṭ*, vol. 1, 474.18).

94. The garden (*bustān*) was surrounded by a wall that was overarched on both sides by orange trees; the branches had grown together and provided shade. They bore fruit simultaneously of two seasons—one ending and the other beginning.

95. In 516/1122, Ibn al-Ma'mūn mentions simply that Ibn Abi'l-Raddād and the captains of the Nile boats received robes of honor and

that many things, too numerous to recount, were taken to the Nilometer for the overnight stay (*al-mabīt*) and the caliph's procession to the pavilion and the Nilometer.

96. The Pearl Pavilion was also called the "Pearl Palace" (*qaṣr al-lu'lu'a*) and was on the canal near Bāb al-Qanṭara. To the east, it had a view of the Kāfūrī Garden; to the west, a view of the canal. At that time, there were no buildings on the west bank of the canal but, rather, magnificent gardens and a lake (see *Khiṭaṭ*, vol. 1, 467.32ff.).

The Gold House was next to the *manẓarat al-ghazāla*, located in al-Maqrīzi's time between Bāb al-Khawkha and Bāb al-Saʿāda, overlooking the canal. The Gold House (*dār al-dhahab*) was built by al-Afḍal, who used to stay there when the caliph stayed in the Pearl Pavilion. According to Ibn ʿAbd al-Ẓāhir, the Gold House was guarded by Wazīrīya troops who were quartered at Bāb al-Saʿāda and by Maṣāmida troops at Bāb al-Khawkha (ibid., 468.3ff. [citing Ibn al-Ma'mūn, *Nuṣūṣ min akhbār miṣr,* ed. Sayyid, pp. 98–100] and 470.10–24).

97. Ibn al-Ṭuwayr notes that the caliph rode in processional costume, but without a parasol or the other insignia that ordinarily accompany him. I have not been able to determine the significance of the procession without a parasol or insignia.

98. This was the main Nile port of Fustat in Fatimid times, where customs dues were collected. It also housed the Office of the Fleet. See Goitein, *Mediterranean Society*, vol. 1, pp. 340–41; vol. 4, p. 34.

99. Identified with *al-dār al-fāḍiliyyāt* by Paul Casanova (*Essai de reconstitution topographique de la ville d'al-Foustat ou Misr* [Paris, 1913–19], pp. 219–22).

100. On the *qaysāriyya*, a building devoted to a single type of commercial transaction, see Goitein, *Mediterranean Society*, vol. 1, p. 194.

101. Thus in the description of the procession route. Elsewhere, in *Khiṭaṭ*, vol. 2, 197, we read that it was the arsenal (*ṣināʿa*) that had the vestibule with the benches. The Office of the Fleet (*dīwān al-jihād* or *dīwān al-ʿamā'ir*) was also located at the arsenal. No one was permitted during the Fatimid era to enter there mounted except the caliph and the wazir, who rode through there on the day of the opening of the canal (which is confirmed in Ibn al-Ṭuwayr's description of the cutting of the canal), when the caliph and wazir crossed from there to the Nilometer. This brief account of the arsenal appears to conflate the two processions, one to perfume the Nilometer and the other to open the canal. There seems to be some confusion here. The arsenal was not the site of the opening of the canal. Ibn al-Ṭuwayr clearly states that the procession route for the opening of the canal was the same as that of the perfuming,

except for the fact that the caliph did not actually enter the streets of Fustat at the Khashshābīn; he took the route on the shore—it would seem, in the direction of the *manẓarat al-sukkara.*

ʿAbbadānī mats, manufactured in the southern Iranian city of ʿAbbadān, are frequently mentioned in the Geniza. They were apparently copied in Egypt and other countries. The ʿAbbadānī mats were stronger than regular mats; fine mats had designs. See Goitein, *Mediterranean Society*, vol. 4, 128.

102. Casanova, *Reconstitution*, p. 221 n. 2, amends the Būlāq text from al-Suyūfiyyīn to al-Suyūriyyīn. On al-Suyūriyyīn, see ibid., pp. 224–27.

103. This residence was built by al-Afḍal in 501/1107–8. He occupied it instead of the *dār al-wizāra* ("Seat of the Wazirate") adjacent to the palace in Cairo. *Dār al-mulk* faced the Nilometer, located at the southern tip of Rawda Island. After the death of al-Afḍal, it became one of the caliph's pleasure pavilions. See ibid., pp. 103–4.

104. Ar. *sutūr dabīqī mulawwana.* This detail is reported in the description of the perfuming (*takhlīq*) for the year 518/1124. On the meaning of the term *mulawwana*, fabric of different colors, see Goitein, *Mediterranean Society*, vol. 4, p. 113 and n. 30.

105. According to Ibn al-Ma'mūn, in 517/1123, the investiture of the robe of honor (*khilʿa*) took place on the same day; Ibn al-Ṭuwayr, however, says that it occurred early the following day.

106. Ar. *badla mudhahhaba wa-thawb dabīqī ḥarīrī.* For an explanation of the term *dabīqī ḥarīrī*, see Goitein, ibid., Appendix D, passim.

107. I am uncertain how to translate this term. Serjeant, *Islamic Textiles*, p. 107, has a single reference to *ṭayālisa muḳawwara*, which he translates tentatively as "ṭailasans which are made with hollows (. . . i.e., possibly with some kind of raised pile or embroidery which gave the appearance of hollows?)." Ibn al-Ṭuwayr also notes this piece of costuming specifically, and a white costume with gold threads, as well as cloths of various materials: siglaton, superior quality (*khazz*) silk, and *dabīqī* linen. On the term *khazz*, see Goitein, *Mediterranean Society*, vol. 1, pp. 337, 454.

108. Ibn al-Ṭuwayr says in one place that the *mabīt* was in the *miqyās* and in another that it was in the Mosque of the Nilometer. Ibn al-Ma'mūn designates only the Nilometer, but we might assume from the description of the occasion as well as the list of participants that it took place in all cases in the Mosque of the Nilometer.

109. According to Ibn al-Ṭuwayr. Ibn al-Ma'mūn, on the other

hand, mentions the professors and the witnesses, but not the Qur'an readers. I assume, however, that they attended in his day, as well.

110. Jawhar bestows a robe of honor on him in 360/970–71, before al-Muʿizz's arrival (*Ittiʿāẓ*, vol. 1, 129); robes of honor in 363/973–74 and 364/974–75, during reign of al-Muʿizz (*Ittiʿāẓ*, vol. 1, 215, 224); in 399/1008–9, reign of al-Ḥākim (*Ittiʿāẓ*, vol. 2, 76).

111. William Popper, *The Cairo Nilometer: Studies in Ibn Taghri Birdi's* Chronicle of Egypt (Berkeley, 1951), p. 85, maintains that the ceremony was instituted sometime around the beginning of the twelfth century and notes that the first record is the account of Ibn al-Ma'mūn for 516/1122.

112. For a complete history of this and other Nilometers, see Popper, *Cairo Nilometer.*

113. See Popper, *Cairo Nilometer*, p. 25.

114. The flood occurred in 481/1088: *fa-halakat al-zurūʿ wa'l-ghilāt wa'l-makhāzin min kathrat al-mā'* (*Nujūm*, vol. 5, 128). Is this what inspired the letter from a worried father in Salonica to his son in Egypt, in which he wrote: "My boy Ismaʿīl, I was informed in the year 48 [1087–88] about the inundation of the Nile. I was terrified and had no rest either by day or by night. For God's sake, make an effort and write me about your well-being . . ." (T-S Arabic Box 53, f. 37, translated in Goitein, *Mediterranean Society*, vol. 5, 440 and n. 126).

115. See Popper, *Cairo Nilometer*, pp. 50–56.

116. Popper, *Cairo Nilometer*, p. 55, citing Marcel, *Déscription d'Egypte.*

117. Ibn Taghrībirdī cites *Mirāt al-zamān*, attributing to it the demise of the Seljuq Malikshāh and the murder of his wazir Niẓām al-mulk, *Nujūm*, vol. 5, 134. Ibn Khaldūn treats it in his discussion of astrology in the *Muqaddimah*, vol. 2, 213: "There occurs the conjunction of the two unlucky planets [Saturn and Mars], in the sign of Cancer once every thirty years. It is called *ar-rābiʿ* [the fourth]. The sign of Cancer is the ascendant of the world. It is the detriment of Saturn and the dejection of Mars. This conjunction strongly indicates disturbances, wars, bloodshed, the appearance of rebels, the movement of armies, the disobedience of soldiers, plagues, and drought. These things persist, or come to an end, depending on the luck or ill luck [prevailing] at the time of conjunction [of the two unlucky planets]."

118. On shipping seasons, see Goitein, *Mediterranean Society*, vol. 1, pp. 316–17.

119. This point is discussed in a different context by A. L.

Udovitch, "Merchants and *Amīrs*: Government and Trade in Eleventh Century Egypt," *Asian and African Studies* (1988): 53–72.

120. For details, see *Khiṭaṭ*, vol. 1, 468ff.

CHAPTER 6

1. The variants to this short but pithy text are seemingly innumerable, and the discussion that it engendered is seemingly inexhaustable. The history of the event is recounted in summary form in *EI2*, s.v. "Ghadīr Khumm." References to the *ḥadīth* literature may be found in A. J. Wensinck, *A Handbook of Early Muhammadan Tradition* (Leiden, 1927), s.v. "ghadīr khumm."

2. Al-Qāḍī al-Nuʿmān considered the *waṣiyya* as the equivalent of an oath of allegiance (*bayʿa*): "What *bayʿa* could be more certain [*akīd*] than this *bayʿa* and *wilāya*?" See *Daʿā'im al-islām*, vol. 1, 20.

3. The different versions of the circumstances surrounding the death of Muḥammad were used to support various claims to political authority in the Islamic community. They therefore present complicated problems of interpretation. For a discussion of the Prophet's death in the context of early Abbasid historiography, see Jacob Lassner, *Islamic Revolution and Historical Memory* (New Haven, 1986), pp. 15–19; also Mottahedeh, *Loyalty and Leadership*, pp. 7ff.

4. In the writings of al-Mu'ayyad fi'l-dīn al-Shīrāzī, chief missionary under the caliph al-Mustanṣir, the *farā'iḍ* also include holy war (*jihād*).

5. *Daʿā'im al-islām*, vol. 1, 14.

6. Ismaʿilis interpreted the Qur'anic verse, "Your friend is only God and His Messenger and the believers who perform the prayer and pay the alms, and bow them down" (5:55) to mean both that God had imposed the duty of *walāya* and that this duty was bound up with the other religious duties. The rest of the verse reads, "Whoever makes God his friend, and His Messenger, and the believers—the party of God, they are the victors." The refrain of the Prophet's speech at Ghadīr Khumm, imploring God to befriend those who are ʿAlī's friends, etc., so reminiscent of this half of the verse, must have had much resonance for those living at a time when one knew the Qur'an and much of the hadith by heart. See *Daʿa'im al-islām*, vol. 1, 14–16.

7. Ar. *amrun amaranī bihi rabbī wa-ʿahdun ʿahidahu ilayya wa-amaranī an uballighakumuhu ʿanhu* (ibid.).

8. In *Al-Majālis al-Mu'ayyadiyya, majlis* 6, the missionary al-Mu'ayyad fi'l-dīn al-Shīrāzī, states that allegiance to the Prophet (*walāyat al-rasūl*) is like "the center (*markaz*) around which the circle of the religious duties revolves."

9. "Knowing the imam is the perfection of belief," *Al-Majālis al-Mustanṣiriyya*, p. 25, cited in Makarem, *Political Doctrine of the Ismailis*, p. 14.

10. See also Makarem, *Political Doctrine of the Ismailis*, p. 26 (Ar. text pp. 8–9 [time of al-Ḥākim]); *al-Majālis al-Mu'ayyadiyya, majlis* no. 6 (time of al-Mustanṣir).

11. *Da'ā'im al-islām*, vol. 1, 20.

12. Ibid., 25.

13. 'Izz al-dīn Ibn al-Athīr, *Al-Kāmil fi'l-tarīkh,* vol. 9 (Beirut, 1965–67), 407, s.a. 352.

14. *Khiṭaṭ*, vol. 1, 389.6; *Itti'āẓ*, vol. 1, 142.

15. This is a typical Shi'i practice (*Khiṭaṭ*, vol. 2, 340.6; al-Maqrīzī does not identify his source; perhaps it was Ibn Zūlāq).

16. M. Kamil Hussein, "Shiism in Egypt before the Fatimids," Islamic Research Association, series no. 11, vol. 1 (1948) (Oxford, 1949).

17. Ibn al-Athīr, *Al-Kāmil fi'l-tarīkh,* vol. 9, 110, s.a. 389; Abu'l-Faraj Ibn al-Jawzī, *Al-Muntaẓam fī ta'rīkh al-mulūk wa'l-umam*, 6 vols. [= vols. 5–10] (Hyderabad, 1938–40), vol. 7, 206, s.a. 389, where he adds that the people visited the grave of Mus'ab b. al-Zubayr just as the grave of Ḥusayn was visited.

18. *Itti'āẓ*, vol. 1, 273, 276, 280, 284 for the years 381/992, 382/993, 383/994, 384/995; vol. 2, 24, 74, 91 for the years 389/999, 398/1008, 402/1012.

19. The *munshidūn* are singers of religious music, particularly songs in praise of the Prophet and the imam. They came to be a fundamental element in Sufi ceremonies in Egypt. Earle H. Waugh has published a study of the *munshidūn* in modern Egypt, *The Munshidīn of Egypt: Their World and Their Song* (Columbia, S.C., 1989).

20. *Khiṭaṭ*, vol. 1, 389.

21. *Itti'āẓ*, vol. 2, 67 and *Khiṭaṭ*, vol. 1, 431.

22. *Itti'āẓ*, vol. 2, 168 and al-Musabbiḥī, *Akhbār Miṣr*, p. 85. Note that this is only a few days after the *'abīd* (black slaves) had plundered

the banquet for the Sacrificial Festival (*simāṭ al-ʿīd*), *Ittiʿāẓ*, vol. 2, 167. Even nineteen years after ʿAbd al-ʿAzīz b. al-Nuʿmān's injunction against public Shiʿi practices that might antagonize a largely Sunni population, it was still in force and noted by al-Musabbiḥī, although al-Maqrīzī, writing several hundred years later, did not deem this fact worth transmitting.

23. *Ittiʿāẓ*, vol. 2, 79.

24. After 415/1025, a century passes without a report of the celebration of Ghadīr Khumm. But for the year 516/1122–3, we have the detailed report by the historian Ibn al-Ma'mūn al-Baṭā'iḥī, who chronicled his father's wazirate under al-Āmir. Like all of the descriptions of Ibn al-Ma'mūn, this one emphasizes the role of the wazir, who had become the real ruler of the Fatimid state during the years of Badr and al-Afḍal, a change that was reflected in ceremonial as well as in titulature.

25. *Khiṭaṭ*, vol. 1, 436.1, 15.

26. See *Daʿā'im al-islām*, section on festival prayer (*ṣalāt al-ʿīd*), where women are encouraged to seek husbands on the Sacrificial Festival.

27. The wardrobe (*kiswa*) is described by Ibn al-Ma'mūn under the section on *ʿīd al-naḥr* in *Khiṭaṭ*, vol. 1, 436.22–23.

28. The Arabic text designates this by the term *al-khuṣūṣ*, not the *ʿumūm*. It is possible that, following a common Ismaʿili usage of *ʿumūm* to mean non-Ismaʿilis, the phrase means "Ismaʿilis, not non-Ismaʿilis," but the sense here seems to be those attached to the court, as opposed to the general public.

29. The *manẓara* must be the belvedere over the Gold Gate (*bāb al-dhahab*), cf. *Khiṭaṭ*, vol. 1, 452, under *ṣalāt al-ʿīd*.

30. Ar. *khilʿa mukammala min badalāt al-naḥr*. According to the inventory list for the wardrobe (*kiswa*) of 516/1122, the caliph's costume for the procession consisted of a suit (*badla*) comprising eleven pieces. Of these, two pieces are described as robe (*thawb*), but no color is indicated. Red was a royal color, so it might be concluded that the suit itself was that color. See *Khiṭaṭ*, vol. 1, 410–13, reproduced in Sayyid, *Nuṣūṣ min akhbār miṣr*, pp. 48–55.

31. On *niʿma*, see Mottahedeh, *Loyalty and Leadership*, pp. 73–79. Such benefits carried with them the obligation of gratitude and loyalty.

32. This is not a gate of the palace but, rather, a private door within the palace used only by the caliph.

33. Ibn al-Ma'mūn consistently uses the term *muqri'ūn* for Qur'an reciters, instead of the more common *qurrā'* or *qurrā' al-ḥaḍra.*

34. The caliph ordered music to be played in the streets and at the gates of the palaces, and issued new clothes to the armies. The Iwan was decorated with tapestries and various gold and silver ornaments brought from the treasuries. After two weeks of celebration, the *'aqīqa* ceremony was held. The ram for the *'aqīqa* sacrifice was covered with embroideries and silver collars. An elaborate banquet was laid out with fruits brought from the provinces of the Fayyūm, Qalyūbiyya, and Sharqiyya, and gold dinars were thrown to those in attendance. S. M. Stern, "Succession to the Fatimid Imam al-Āmir, the claims of the later Fatimids to the Imamate, and the rise of Ṭayyibī Ismailism," *Oriens* 4 (1951): 196–97, reports these celebrations as part of his evidence for the historical reality of the infant al-Ṭayyib. The account, based on Ibn Muyassar's *Akhbār Miṣr* (Massé ed., p. 72), is also reported by al-Maqrīzī (*Itti'āẓ*, vol. 3, 128). As Stern notes (p. 197), this is "not the special pleading of a dogmatic theologian defending his doctrines, but the straightforward entry of an annalist recording, in the manner usual in such works, a great public occasion. . . One can see little grounds for impugning the evidence of such a text."

35. Ibn Muyassar, *Akhbār Miṣr* (Massé ed., p. 74; Sayyid ed., p. 113) simply states, "When al-Āmir was killed, al-Ḥāfiẓ concealed the matter of the child born to al-Āmir that year." Al-Maqrīzī does not mention the later concealment of al-Ṭayyib's birth or his disappearance at all.

We may ask why the account of the child's birth was even retained in the official histories of the Fatimid caliphate when it implicitly contradicted the claim of al-Ḥāfiẓ to the imamate. The account of Ibn Muyassar and al-Maqrīzī is probably based upon the lost chronicle of Ibn al-Muḥannak (d. 549/1154). Stern discusses all of the evidence, including the problematic accounts in Syrian, Yemenī, and Ṭayyibī sources, in "Succession," pp. 197–202. The fact that the matter-of-fact account of al-Ṭayyib's birth was retained by Mamluk historians has no particular significance. The Mamluks were unconcerned with the internal disputes of the Fatimid house. The one exception to this is the Mamluk reconstruction of the Nizārī schism. The Mamluk historians had an identifiably Musta'lian perspective on this issue.

36. Stern asserts that 'Abd al-Majīd was never the regent for al-Ṭayyib, whose claim was discounted from the very beginning of al-Ḥāfiẓ's tenure.

37. *Itti'āẓ*, vol. 3, 137.

38. *Ibid.*, 141. The unnamed child is *not* to be identified with al-

Ṭayyib. Such incidental references provide powerful evidence that, as Stern says, the claims of al-Ṭayyib were discounted almost immediately after al-Āmir's death.

39. See ibid., 111–12 for the account of the murder of the male progeny of al-Afḍal and his brothers. According to this account, Abū ʿAlī was the sole survivor, spared only because he was considered to be too sickly to pose a threat.

40. We do not really know why. Perhaps his support in the palace was too firm or Abu Ali's support within the army was too fragile.

41. Stern notes that this was to fill the vacuum left by the extinction of the Fatimid line. But the more complete account of ibid., 140–41 (which was unavailable when Stern wrote his article) throws new light on the matter. Al-Maqrīzī reports (on unknown authority) that Kutayfāt was a zealous Twelver who was pressed by a powerful Twelver faction in the army to display the Twelver *madhhab* openly. They were, finally, successful. He introduced the Twelver call to prayer (*adhān*), struck dirhems in the name of the Expected One, and had the *khuṭba* pronounced in his own name on Fridays. This version contradicts the assertion of Ibn Taghrī Birdī (*Nujūm*, vol. 5, 239) that Abū ʿAlī was a Sunnī like his father.

42. *Ittiʿāẓ*, vol. 3, 146, reports that a second *bayʿa* was taken to al-Ḥāfiẓ (clearly in his capacity as regent) when the unnamed child whose birth was prophesized in al-Āmir's dream arrived. But he also reports that this child's birth was concealed and that he was killed. This is clearly *not* the infant al-Ṭayyib, whose birth and designation was reported in such detail in ibid., 128 and who is not mentioned again by al-Maqrīzī. What can we make of these textual complications, which carry the story of al-Ṭayyib's birth, the dream prophesy of al-Āmir, and the killing of the unnamed infant heir without attempting to resolve any of the contradictions between the various versions?

They are the remnants of two distinct historiographical traditions that Mamluk historians, writing from a distance of several hundred years, were unable to distinguish. The straightforward account of al-Ṭayyib's birth reflects the Ṭayyibī claim that al-Āmir had designated this child as his heir to the imamate; however, the Mamluks did not incorporate later Ṭayyibī arguments about the child's occultation in the Yemen. Perhaps this is because the birth of al-Ṭayyib was included in official Fatimid histories, whereas his disappearance after al-Ḥāfiẓ declared his regency in the name of an unborn child was not. Al-Ṭayyib, at that point, simply disappeared from official Fatimid historiography.

The stories of the dream prophesy and the later fate of the child in whose name al-Ḥāfiẓ ruled as regent are the contributions of the Ḥāfiẓī historiographical tradition. While we may wonder why an official Ḥāfiẓī history would have reported the murder of this child, an event not likely to enhance the claims of al-Ḥāfiẓ to the imamate, the story does provide further evidence for Stern's assertion that al-Ḥāfiẓ never assumed the regency for al-Ṭayyib; his claims as regent were, from the beginning, based on the dream-prophesy and the expected birth of the child. Although not all of the complications of these versions can be resolved, they do point to the unmistakable influence of an incipient Ḥāfiẓī historiography.

It is not surprising that the Mamluk historians retained all of these stories uncritically. Al-Maqrīzī and the Mamluk authors seem to have preserved stories from different phases in the development of Ḥāfiẓī historiography that represent different arguments and rhetorical strategies. They transmitted these versions, giving each of them equal weight, apparently untroubled by the contradictory nature of the claims that each of them made, and certainly unaware of what Jacob Lassner has called the "stratigraphy of historical traditions." (See Lassner, *Islamic Revolution and Historical Memory*, pp. 3–36, for a far-reaching discussion of similar historiographical problems of the early Abbasid period.) It is likely that Mamluk authors, knowing of the birth of al-Ṭayyib, *assumed* that he was identical with the unnamed child of whom Fatimid historians were speaking. At the very least, they probably conflated the child al-Ṭayyib and the child mentioned in the dream. A Fatimid audience, of course, would have understood that this second child was not identical to al-Ṭayyib.

43. See *Khiṭaṭ*, vol. 1, 357.14–15, 390.1–10 (full details), and 490.36–491.4. The festival was celebrated without a procession in the Iwan, which was still decorated with the furniture and drapes from the Festival of Ghadīr Khumm. The audience hall known as *al-muḥawwal* was also decorated. A *martaba* was set up close to the windcatcher (*bādhanj*) and the military and civilian officials of the state gathered at the Royal Entrance (*bāb al-mulk*) next to the grilled loge (*shubbāk*). The caliph rode mounted to the audience hall and dismounted at the door. His personal entourage (*al-khawāṣṣ*) stood before him as he sat on the *martaba*. In front of him, two rows of men extended to the door of the audience hall (*bāb al-majlis*). The *kursī al-daʿwa*, covered with a Qurqūbī cloth, was set up opposite this door and various high-ranking amirs stood around it. Then the chief judge (*qāḍī al-quḍāt*) stepped up on the minbar and took a notebook from his sleeve that contained texts of stories of "Relief after Adversity" (*faraj baʿd al-shidda*). He read various stories of the prophets and kings until he got to al-Ḥāfiẓ. The chief judge wore a fine suit of clothes that had been prepared specially for him (*badla mumayyaza*) and received fifty dinars.

Gaston Wiet, *Matériaux pour un Corpus inscriptionum arabicarum*, in Mémoires publiés par les membres de l'Institut Français d'Archéologie Orientale, vol. 52 (Cairo, 1930), p. 87, also discusses the festival.

44. Ibn Muyassar, *Akhbār Miṣr* (Massé ed.), p. 63. Al-Maqrīzī says Rabīʿ I (*Ittiʿāẓ*, vol. 3, 146); in *Nujūm*, Ibn Taghrī Birdī, quoting Ibn Khallikan, gives no date.

45. Translation based partially on Stern. Cf. *Nujūm*, vol. 5, 238–39. Proclamation preserved in *Ṣubḥ*, vol. 9, 291–97.

46. S. M. Stern, "Succession," pp. 209–10.

47. For a full discussion of the rhetoric of this proclamation and its implications for Fatimid historiography, see Paula Sanders, "Claiming the Past: Ghadīr Khumm and the Rise of Ḥāfiẓī Historiography in Late Fāṭimid Egypt," *Studia Islamica* 75 (1992): 81–104.

48. See *EI2*, s.v. "Ascalon," as well as *Ṣubḥ*, vol. 3, 347, and *Khiṭaṭ*, vol. 1, 427–30.

49. The lamentations and banquets on ʿĀshūrā also were moved to the new *mashhad* (see *Khiṭaṭ*, vol. 1, 431).

50. See the explanation of the *makān* of the wazir—i.e., the place in the palace where he mounted and dismounted—in the discussion of the New Year's procession.

51. Ibn al-Ṭuwayr adds that his back was turned toward the residence of what was the Residence of Fakhr al-Dīn Jahārakis (d. 608/1211), a contemporary of Ibn al-Ṭuwayr. It is worth noting that in al-Maqrīzī's day the same place was known as Dār al-Quṭbiyya and later al-Māristān al-Manṣūrī (see ibid., 433 and *Khiṭaṭ*, vol. 2, 379–80. Thus, the remark is not a gloss from al-Maqrīzī, as one might first suspect; it is transmitted from Ibn al-Ṭuwayr himself—a small, but important piece of evidence for the authenticity of the text that al-Maqrīzī transmitted.

CHAPTER 7

1. Cited in *Khiṭaṭ*, vol. 1, 495–96.

SELECTED BIBLIOGRAPHY

FATIMID, AYYUBID, AND MAMLUK SOURCES

al-ʿAbbāsī, al-Ḥasan b. ʿAbd Allāh. *Athār al-uwal fī tartīb al-duwal.* Bulaq, n.d.

Aḥmad b. Yaʿqūb. *Al-Risāla fi'l-imāma* (The political doctrine of the Ismaʿilis]. Edited and translated by Sami Makarem. New York, 1977.

ʿAlī Mubārak. *al-Khiṭaṭ al-tawfīqiyya al-jadīda.* Reprint. Cairo, 1969.

al-ʿAmidī, *Rasā'il al-ʿAmīdī,* Princeton University Library, Yahuda Collection, no. 1877 (Cat. 4365).

al-Āmir bi-aḥkām Allāh [Fatimid caliph]. *Al-Hidāyatu'l-Amiriyya.* Edited by A. A. A. Fyzee. Islamic Research Association Series, no. 7. Oxford, 1938.

Ibn al-Athīr [d. 1233]. *Al-Kāmil fi'l-tarīkh.* 13 vols. Beirut, 1965–67.

Ibn Aybak al-Dawādārī [d. 1335]. *Kanz al-durar wa-jāmiʿ al-ghurar.* Vol. 6, *Al-Durra al-muḍiyya fī akhbār al-dawla al-fāṭimiyya.* Edited by Ṣalāḥ al-Dīn al-Munajjid. Cairo, 1961.

Ibn Baʿra. *Kashf al-asrār al-ʿilmiyya bi-dār al-ḍarb al-miṣriyya.* Edited by ʿAbd al-Raḥmān Fahmī. Cairo, 1966.

Ibn Duqmāq, Ibrāhīm b. M. [d. 1406]. *Kitāb al-intiṣār li-wāsiṭat ʿiqd al-amṣār* (Description de l'Egypte). Vols. 4, 5. Edited by Karl Vollers. 1893. Reprint. Beirut, n.d.

Ibn al-Furāt, M. b. ʿAbd al-Raḥīm [d. 1405]. *Tarīkh al-duwal wa'l-mulūk.* Vol. 4, pt. 1. Edited by H. M. al-Shammāʿ. Basra, 1967.

Ibn Ḥammād b. ʿAlī [d. 1230]. *Akhbār mulūk banī ʿUbayd* (Histoire des rois ʿObaidides). Edited and translated by M. Vonderheyden. Algiers-Paris, 1927.

Ibn Hāni'. *Dīwān.* Edited by Zāhid ʿAli. Cairo, 1933.

Ibn Ḥawqal, Abu'l-Qāsim. *K. ṣūrat al-arḍ.* 2nd ed., edited by J. H. Kramers. Leiden, 1938–39.

Ibn Mammātī. *Qawānīn al-dawāwīn.* Edited by A. S. Atiya. Cairo, 1943.

Ibn al-Ma'mūn al-Baṭā'iḥī. *Passages de la Chronique d'Egypte d'Ibn al-Ma'mūn.* Edited by Ayman Fu'ād Sayyid. Cairo, 1983.

Ibn Khaldun. *The Muqaddimah.* Translated by Franz Rosenthal. 3 vols. New York, 1958.

Ibn al-Muqaffaʿ, Sawīrus [d. 1000]. *Ta'rīkh baṭārika al-kanīsa al-*

miṣriyya (History of the patriarchs of the Egyptian church). Vol. 2, pt. 3, edited and translated by Aziz Suryal Atiya et al., Cairo, 1959.

———. *Ta'rikh baṭārika al-kanīsa al-miṣriyya* (History of the patriarchs of the egyptian church). Vol. 3, pt. 1, edited and translated by Antoine Khater and O. H. E. KHS-Burmester. Cairo, 1968.

Ibn Muyassar, M. b. ʿAli [d. 1278]. *Akhbār Miṣr* (Annales d'Egypte). Edited by H. Massé. Cairo, 1919.

———. *Akhbār Miṣr*. Edited by Ayman Fu'ād Sayyid. Cairo, 1981.

Ibn Saʿīd, ʿAlī b. Mūsā [d. 1274 or 1286]. *K. al-mughrib fī ḥulā al-maghrib*. Vol. 4, edited by Knut L. Tallquist. Leiden, 1899.

———. *al-Nujūm al-zāhira fī ḥulā ḥaḍrat al-qāhira*. Edited by Ḥusayn Naṣṣār. Cairo, 1970.

Ibn al-Ṣayrafī, Abu'l-Qāsim ʿAlī b. Munjib [d. ca. 1155]. *Al-Ishāra ilā man nāla al-wizāra*. Edited by ʿAbd Allāh Mukhliṣ. Cairo, 1924–25. Also published in *BIFAO* 25 (1925): 49–112; 26 (1926): 49–70.

———. "Code de la chancellerie d'état" (Qanūn dīwān al-rasā'il). Translated by Henri Massé. *BIFAO* 9 (1914): 65–119.

———. *Qanūn dīwān al-rasā'il*. Edited by Alī Bahjat. Cairo, 1905.

Ibn Taghrī Birdī, Abu'l-Maḥāsin [d. 1470]. *Al-Nujūm al-zāhira fī mulūk miṣr wa'l-qāhira*. 12 vols. Cairo, 1929–55.

Ibn Ẓāfir al-Azdī, Abu'l-Ḥasan ʿAlī [d. 1216]. *Akhbār al-duwal al-munqaṭiʿa: La section consacrée aux Fatimides*. Edited by A. Ferré. Cairo, 1972.

Ibn al-Zubayr. *Kitāb al-dhakhā'ir wa'l-tuḥaf*. Edited by M. Hamid Allah. Kuwait, 1959.

Ibn Zūlāq, al-Ḥasan b. Ibrāhīm. *K. akhbār Sībawayh al-miṣrī*. Edited by M. Ibrāhīm Saʿd and Ḥusayn al-Ḍīb. Cairo, n.d.

Idrīs ʿImād al-dīn b. al-Ḥasan. *ʿUyūn al-akhbār wa-funūn al-athār*. Vols. 4–6. Edited by Muṣṭafā Ghālib. Beirut, 1973–78.

[al-Jahiz?] *K. al-tāj fī akhlāq al-mulūk*. Edited by Ahmed Zaki Pasha. Cairo, 1914.

———. *Le Livre de la couronne*. (K. al-tāj fī akhlāq al-mulūk). Translated by Charles Pellat. Paris, 1954.

al-Jūdharī, Abū ʿAlī Manṣūr. *Sīrat al-ustādh jūdhar (Jawdhar)*. Edited by M. Kāmil Ḥusayn and M. ʿAbd al-Hādī Shaʿīra. Cairo, 1954.

———. *Vie de l'ustadh Jaudhar* (Sīrat al-ustādh jūdhar [Jawdhar]). Translated by Marius Canard. Algiers, 1958.

al-Kindī. *Kitāb al-wulāt wa-kitāb al-quḍāt*. Edited by Rhuvon Guest. Beirut, 1908.

al-Makhzūmī, Abu'l-ḥasan ʿAlī b. ʿUthmān [d. 1189]. *Kitāb al-minhāj fī ʿilm kharāj miṣr*. Partial edition by Claude Cahen and Y. Rāghib. Cairo, 1986.

al-Malījī, Abu'l-Qāsim ʿAbd al-Ḥakīm b. Wahb. *Al-Majālis al-mustanṣiriyya*. Edited by M. Kāmil Ḥusayn. Cairo, [1947].

al-Maqrīzī, Taqī al-dīn [d. 1442]. *Itti'āẓ al-ḥunafā bi-akhbār al-a'imma al-fāṭimiyyīn al-khulafā*. Vol. 1, edited by Jamāl al-dīn al-Shayyāl. Cairo, 1967.

———. *Itti'āẓ al-ḥunafā bi-akhbār al-a'imma al-fātimiyyīn al-khulafā*. Vols. 2 and 3, edited by M. Ḥilmī M. Aḥmad. Cairo, 1971–73.

———. *K. ighāthat al-umma bi-kashf al-ghumma*. Edited by M. M. Ziyāda and Jamāl al-dīn al-Shayyāl. Cairo, 1940.

———. "Le traité des famines de Maqrizi" (K. ighāthat al-umma bi-kashf al-ghumma). Translated by G. Wiet. *JESHO* 5 (1962): 1–90.

———. *Kitāb al-mawā'iẓ wa'l-i'tibār bi-dhikr al-khiṭaṭ wa'l-athār*. 2 vols. Būlāq, 1853. Reprint. Beirut, n.d.

al-Mu'ayyad fi'l-dīn al-Shīrāzī, Abū Naṣr Hibat Allāh. *Dīwān*. Edited by M. Kāmil Ḥusayn. Cairo, 1949.

———. *Al-Majālis al-Mu'ayyadiyya*. Vols. 1 and 3. Edited by Muṣṭafā Ghālib. Beirut, 1974–84.

———. *Sīrat al-mu'ayyad fi'l-dīn dā'ī al-du'āt*. Edited by M. Kāmil Ḥusayn. Cairo, 1949.

al-Muqaddasī [al-Maqdisī], M. b. Aḥmad. *Aḥsan al-taqāsīm*. 2nd ed. Edited by M. J. de Goeje. Leiden, 1906.

al-Musabbiḥī, al-Amīr al-Mukhtār 'Izz al-mulk b. Aḥmad [d. 1029]. *Akhbār Miṣr* [Tome Quarantième de la Chronique d'Egypte de Musabbiḥī]. Edited by Ayman Fu'ād Sayyid and Thierry Bianquis. Cairo, 1978.

al-Mustanṣir billāh, Abū Tamīm Ma'add. *Al-Sijillāt al-mustanṣiriyya*. Edited by A. M. Mājid. Cairo, 1954.

Nasir-i Khusrau [d. after 1087). *Nāṣer-e Khosraw's Book of Travels* (Safarnāma). Translated by W. M. Thackson, Jr. New York, 1986.

———. *Sefer Nameh: Relation des voyages de Nasiri Khosrau en Syrie, en Palestine, en Egypte, en Arabie et en Perse* (Safar-nāma). Translated by Charles Schefer. Paris, 1881.

al-Nu'mān b. Muḥammad, al-Qāḍī Abū Ḥanīfa b. M. [d. 974]. *Da'ā'im al-islām wa-dhikr al-ḥalāl wa'l-ḥarām wa'l-qaḍāya wa'l-aḥkām*. Edited by A. A. A. Fyzee. 2 vols. Cairo, 1951–60.

———. *K. al-himma fī adab ittibā' al-a'imma*. Edited by M. Kāmil Ḥusayn. Cairo, n.d.

———. *K. al-majālis wa'l-musāyarāt*. Edited by al-Ḥabīb al-Faqī, Ibrāhīm Shabbūḥ, and Muḥammad al-Ya'lāwī. Tunis, 1978.

———. *Risālat iftitāḥ al-da'wa*. Edited by Farhat Dachraoui. Tunis, 1975.

———. *Ta'wīl al-da'ā'im*. Edited by M. Ḥasan al-A'zamī. 3 vols. Cairo, 1967–72.

al-Qalqashandī, Aḥmad b. 'Alī [d. 1418]. *K. Ṣubḥ al-a'shā fī ṣinā'at al-inshā*. 14 vols. Cairo, 1913–19.

al-Ṣābi', Hilāl [d. 448/1056]. *The Rules and Regulations of the 'Abbasid Court*. Translated by Elie A. Salem. Beirut, 1977.

———. *Rusūm dār al-khilāfa*. Edited by Mikhā'īl 'Awwād. Baghdad, 1964.

al-Shayyāl, Jamāl al-dīn, ed. *Majmū'at al-wathā'iq al-fāṭimiyya*. Vol. 1. Cairo, 1965.

al-Ṭurṭūshī. *Sirāj al-mulūk wa'l-khulafā' wa-minhaj al-wulāt wa'l-wuzarā'*. Cairo, n.d.

'Umāra b. 'Alī al-Ḥakamī. *Yaman, Its Early Medieval History* (Ta'rīkh al-Yaman). Edited and translated by Henry C. Kay. London, 1892.

al-Walīd, 'Alī b. Muḥammad. *Tāj al-'aqā'id*. Edited by 'A. Tāmir. Beirut, 1967.

al-Yamanī, M. b. M. "L'autobiographie d'un chambellan du Mahdī 'Obeidallāh le Fāṭimide." (Sīrat al-ḥājib Ja'far b. 'Alī). Translated by M. Canard. *Hespéris* 39 (1952): 279–324.

———. *Sīrat al-ḥājib Ja'far b. 'Alī*. Edited by W. Ivanow. *Bulletin of the Faculty of Letters, University of Egypt* 4, pt. 2 (1936), Arabic section: 107–33.

———. *Sīrat al-ḥājib Ja'far b. 'Alī*. Translated by W. Ivanow. In *Ismaili Tradition Concerning the Rise of the Fatimids*, pp. 184–223. London, 1942.

STUDIES

Assaad, Sadik A. *The Reign of al-Hakim bi Amr Allah (386/996–411/1021): A Political Study*. Beirut, 1974.

Bacharach, Jere L. "African Military Slaves in the Medieval Middle East: The Cases of Iraq (869–955) and Egypt (868–1171)." *IJMES* 13 (1981): 471–95.

Berchem, Max von. *Materiaux pour un corpus inscriptionum arabicarum*. (Mémoires de la Mission Archéologique Française au Caire), vol. 19. Cairo, 1894–1903.

Beshir, B. J. "Fatimid Military Organization." *Der Islam* 55 (1978): 37–56.

Bianquis, Thierry. "La prise de pouvoir par les Fatimides en Égypte." *Annales Islamologiques* 11 (1972): 49–108.

Bierman, Irene. *Writing Signs*. Forthcoming.

Bloom, Jonathan Max. "Meaning in Early Fatimid Architecture: Islamic Art in North Africa and Egypt in the Fourth Century A.H. (Tenth century A.D.)." Ph.D. diss., Harvard, 1980.

———. "The Mosque of al-Hakim in Cairo." *Muqarnas* 1 (1982): 15–36.

Bonneau, Danielle. *La Crue du Nil, Divinité Égyptienne*. Paris, 1967.

Bousquet, G.-H. *Les grandes pratiques rituelles de l'Islam*. Paris, 1949.

Brunschvig, Robert. "Fiqh fatimide et histoire de l'Ifriqiya." *Etudes Islamologique*. Vol. 1, pp. 63–69. Paris, 1969.

Cahen, Claude. "L'Administration financière de l'armée fatimide d'après al-Makhzūmī." *Makhzūmiyyāt*, pp. 155–74. Leiden, 1977.

———. "Histoires coptes d'un cadi médiévale." *BIFAO* 59 (1960): 133–50.

———. *Makhzūmiyyāt: Études sur l'histoire économique et financière de l'Égypte médiévale*. Leiden, 1977.

———. "Quelques chroniques anciennes relatives aux derniers Fatimides." *BIFAO* 37 (1937–38): 1–27.

———. "Un texte inédit relatif au Ṭirāz égyptien." *Arts Asiatiques* 11 (1965): 165–68. Reprinted in *Makhzūmiyyāt*, pp. 190–93.

———. "Un traité financier inédit d'époque fatimide-ayyubide." *JESHO* 5, no. 2 (1962), 139–59. Reprinted in *Makhzūmiyyāt*, pp. 1–21.

Canard, Marius. "Le Cérémonial fatimite et le cérémonial byzantin: Essai de comparaison." *Byzantion* 21 (1951): 355–420.

———. "Fatimids." *Encyclopaedia of Islam*. New ed. Vol. 2, pp. 850–62.

———. "L'Impérialism des Fatimides et leur propagande." *Annales de l'Institut d'Etudes Orientales de la Faculté des Lettres d'Alger* 6 (1942–47): 156–93. Reprinted in M. Canard, *Miscellanea Orientalia*, London, 1973.

———. "La Procession du nouvel an chez les Fatimides." *Extrait des Annales de l'Institut d'Études Orientales* 1952: 364–98.

Casanova, Paul. *Essai de reconstitution topographique de la ville d'al-Foustat ou Misr*. Paris, 1913–19.

Chelhod, Joseph. *Le sacrifice chez les arabes*. Paris, 1955.

Cohen, Mark R. *Jewish Self-Government in Medieval Egypt: The Origins of the Office of Head of the Jews, ca. 1065–1126*. Princeton, 1980.

Colloque international sur l'histoire du Caire. Cairo, 1972.

Creswell, K. A. C. *The Muslim Architecture of Egypt*. Vol. 1, Ikhshids and Fatimids. Oxford, 1952.

Dachraoui, Farhat. *Le Califat fatimide au maghreb, 296–365 H./909–975 J.-C.: Histoire politique et institutions*. Tunis, 1981.

Daftary, Farhad. *The Ismāʿīlīs: Their History and Doctrines*. Cambridge, 1990.

Dozy, R. *Dictionnaire détaillé des noms des vêtements chez les Arabes*. Amsterdam, 1845. Reprint. Beirut, n.d.

———. *Supplément aux Dictionnaires Arabes*. 2 vols. Leiden, 1881.

Ehrenkreutz, A. S. "Arabic *Dīnārs* Struck by the Crusaders: A Case of Ignorance or of Economic Subversion." *JESHO* 7 (1964): 167–82.

———. "Contributions to the Knowledge of the Fiscal Administration of Egypt in the Middle Ages." *BSOAS* 16 (1954): 502–14.

———. "The Crisis of *Dīnār* in the Egypt of Saladin." *JAOS* 71 (1956): 178–84.

———. "Extracts from the Technical Manual on the Ayyūbid Mint in Cairo." *BSOAS* 15 (1953): 423–47.

Ess, Josef van. *Chiliastische Erwartungen und die Versuchung der Göttlichkeit: Der Kalif al-Ḥākim (386–411 H.).* Heidelberg,1977.

Fischel, Walter J. *Jews in the Economic and Political Life of Medieval Islam.* London, 1937.

Fyzee, Asaf A. A. "Qadi an-Nu'man, the Fatimid Jurist and Author." *JRAS* (1934): 1–32.

———. "The Study of the Literature of the Fatimid Da'wa." In *Arabic and Islamic Studies in Honor of Hamilton A. R. Gibb*, edited by G. Makdisi, pp. 232–49. Leiden, 1965.

Geertz, Clifford. *Islam Observed.* Chicago, 1968.

———. *Negara: The Theatre State in Nineteenth-Century Bali.* Princeton, 1980.

Goitein, S. D. "Cairo: An Islamic City in the Light of the Geniza Documents." In *Middle Eastern Cities*, edited by Ira Lapidus, pp. 80–96. Berkeley and Los Angeles, 1969.

———. "Formal Friendship in the Medieval Near East." *Proceedings of the American Philosophical Society* 115, no. 6 (1971): 484–89.

———. *A Mediterranean Society: The Jewish Communities of the Arab World as Portrayed in the Documents of the Cairo Geniza.* 5 vols. Berkeley and Los Angeles, 1967–88.

———. "Prayers from the Geniza for Fatimid Caliphs, the Head of the Jerusalem Yeshiva, the Jewish Community and the Local Congregation." In *Studies in Judaica, Karaitica and Islamica*, edited by Sheldon R. Brunswick, pp. 47–58. Ramat-Gan, Israel, 1982.

Grabar, Oleg. *Ceremonial and Art at the Umayyad Court.* Ph.D. diss., Princeton University, 1954.

———. "Notes sur les cérémonies umayyades." In *Studies in Memory of Gaston Wiet*, pp. 51–60. Edited by Miriam Rosen-Ayalon. Jerusalem, 1977.

Grunebaum, G. E. von. *Medieval Islam.* Chicago, 1945.

Guest, A. R. "The Foundation of Fustat and the Khittas of that Town." *JRAS* (1907): 49–83.

———. "A List of Writers, Books, and other Authorities Mentioned by El Maqrizi in His Khitat." *JRAS* (1902): 103–25.

Hamblin, William. "The Fāṭimid Army during the Early Crusades." Ph.D. diss., University of Michigan, 1984.

Hamdani, Abbas. "The Dā'ī Ḥātim Ibn Ibrāhīm al-Ḥāmidī (d. 596 H./1199 A.D.) and his book *Tuḥfat al-Qulūb.*" *Oriens* 23–24 (1970–1971): 258–300.

———. "Evolution of the Organisational Structure of the Fāṭimī Da'wah." *Arabian Studies* 3 (1976): 85–114.

———. "The Ṭayyibī-Fāṭimid Community of the Yaman at the Time of the Ayyūbid Conquest of Southern Arabia." *Arabian Studies* 7 (1985): 151–60.

Hamdani, Abbas, and de Blois, F. "A Re-Examination of al-Mahdī's Letter to the Yemenites on the Genealogy of the Fatimid Caliphs." *JRAS* (1983): 173–207.

al-Hamdānī, Ḥusain F. "The Letters of al-Mustanṣir bi'llāh." *BSOAS* 7 (1934): 307–24.

Ḥasan, Ḥasan Ibrāhīm. *Ta'rīkh al-dawla al-fāṭimiyya*. Cairo, 1957.

Hodgson, Marshall G. S. *The Order of Assassins; the Struggle of the Early Nizārī Ismā'īlīs against the Islamic World*. The Hague, 1955.

Hussein, M. Kamil. "Shiism in Egypt before the Fatimids." *Islamic Research Association*, series no. 11, vol. 1 (1948): 73–85. Oxford, 1949.

Ivanow, W. *Ismaili Tradition Concerning the Rise of the Fatimids*. Bombay, 1942.

———. "The Organization of the Fatimid Propaganda." *Journal of the Bombay Branch of the Royal Asiatic Society* n.s. 15 (1939): 1–35.

Kahle, P. "Die Schätze der Fatimiden." *ZDMG* 14 (1935): 329ff.

Kay, H. C. "Al-Kahira and Its Gates." *JRAS* (1882): 229–45.

Kister, M. J. "'You Shall Only Set Out for Three Mosques': A Study of an Early Tradition." *Le Muséon* 82 (1969): 173–96. Reprinted with additional notes in M. J. Kister, *Studies in Jāhiliyya and Early Islam*. London, 1980.

Lambton, Ann K. S. *State and Government in Medieval Islam*. Oxford, 1981.

Lane, Edward W. *Manners and Customs of the Modern Egyptians*. London, 1836. Reprint. New York, 1973.

Lapidus, Ira M. "Knowledge, Virtue, and Action: The Classical Muslim Conception of *Adab* and the Nature of Religious Fulfillment in Islam." In *Moral Conduct and Authority: The Place of Adab in South Asian Islam*, edited by Barbara Daly Metcalf, pp. 38–61. Berkeley, 1984.

Lev, Yaacov. "Army, Regime, and Society in Fatimid Egypt, 358–487/968–1094." *IJMES* 19 (1987): 337–66.

———. "The Fāṭimid Army, A.H. 358–427/968–1036 C.E.: Military and Social Aspects." *Asian and African Studies* 14 (1980): 165–92.

———. "The Fāṭimid Imposition of Ismā'īlism on Egypt (358–386/969–996)." *ZDMG* 138, no. 2 (1988): 315–17.

———. "The Fatimid Vizier Ya'qub ibn Killis and the Beginning of the Fatimid Administration in Egypt." *Der Islam* 58, pt. 2 (1981): 237–49.

———. *State and Society in Fatimid Egypt*. Leiden, 1991.

Levey, Martin. "Chemical Aspects of the Medieval Arabic Minting in a Treatise by Manṣūr Ibn Ba'ra." *Japanese Studies in the History of Science*, supp. 1. Tokyo, 1971.

Lewis, Bernard. *The Assassins: A Radical Sect in Islam*. London, 1967.

———. "An Interpretation of Fatimid History." In *Colloque sur l'histoire du Caire (1969)*. pp. 287–95. Cairo, 1972.

———. *Islam from the Prophet Muhammad to the Conquest of Constantinople*. 2 vols. New York and Oxford, 1974.

———. *The Origins of Isma'ilism: A Study of the Historical Background of the Fāṭimid Caliphate*. Cambridge, 1940.

Lopez, R. S. "The Silk Industry in the Byzantine Empire." *Speculum* 20 (1945): 1–42. Reprinted in R. S. Lopez, *Byzantium and the World around It: Economic and Institutional Relations*. London, 1978.

Mājid [Magued], 'Abd al-Mun'im. "Aṣl ḥafalāt al-fāṭimiyyīn fī miṣr." *Ṣaḥīfat al-ma'had al-miṣrī li'l-dirāsāt al-islāmiyya fī Madrid* 2, no. 1–2 (1954), Arabic section: 253–57.

———. *Nuẓum al-fāṭimiyyīn wa-rusūmuhum fī miṣr*. 2 vols. Cairo, 1973.

———. "La personnel de la cour fatimide en Égypte." *Ann. Fac. of Arts 'Ain Shams* 3 (1955): 147–60.

Meinardus, Otto F. *Christian Egypt: Ancient and Modern*. Cairo, 1965.

———. *Chrisian Egypt: Faith and Life*. Cairo, 1970.

Mez, Adam. *The Renaissance of Islam*. Translated by K. Bakhsh and D. S. Margoliouth. Patna, 1937.

Mottahedeh, Roy P. *Loyalty and Leadership in an Early Islamic Society*. Princeton, 1980.

Poonawala, Ismail K. *Biobibliography of Ismā'īlī Literature*. Malibu, 1977.

Popper, William. *The Cairo Nilometer: Studies in Ibn Taghri Birdi's Chronicle of Egypt*. University of California Publications in Semitic Philology, vol. 12, 1951.

al-Qadi, Wadad. "An Early Fāṭimid Political Document." *Studia Islamica* 48 (1978): 71–108.

Rabie, Hassanein. *The Financial System of Egypt*. Oxford, 1972.

———. "Some Technical Aspects of Agriculture in Medieval Egypt." In *The Islamic Middle East, 700–1900*, edited by A. L. Udovitch, pp. 59–90. Princeton, 1981.

Ravaisse, P. *Essai sur l'histoire et sur la topographie du Caire d'apres Maqrizi (Palais des califes fatimids). Mémoires de la Mission Archéologique Française au Caire, 1881–1884*, vol. 1, pt. 3 and vol. 3, pt. 4. Paris, 1887–90.

Sachedina, Abulaziz Abdulhussein. *Islamic Messianism: The Idea of the Mahdi in Twelver Shi'ism*. Albany, N.Y., 1981.

Salmon, Georges. *Etudes sur la topographie du Caire: La Kal'at al-kabch et la Birkat al-fil*. Cairo, 1902.

Sanders, Paula. "From Court Ceremony to Urban Language: Ceremonial in Fatimid Cairo and Fusṭāṭ." In *The Islamic World from Classical to Modern Times*, edited by C. E. Bosworth, Charles Issawi, Roger Savory, and A. L. Udovitch, pp. 311–21. Princeton, N.J., 1989.

———. "A New Source for the History of Fāṭimid Ceremonial: The *Rasā'il al-ʿAmīdī.*" *Annales Islamologiques* 25 (1990): 127–31.

Sayyid, Ayman Fu'ād. "Al-Qāhira et al-Fusṭāṭ: Essai de reconstitution topographique." 3 vols. Ph.D. diss., University of Paris, 1986.

Scanlon, George. *A Muslim Manual of War.* Cairo, 1961.

Serjeant, R. B. *Islamic Textiles: Material for a History up to the Mongol Conquest.* Beirut, 1972.

Shoshan, Boaz. "On Costume and Social History in Medieval Islam." *Asian and African Studies* 22 (1988): 35–51.

Sourdel, D., "Questions de Cérémonial ʿAbbaside." *Revue des Etudes Islamiques* 1960: 121–48.

Stern, S. M. "Cairo as the Centre of the Ismāʿīlī Movement." *Colloque* 1969: 437–50. Reprinted in S. M. Stern, *Studies in Early Ismaʿilism,* pp. 234–56. Jerusalem [Leiden], 1983.

———. "The Epistle of the Fatimid Caliph al-Amir (al-Hidāya al-Amiriyya)—its Date and Purpose." *JRAS* 1950: 20–31. Reprinted in S. M. Stern, *History and Culture in the Medieval Muslim World.* London, 1984.

———. *Fāṭimid Decrees: Original Documents from the Fāṭimid Chancery.* London, 1964.

———. "Heterodox Ismāʿīlism at the time of al-Muʿizz." *BSOAS* 17 (1955): 10–33. Reprinted in S. M. Stern, *Studies in Early Ismaʿilism,* pp. 257–88. Jerusalem [Leiden], 1983.

———. *History and Culture in the Medieval Muslim World.* London, 1984.

———. "Ismāʿīlīs and Qarmatians." In *L'elaboration de l'Islam,* edited by Claude Cahen, pp. 99–108. Paris, 1961. Reprinted in S. M. Stern, *Studies in Early Ismāʿīlism,* pp. 289–98. Jerusalem [Leiden], 1983.

———. *Studies in Early Ismāʿīlism.* Jerusalem: [Leiden], 1983.

———. "The Succession to the Fatimid Imam al-Amir, The Claims of the Later Fatimids to the Imamate, and the Rise of Ṭayyibī Ismailism." *Oriens* 4 (1951): 193–255. Reprinted in S. M. Stern, *History and Culture in the Medieval Muslim World.* London, 1984.

Stillman, Norman A. "Charity and Social Service in Medieval Islam." *Societas* 5 (1975): 105–15.

Toussoun, Omar. "Mémoire sur l'histoire du Nil." In *Mémoires de l'Institut d'Egypt,* vol. 8, pp. 195–264. Cairo, 1925.

Trexler, Richard. "Ritual Behavior in Renaissance Florence: The Setting." *Medievalia et Humanistica,* n.s. no. 4 (1973): 125–44.

Tyan, E. *Institutions de droit publique musulmane.* 2 vols. Paris, 1954–56.

Udovitch, A. L. "Formalism and Informalism in the Social and Economic Institutions of the Medieval Islamic World." In *Individualism and conformity in classical Islam*, edited by Amin Banani and Speros Vryonis, Jr., pp. 61–81. Wiesbaden, 1977.

Watson, Andrew. *Agricultural Innovation in the Early Islamic World.* Cambridge, 1983.

———. "A Medieval Green Revolution: New Crops and Farming Techniques in the Early Islamic World." In *The Islamic Middle East, 700–1900*, edited by A. L. Udovitch, pp. 29–50. Princeton, 1981.

Wensinck, A. J. "Arabic New Year and the Feast of Tabernacles." *Verhandelingen der Koninklijke Akademie van Wetenschappen te Amsterdam*, Afdeeling Letterkunde, n.r. 25, no. 2 (1925): 1–41.

———. "Some Semitic Rites of Mourning and Religion." *Verhandelingen der Koninklijke Akademie van Wetenschappen te Amsterdam*, Afdeeling Letterkunde 18, no. 1 (1917): 1–101.

Wiet, Gaston. *Matériaux pour un Corpus Inscriptionum Arabicarum.* Mémoires publiés par les membres de l'Institut Français d'Archéologie Orientale, vol. 52. Cairo, 1930.

Williams, Caroline. "The Cult of ʿAlid Saints in the Fatimid Monuments of Cairo." *Muqarnas* 1 (1983): 37–52; 3 (1985): 39–60.

Zaki, M. Hasan. *Kunūz al-fāṭimiyyīn.* Cairo, 1937.

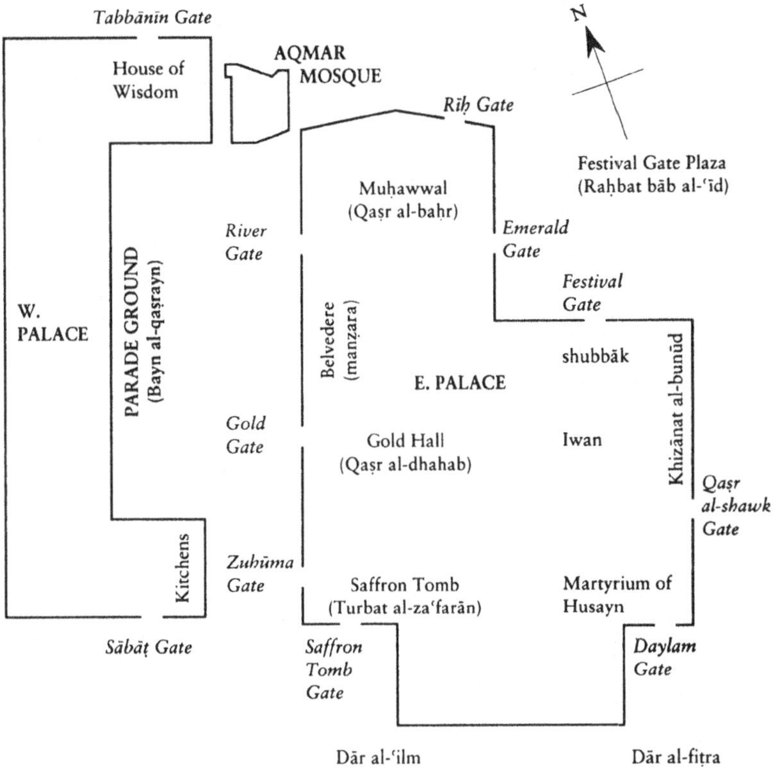

PALACES AND MOSQUES
Palace Gates
Other Palace Locations

THE FATIMID PALACES

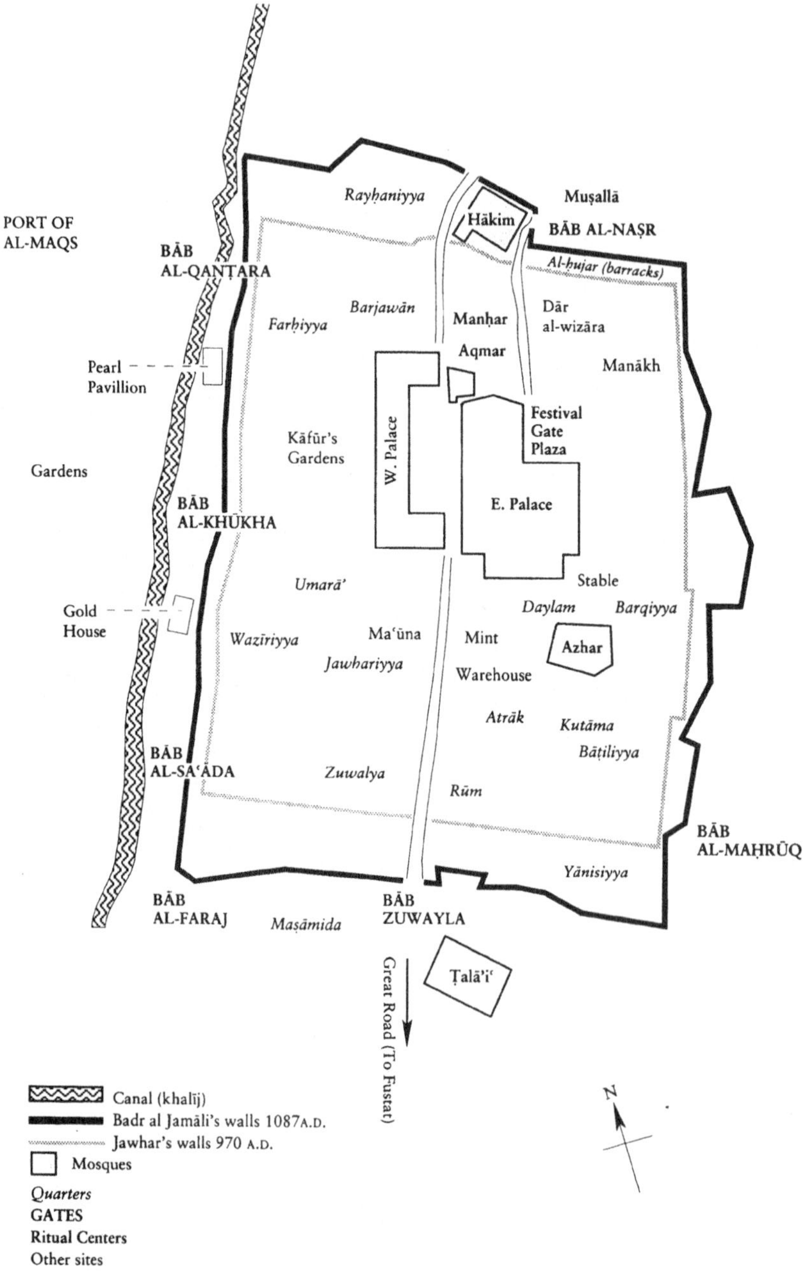

FATIMID CAIRO

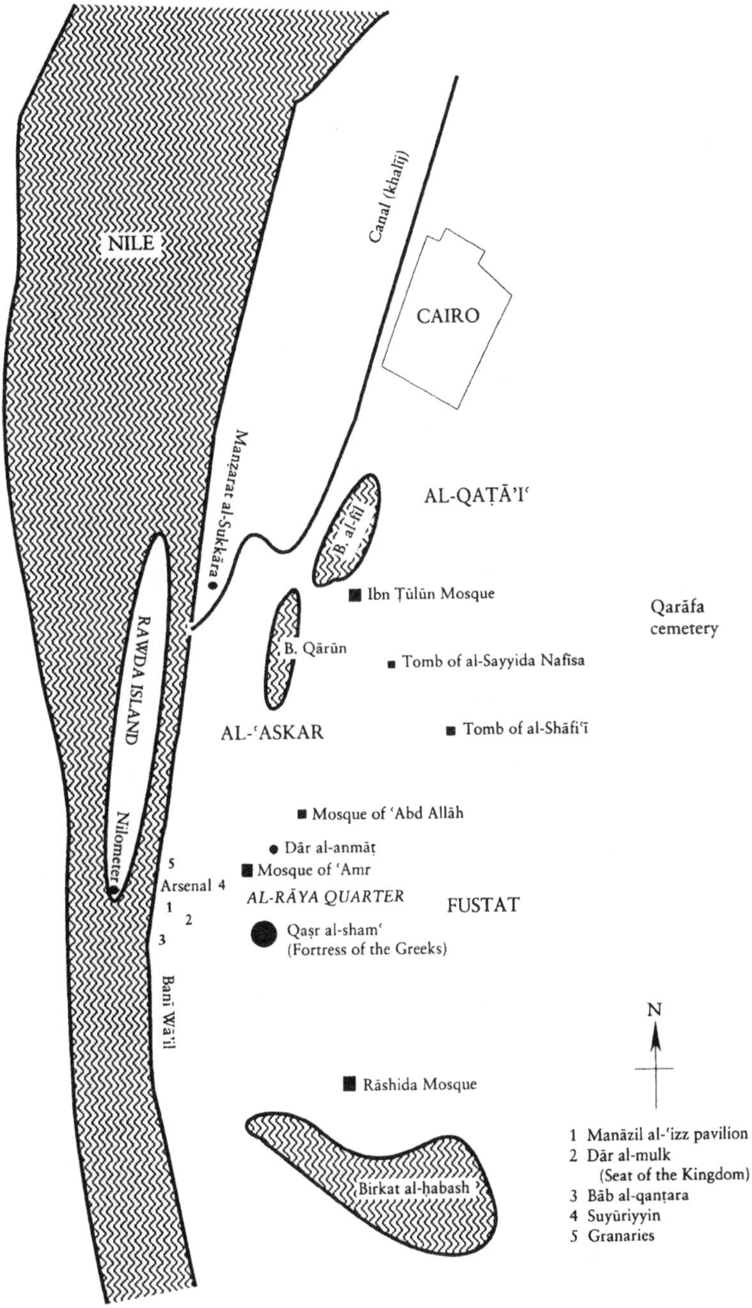
NILE
Canal (khalīj)
CAIRO
Manẓarat al-Sukkāra
AL-QAṬĀ'I'
B. al-fīl
Ibn Ṭūlūn Mosque
Qarāfa cemetery
RAWDA ISLAND
B. Qārūn
Tomb of al-Sayyida Nafīsa
AL-'ASKAR
Tomb of al-Shāfi'ī
Mosque of 'Abd Allāh
Nilometer
Dār al-anmāṭ
5
Mosque of 'Amr
Arsenal 4
AL-RĀYA QUARTER
FUSTAT
1
2
3
Qaṣr al-sham'
(Fortress of the Greeks)
Banī Wā'il
N
Rāshida Mosque
Birkat al-ḥabash
1 Manāzil al-'izz pavilion
2 Dār al-mulk
(Seat of the Kingdom)
3 Bāb al-qanṭara
4 Suyūriyyin
5 Granaries

FATIMID CAIRO AND FUSTAT

INDEX

Printed in Great Britain
by Amazon

46664777R00139